DAVE WHITLOCK'S

Guide to
AQUATIC
TROUT FOODS

DAVE WHITLOCK'S

Guide to
AQUATIC
TROUT FOODS

Nick Lyons Books

Printed in the United States of America

10 9 8 7 6 5 4 3 2

Library of Congress Cataloging in Publication Data
Whitlock, Dave.
    Dave Whitlock's Guide to aquatic trout foods.

    1. Trout—Food.   2. Insects, Aquatic.   3. Fly tying.   4. Trout fishing.   I.
Title.   II. Title: Guide to aquatic trout foods.
QL638.S2W47   799.1'755   82-4834
ISBN: 0-941130-64-9   AACR2

CONTENTS

To my wife Joan and sons Alan and Joel,
who have supported me with their total confidence,
infinite patience, and sacrifice of security
that has permitted me to make a second career
in the arts of fly fishing

I would like to express my sincerest appreciation and thanks to the Scientific Anglers/3M Company and the late Lew Jewett for providing me with the opportunity and encouragement to develop a major portion of this text and the graphic aquatic-insect illustrations.

To Gary Borger, for his counsel and unique perspective on aquatic insects.

To Jim Cook, Fred Oswalt, Doug Swisher, Carl Richards, Darrel Martin, Wayne Moore, Dan Abrams, Kathy and Jay Buchner, Bob Krumm, Fred Horvath, Rene Harrop, Howard West, and Virginia Buzeck Perry for their advice, assistance, and encouragement while developing the knowledge and perspectives of this book.

To Joe Brooks and Lefty Kreh, for their positive influence and counsel throughout my career.

PREFACE

Trout, in a local stream or anywhere throughout the world, feed on a surprisingly great variety of aquatic and terrestrial foods. The fly fisherman who understands the nature of these foods and how and when trout react to them may design and fish artificial flies that successfully imitate these foods and thus gull the trout. There are no higher pleasures in outdoor sport than the challenge and reward of catching beautiful wild trout on flies you have chosen or made to match specific trout foods.

The study, identification, and matching of trout foods goes back in time past Walton, Cotton, and Dame Juliana Berners. Since then, first in England, then in America, these skills have advanced. Fly fishers have been so moved by their personal discoveries and experiences that they have written hundreds of volumes full of colorful prose and detailed text on practically every conceivable aspect of the sport. The sum of these books provides fly-fishing with a rich legacy of history, tradition, and knowledge—and also a good dose of confusion. So much has been done in fly-fishing and so much as been spoken and written on the sport that I have often heard it said that there is nothing truly new about flies and fly-fishing today.

Though it may seem that way to some fly fishermen, fly-fishing is now in the middle of a new revolution characterized by man's technological advances, the changing wildlife environment, and the increasing thousands of fly fishers. The new emphasis on matching *all* food forms in *all* types of waters for *all* species has drastically altered the philosophy of fly-fishing and fly-tying. The expansion of fly-fishing from East to West and, as importantly, from North to South in North America and its expansion throughout the world has brought saltwater gamefish, bass, pike, and even such species as carp and catfish into the fly fisher's ken.

This revolution in fly-fishing has naturally attracted many new minds. It has reopened old dialogues and required that contemporary spokesmen be more objective. The advances made in these new areas of fly-fishing have then circled back to fly-fishing for salmonids and have led to a great many new approaches to matching trout foods with the artificial fly. This has generated an overwhelming amount of published material, some of excellent quality, some muddy or quite poor.

Frankly, today's fly fishers and fly tiers never had it so good—*if* they can utilize this mass of information. But in my travels throughout the world of fly-fishing these past ten years, I have been constantly astounded at how few of today's fly fishers exploit what is available to them. Is this because only a few of the books and articles have really related well to the masses for whom they were composed? Perhaps. Most books confuse or perplex the newcomer or average fly fisher because they fail to relate to the actual levels, problems, questions, and needs of these anglers.

I was born in 1934 *without* a fly rod in my hand or one in my family, and it was seven hundred miles from Muskogee, Oklahoma, to the nearest wild trout. I first became interested in fly-fishing and read about it when it was still in the grips of tradition and the well-heeled purist minority. The mystique, tradition, and downright bullshit scared me to death. I wondered if I would ever be worthy enough to fly-fish for trout. Coming from the very bottom, I can certainly relate to how most of today's fly fishers must feel.

But thanks to the fine works of Ray Bergman, Ted Trueblood, Lee Wulff, Al McClane, and Joe Brooks, I was able to start myself in fly-fishing. Since then this new revolution has begun and the techniques, teachings, articles, and books of Art Flick, Lefty Kreh, Carl Richards, and Doug Swisher have not only helped me to advance but also to become a part of this exciting new era in fly-fishing. Most of all, my ten-year association with thousands of fly-fishing friends from all over the world, especially through the Federation of Fly Fishermen and Trout Unlimited, has given me the clearest perspectives on what fly-fishing really is about.

Several years ago, Lew Jewett, the late, personable head of 3M's Scientific Anglers Division, challenged me to develop a slide show, on a basic level, on understanding and matching hatches of the six aquatic insects most important to the trout and to fly fishers of trout. A project that was to have taken six months instead took three years to develop. Thanks to Lew's patience and confidence in me, I had that opportunity to develop a unique perspective on aquatic-insect life cycles as they related to the trout's interest in them; and in turn, I explored the fly tier's and fly fisher's roles in matching these insects to catch the trout feeding on them. Such a basic work was difficult to do for I had to relate to beginners as well as to advanced entomologist-anglers. But it qualified and conditioned me to see *all* trout foods in a bright true light so that the flies I have since tied and the ways I have fished them have proved enormously successful.

This book deals principally with the significant waterborn-aquatic trout foods; although it is well to realize that many significant landborn-terrestrial trout foods exist: grasshoppers, ants, moths (insects), mice, voles (rodents), earthworms, lizards, etc. However, I have chosen not to complicate this text by adding these nonaquatic foods, a subject that, if given the attention it deserves, would comprise a second complete book.

Now I want to share what I have learned—in my underwater studies, peering into a microscope, at my tying vise, and in thousands of hours along trout waters in every part of the country. I want to help fly fishermen learn the basic techniques of recognizing, studying, and matching all aquatic trout foods, for I want to encourage you to use your own skills and common sense as you seek to identify, match, and fish them. I feel positive that this book will enrich *any* fly fisher's skill and pleasure.

And isn't that what it's all about?

1
CONCEPTS OF IMITATION

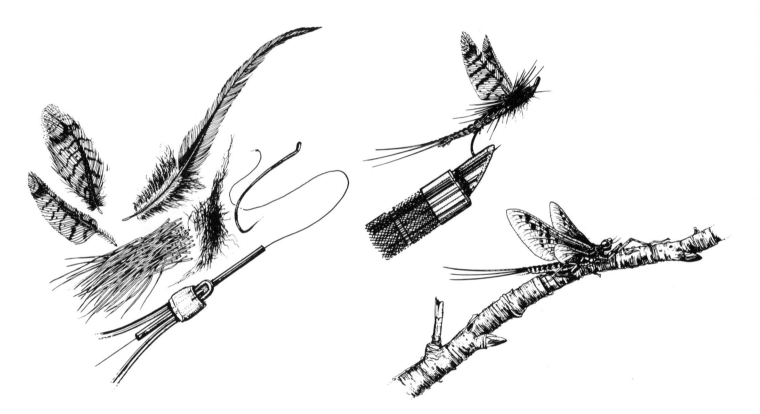

All the natural foods upon which trout feed—such as aquatic and terrestrial insects, minnows, worms, crustaceans, shellfish, amphibians, rodents, and reptiles—can be imitated by today's fly-tying methods and then cast and fished most effectively with a fly rod. Trout undoubtedly eat the greatest range of food types and sizes of any gamefish, and this wide range makes them the most desirable of all fish to catch on flies. Imitation is best accomplished when these foods are properly identified and their life cycles clearly understood. "How and when do they interest the trout?" we must ask before we can make or obtain fly designs and

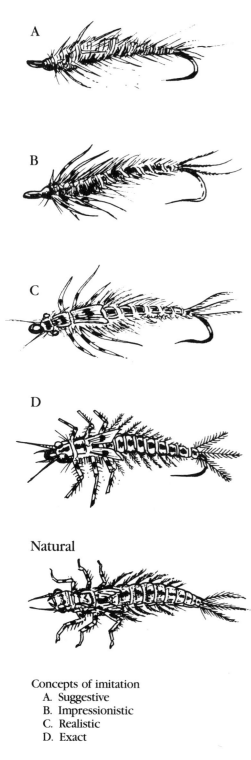

Concepts of imitation
A. Suggestive
B. Impressionistic
C. Realistic
D. Exact

patterns that best simulate these foods and then fish the flies to simulate their subtlest movements at their most vulnerable periods to the trout.

Size, action, texture, shape, and color come directly into play when the fly tier makes an artificial and the fly fisher then manipulates it to the trout. A critical balance between these important characteristics will determine whether the fly should be suggestive, impressionistic, realistic, or exact.

Fly fishermen and fly tiers often loosely use the descriptive terms of suggestive, impressionistic, realistic, and exact to describe the concept of artificial imitations in relation to their natural trout foods. I feel, for the sake of clarity, that these terms be described as I define and use them in my writings, lectures, and fly tying.

Suggestive—a particular form of artificial fly that depicts a simple, crude, almost nondescript live natural food.
Impressionistic—a particular form of artificial fly that gives a more distinct illusion of a general food form, such as a snail, mayfly nymph, or sculpin minnow.
Realistic—a particular form of artificial fly that more closely imitates a particular live species in which the major imitation characteristics—size, shape, color, and texture—are observed.
Exact—a particular form of artificial imitation that seeks to duplicate an existing aquatic food by being its best possible copy.

Size, action, texture, shape, and color—in that order—are the most critical elements in matching trout foods with the fly. I will advocate a "suggestive realism." Suggestive or impressionistic flies provide the greatest latitude for forgiving error, and they much more easily deceive the trout. Conversely, exact realism leaves little or no room for error in identifying and matching a specific trout food at a particular time. What we want, of course, is the best possible chance to take the most selective trout.

Throughout this book I will follow this line of reasoning for the Whitlock fly designs. But *you* must also develop your ability to recognize a trout food, and if it is in some way unique you must produce a design and pattern that will cope best with that uniqueness. No two waters, no two trout, no two days are exactly alike. But you can quickly adjust to differences if you have trained yourself to evaluate them and to react accordingly. That has been my single most important concept in designing and fishing the Whitlock series of flies.

Like the sculptor or painter, the fly tier has a variety of tools at his disposal; the bottom line is always how well he uses them to create. A couple of years ago I became interested in the differ-

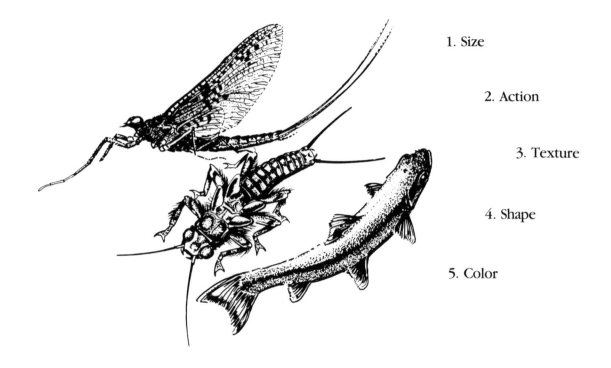

1. Size

2. Action

3. Texture

4. Shape

5. Color

The five major elements of imitation

DEFINITIONS OF TERMS SIZE,
ACTION, TEXTURE, COLOR AND SHAPE

1. SIZE - The length, width, and thickness of a natural aquatic food or the imitation of this food. Generally the exact length is most important to imitate with the smallest foods (⅛″ to ½″), then width and thickness becomes more important as overall size increases (over ½″).

2. ACTION - The movement or degree of movement of a natural or imitation including its own muscular movement and what the water or entrapment on the water gives it. The imitation when fished is given proper live imitative action by the angler's manipulation of cast, rod, line, leader, general design or shape of imitation and water's movement. Action thus depicts living movement, vulnerability, and proper attitude of the imitation to a trout.

3. TEXTURE - The overall *feel*, softness or rigidity, of a natural or imitation. Each natural food has a particular identifiable texture or *feel* when touched or bitten by a trout. So an imitation of such foods should have this same general feel. The tying material considered or used for an imitation should be chosen with the same feel or texture. Very hard or very soft imitations seldom fall into this realistic texture range.

4. SHAPE - The overall outline or silhouette of an aquatic trout food within its *three dimensional size*. Shape should be considered closely when fly imitation designing is done. The best or most versatile imitations usually have the more impressionistic shapes which give the idea of many possible aquatic trout foods.

5. COLOR - Natural aquatic trout foods have distinctive shades and tones of many colors as well as specific *patterns* of these colors. Normally exact duplication of chroma or color is not necessary because even within a common group of naturals there will be wide variations in shades and tones of these colors. Imitations usually are effective if they are generally color pattern imitative.

ences between the original natural tying materials, substitute natural tying materials, and the new synthetics. My study revealed that most of the original fly-tying materials were simply used because they were what was most available that looked like the parts of the insect or minnow being imitated. It is a foolish restriction if we continue to use these materials simply because they are traditionally called for. There is absolutely no reason why *any* material—if it meets the standards of size, action, texture, shape, and color—cannot be used effectively to match any trout foods. There are thousands of interesting materials available today, each with its own best uses, and there are more made available to the serious fly tier each year. My guide in selecting a material is always: "will it do the job best?"

The chief difference between the angler who fly-fishes for trout and the angler who uses bait or who spin-fishes is that the fly fisher enjoys a much greater latitude for self-expression. The more one learns about the life in the stream, and the life above and below the trout stream, the more rewarding the pastime becomes. The greatest fascination and reward of fly-fishing for trout comes when you become totally aware of these factors. They then materialize into a complete scheme of the living stream. Catching trout on imitations of their foods is just one part of what you can derive from the study of this whole picture. You do not have to be a biologist or an entomologist or even know one word of Latin to know about these creatures and their environment. Since I learned to study these natural foods, their life cycles, and their roles in the trout's environment, my angling success has been considerably better. Even on poor days, I now find it easier to explain why trout do not strike.

Suggestive realism—
natural and imitations

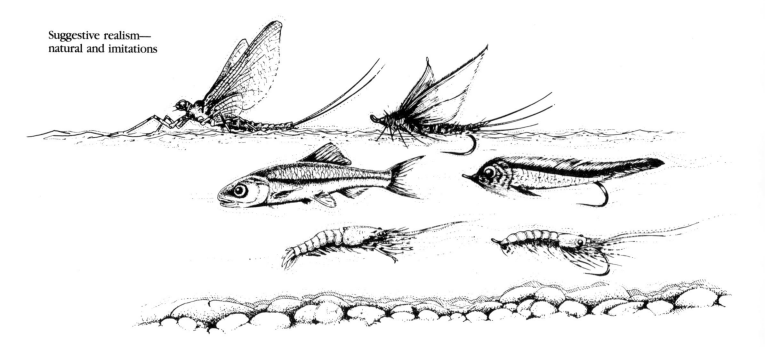

Wild trout are creatures that predictably react to their environment's conditions and seasons. To a lesser degree, tame, stocked trout also seem to follow these stimuli. The water in which trout live cycles daily and seasonally. It varies in temperature, volume, clarity, and chemical composition. The sum of these environmental factors will determine how the trout reacts to his foods, which have a similar environmental response themselves. Unusual weather conditions, unnatural interruptions by predators, disease, parasites, and spawning will all drastically alter the seasonal feeding routines and residency of trout. Recognizing these factors is important for locating fish, choosing the right fly, and using the right technique on normal days.

Each natural trout food has unique physical properties. Each has a definite shape, color, size range, action, texture, and even odor. And each of these properties is sensed by a trout's sight, hearing, smell, and touch. To tie the most effective imitations I try to incorporate and utilize as many of a food's properties as practical.

As I tie a fly, I seriously consider its size, shape, color, texture, and eventual action when in the water. Always foremost in my mind is the fly's capacity to fish well. It must be able to *look alive* in the water where I intend to fish it. And to design the best pattern to match the food, I must have seen and studied the live creature in its natural environment.

For many years I was negligent in doing this field study of live naturals, shortcutting and thus shortchanging myself by too often accepting what others have said or written about the food. Often, too, we do not objectively test the artificials in aquariums, or study how they respond at the end of a cast. Recently I ran some tests on how a popular western dry fly landed and rode on the water. What I envisioned would happen and what actually happened were radically different. Our imaginations often mislead us drastically.

I am so convinced of this that I believe most fly designs and patterns are incorrectly tied and fished, and trout strike them for a completely different reason than we think. Or, in plainer terms, many trout are caught *accidentally*.

Those times when I felt sure the trout were striking my fly for exactly what it was supposed to imitate were fantastic experiences. Carl Richards has often told me that if you have the right fly and fish it right you should take most of the feeding trout to which you cast. I now think this is so.

Most wild fish taken on poor imitations or poorly fished imitations have merely responded to their natural curiosity. Trout do this regularly, and will often attack *any* unnatural invaders into their territory. I cannot remember ever having investigated the

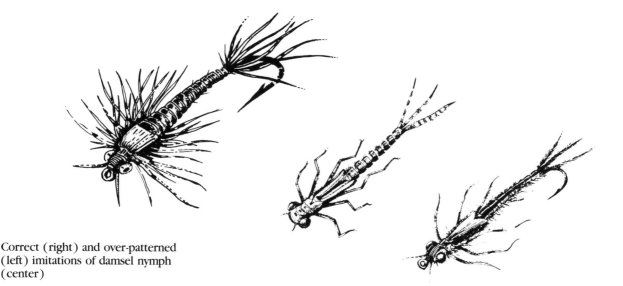

Correct (right) and over-patterned (left) imitations of damsel nymph (center)

contents of a trout's stomach when I was not surprised at one or two of the odd things I found there. My observations convince me that trout also make *playful responses.* Many writers have said otherwise, stating that the natural struggle for food and survival does not allow trout this playfulness. But it would be hard, then, to explain some of the erratic antics I have seen trout go through with other trout and with various creatures and even with inanimate objects if it was not for their own amusement or exercise!

Most fly designs that are made to imitate specific trout foods—especially those for insects, crustaceans, and minnows—are grossly overpatterned. They are too large, they use too many materials, and their form is exaggerated. For instance, no aquatic insect has more than six legs and three tails and two antennae. Yet wet flies and nymphs used to match them may have a dozen tails and three or four dozen legs. Such overdressed flies seldom deceive trout, but a trout's unselective strike may easily deceive the angler. The first mistake most fly fishers make, then, is to fish overdressed flies.

The second mistake most fly fishers make is to cause the fly to overact the part of a real food. Causing or allowing a fly to move faster than a naturally possible swimming action, or at angles to the current that are unnatural or impossible for the real food to accomplish, are examples of this.

So we have oversized, out-of-proportion flies reacting in strange ways, unlike the food of the day. But they catch some trout. Why? Because they are attractors that entice the trout's natural curiosity, threaten its territory, or depict an unknown creature in distress. In some ways these trout are responding to these lures the way a salmon does to a fly. In fact, such riseforms, strikes, and refusals are exact duplicates of the Atlantic salmon's responses to dry and wet salmon flies.

Of course the most flagrant mismatches occur when imitating aquatic insects. But other major foods—terrestrials, crustaceans such as shrimp, scud, or crayfish, and various baitfish minnows—all suffer, too; their sizes, shapes, and actions are often greatly out of proportion. Less common foods, such as leeches, mice, and frogs, do not generally require the degree of refinement in tying or fishing as the more regularly seen and eaten foods—and each of these foods will include individuals of radically different size.

As long as we are aware of this misconception, it is all right to enlist it to catch trout. Otherwise, the hatch-matcher will be sorely frustrated. And the problem is so easily corrected that there is no reason to tolerate it if you have a sincere desire to match the natural foods. Just become a new student of the water. Do not look at things with an emotional eye, but learn to see with an objective eye and understand what is really there.

Hopefully, this guide to aquatic trout foods and my best imitations of them will help you do just that.

2 WATER

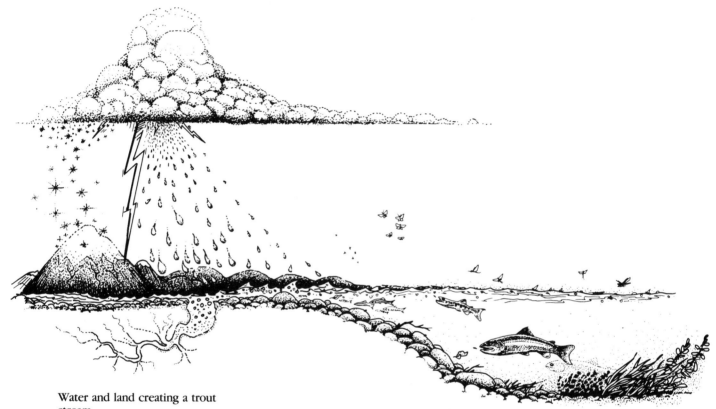

Water and land creating a trout stream

The water in which trout live, feed, and reproduce is the most important element in their lives and in the lives of their foods. Fly fishermen must study water carefully before they can possibly understand trout and their feeding.

No two streams or lakes are completely alike, but all have certain similarities. The amount of water and chemical quality of the water greatly influence how many trout and what size of trout live there; this mostly depends upon how much food is generated annually from a river's or lake's volume and richness. The source of the water and what it comes in contact with from the environment determines what these properties will be. For instance, water from melting snow runoff, underground limestone springs, and swamp runoff will all be drastically different in chemical makeup and pH.

ACID	ALKALINE
0	7.5	15
Softer and less rich in trout food production	*Harder and more rich in trout food production*

Dissolved ground minerals and organic compounds from dead plants and animals in water react with the sunlight, air, and temperature to create a suitable or unsuitable environment for trout and their food chains. The master scheme of a living stream is formed by the utilization of water; its dissolved chemical contents, given energy by the sun, create life. Beginning with the simplest one-cell animal and plant, a series of increasingly complex life forms builds from the next lower to create the food chain of plants and animals. The trout is at the top. There is a natural adjustment or evolution to this if man does not seriously interfere with the species' adaptation processes. This natural adaptation to the water environment is rather slow but produces a true genetic imprint on the species that survive and thrive. Adaptation to chemical content, temperature extremes, diseases, parasites, predators, and food forms is little less than a miracle. The angler who recognizes these mechanisms is enriched, rewarded, and certainly set on the road to becoming knowledgeable about trout and their foods.

Water Types

Water that creates trout steams and lakes comes from the condensation of the world's seas as the condensation moves over land in the form of rainfall or snowfall. It either runs off directly or indirectly, pulled by gravity into a network of veinlike streams. Rivers and lakes are formed, and eventually all water returns to the sea to recycle again.

Water flowing downhill moves at a rate, rhythm, and in a pattern determined by the shape of land it flows over or through. All flowing waters develop the same general physical properties regardless of the amount or size of the stream. These are commonly termed riffles, runs, pools, flats, and tails, and they occur naturally in that order. Even water in a straight concrete ditch or pipe, carrying silt particles, will set up this physical structure. The variation of gradient and friction created by the bottom's resistance to the water's flow determines the size and frequency of these physical characteristics.

In any gradient there is a variation in current speed due to the friction of water against itself and the stationary surface it flows past. In a steam there is a common layering of current speed that is most rapid at the surface (where air and water meet) and slowest at the bottom, where friction against the streambed is greatest. This occurs in all parts of a stream in which the water is allowed to flow. This variation is one of the most important factors you can know about stream water; it holds the key to how most life forms in a stream cope with life there.

Each part of a stream represents a particular gradient or bottom that is the cause of the water's response. The makeup of the bedrock and the extent of contribution from water and land erosion creates these bottom structures. Silt, sand, gravel, rock rubble, and terrestrial structures (such as trees and shrubs) are the building materials that shape or create the anatomy of streams. This flow pattern is shaped much like a crude sine wave.

Aquatic vegetation comes to a stream as water properties allow. When conditions are right, aquatic plants establish themselves and form the last significant anatomical structure that shapes the

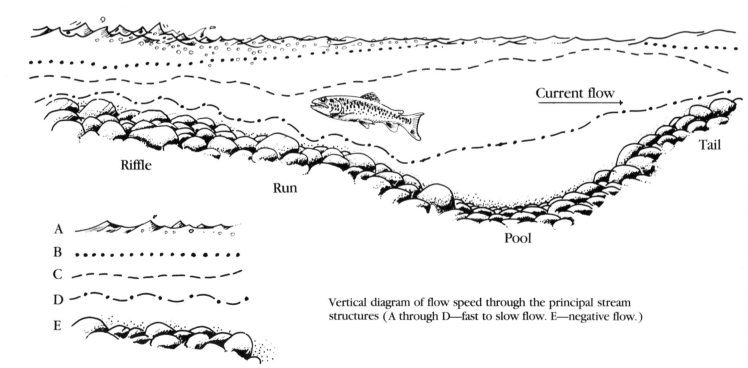

Vertical diagram of flow speed through the principal stream structures (A through D—fast to slow flow. E—negative flow.)

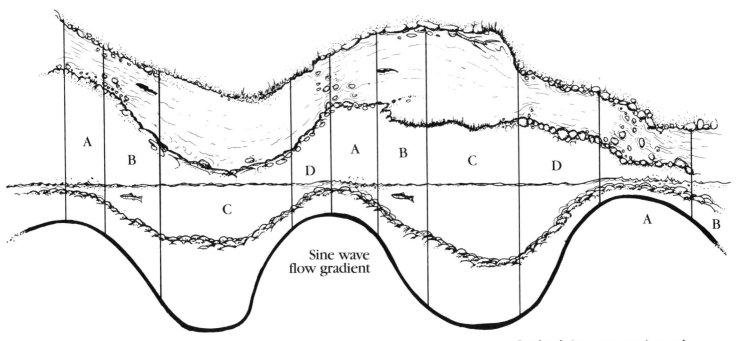

Overhead view, cross section, and
sine wave pattern of flowing trout
stream

A. Riffle
B. Run
C. Pool
D. Tail

stream. However, water fluctuation, clarity (sunlight transmission), chemical content, and the seasons greatly affect plant growth. Algae, the simplest plants, establish themselves first, then the more complex aquatic plants follow in the order of their requirements. High, snow-runoff, freestone streams seldom establish complex water plants. Meadow streams and spring creeks, with their gentler and more temperate flows, often are completely overgrown with multitudes of aquatic and terrestrial plants. Plants are extremely important to the health of waters, and they create a fertile environment for trout foods and trout. Plants are one of the two main sources of free-oxygen and carbon-dioxide absorption. A stream or lake lacking any aquatic plants is dead water.

Knowing water types and the special properties of each will provide the serious fly fisher with immediate clues for selection of the best natural-food imitation. Each section of a stream will have distinctive food forms living there, according to their adaptation. Swimming or crawling mayfly nymphs that live in the fast-water riffles are replaced by burrowing mayflies in the pool. Stoneflies need fast, well-aerated water to survive, so they are seldom found in abundance in the deep or slow waters of the runs, pools, flats, or tails. Highly mobile foods, such as minnows and scuds, move daily to where food and water conditions best suit them.

That part of a stream that has an extreme bottom gradient (other than a rapid) is usually called a *riffle*. This gradient causes the water to move along quickly. Riffles are often turbulent. This turbulence is due to the reluctance of moving water to compress as it strikes rough bottom obstructions such as rocks and boulders. The higher-gradient angle moves the water faster; such water is usually shallow and narrow compared to the water

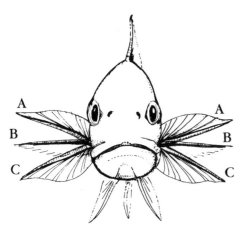

Pectoral fin movement

A—Rise

B—Remain level

C—Dive

Trout in a flow of water—using flow energy to "fly" in the moving water. Note the body and fin attitudes in A, B, and C.

A. Holding a level position

B. Rising trout—water pushes the trout up

C. Descending trout—water pushes the trout down

downstream. It is comparable to the top-down part of the sine wave.

Most trout-stream riffles are recognizable by their irregular, rough, broken, fast-moving surface. Rocks, boulders, and other surface-protruding obstructions as well as those just below the surface cause the water to splash and foam with air. They are usually noisy, exciting, bright areas that appear to dance in the sunlight.

A riffle provides the best opportunity for the water to purify itself by filtration. It expels excess gases such as the carbon dioxide produced by the breakdown of plant and animal waste. Water also best accepts the important oxygen and other gases from the air in a riffle. Such hypercirculation greatly encourages the establishment of the largest colonies of such trout foods as aquatic insects, minnows, snails, and crustaceans. Only large beds of aquatic vegetation approach the riffle for richness in trout foods.

Unless the riffle is excessively deep and turbulent—just a little less than a waterfall—most sizes of trout can live in it since they easily hold in the calm spaces next to the bottom rubble or behind and in front of larger rocks, boulders, moss beds, or logs. Trout in the water are like birds in the sky—by adjusting their swim bladders they can literally fly through the water. By using their pectoral fins they can sail in the current flow. If a riffle is too clean to create natural holds, trout will only move into it temporarily to feed.

Look at the riffle with and without polarizing sunglasses and study its surface and under structure. Watch the bubble line, flow vectors, and color changes. These are all keys to what is going on in this riffle. Try to think "vertically." It is an especially good practice to elevate yourself as high above the stream as possible in order to "read" the water's surface and subsurface best. Standing level or waist deep in a stream or lake almost completely eliminates one or two of your dimension perspectives. Water is deceiving at that angle: its reflective surface and flatness confuses the

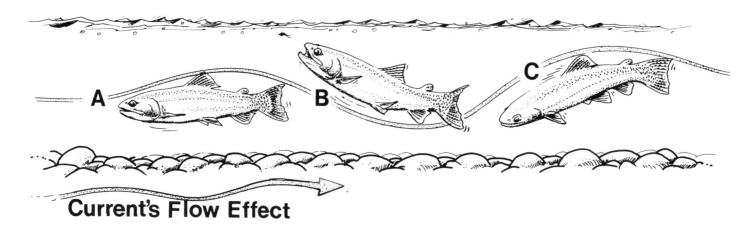

Current's Flow Effect

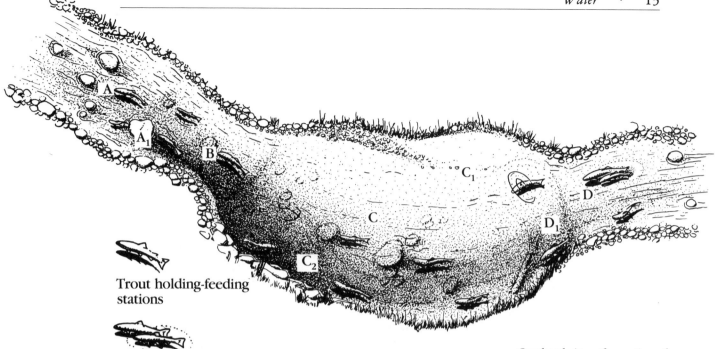

Trout holding-feeding stations

Trout spawning area (D)

eye, and width and depth perception of the streambed are then almost, if not completely, lost. The higher you can get above the water the more these two dimensions return. Even the reflective light on the surface is greatly reduced.

Try to see and understand why the water moves as it does. Wade back and forth through it, using your feet to "see" the design of the bottom. Better yet, a face mask or glass-bottom bucket will help you look below the distorted mirror surface for a true and clear picture of what is there.

This is *reading the water* in its most basic form. Once you make these structural observations in several streams, not merely in the riffles but in all parts of the stream, you can relate accurately to all other streams. In fact, once you understand this natural relationship between the water's movement and the stream bottom, you can even closely estimate the structure of water and the bottom in a stream in which the water is so murky you cannot see into it an inch.

The section of a stream that is usually directly downstream from the riffle is the *run*. Here the water deepens and slows as it moves down toward the third section, the pool. The channel either narrows or spreads wider than the riffle—but it always deepens and slows.

Turbulence here will be less than in the riffle as a result of the slowing effect of the deeper water downstream, which holds it back. At the surface there will be a typical rocking-welling movement from the speed and turbulence of the riffle and the back pressure of the pool.

Overhead view of a section of a typical trout stream with major and minor structures

A—Riffle

A_1—Pockets

B—Run

C—Pool

C_1—Flat

C_2—Back eddy

D—Tail

D_1—Lip of tail

The color of the water darkens as it becomes deeper. If there are no surface protrusions, look for dark objects beneath or rolling-boiling water caused by such large objects as boulders, stumps, or ledges on the bottom to tell you what the bottom is like.

The run is an especially important holding and feeding area for trout, particularly for the larger fish in a stream. The depth, slowness, and less turbulent currents make this area just below the food-rich, water-conditioning riffle nearly perfect for trout. There is nothing like discovering a long, perfect run loaded with feeding trout. Such trout are usually the easiest to catch with all types of flies.

The deepest and widest area in a stream is the *pool*. It is just below the run and riffle. Pools are the result of the riffle's digging and washing turbulence during high-water periods. The sine wave pattern for the pool is the lowest part, or bottom, of the wave. Since the pool is usually wider and deeper than other parts of a stream, the water slows, eddies, and can even back-eddy or stop, according to how much water is coming or going.

Observation, particularly of the shoreline gradients of pools, can tell you a lot about their bottoms, shapes, and depths. Usually, in high-gradient streams that support trout there are large geographical irregularities such as mountains, hills, faults, and ledges. The water cuts away at their sides and the pool will have one high bank and another flat or low bank. The high side will usually be deepest with most of the current flowing through it. The low side will be slower and will carry much more silt, gravel, and terrestrial deposits, which in turn will make it shallower.

Trout will hold and live in various deeper, upper, middle, and lower parts of the pool depending upon the season and cover and food available. Usually they will cruise or patrol in a particular pattern when the feeding period comes. It is common for them to move upstream or downstream from the pool area if food is more available elsewhere, then return to the pool after they have fed.

The area of a stream that usually lies to the side or between the pool and tail is the *flat*. It is a shallow, calm section of the stream. Though the flat is a rich food area, trout do not use it as regularly as they do other areas, especially during daylight hours. Flats are caused by a delta-forming reaction as the pool is dug out by the riffle's turbulence. The wash of sand, silt, gravel, terrestrial and aquatic vegetation, due to the greatly reduced water flow, builds up the bottom. This sedimentation causes the water to spread out. Higher-gradient streams do not have regular or extensive flats. Lower meadow streams, spring creeks, and larger rivers have the best flats.

At night or during exceptional daytime hatches, trout will cruise a flat and feed. Flats are difficult for most fly fishers to fish in daylight, when you must see a cruising fish and intercept it with a fly. The most outstanding "flats" river I have ever fished is the Henrys Fork in Idaho.

The last part of the structural-flow anatomy of a stream is the *tail*. It is the shallow, narrowing section below the pool or flat. It is also called a "slick" since its surface, when not studded with boulders or rubble, is quite oily in appearance. It is the ascending end of the sine wave just before and at the peak.

Tails are interesting places to study—and fascinating places to fish. They show their bottoms well, and feeding fish are usually quite visible at or below the surface. The funneling of the pool's surface film and flow, a first quickening before the next riffle, makes it a prime food and feeding area. Because of its characteristic lip just as it breaks to the head of the riffle, fish can glide and feed or dart easily up or downstream to cover. The smooth, steady flow-pattern of the tail makes it an easy place in which larger trout can hold and forage from bottom to top and from side to side.

But the tail is a fly fisher's nightmare. It is extremely difficult to control the drift and drag of a fly since the downstream acceleration creates havoc; line, leader, tippet, and fly are almost always in different current speeds. The best presentation options are from upstream, downstream, or slightly across stream; careless presentations and excessive line mending over smooth surfaces will put down or panic most trout.

Besides being a good feeding station, the tail is also a staging (mating) and spawning area. Trout pick the tail of the pool to dig their nests and lay their eggs because it offers the most advantages for successful deposit, fertilization, and incubation of eggs. Therefore, just before and during the spawning season, there will be many adult trout in the tail areas.

Wild trout characteristically move upstream from their resident waters to smaller stream sections where the water is more suitable for spawning and fry survival. Even in these smaller waters, the tails are still most frequently used for spawning.

No matter how large a river or how small a brook, all flowing streams have these distinctive areas—riffle, run, pool, flat, and tail. They are extremely important to the lives of trout and their foods, and thus should be prime subjects for the fly fisher's careful study.

Lakes, ponds, and sloughs—impounded bodies of water that are trapped in a depression that is lower than any point on its perimeter—characteristically have low or practically no general water current or movement. Though these types of standing trout waters have many important similarities, like streams, none are identical. With only a few exceptions and shape or size variations, each has an inlet and outlet of water, so in many ways we can relate them to the pool of a stream.

Such trapped bodies of water are identified according to their general shapes and surface areas as ponds, sloughs, or small or large lakes. I call a body of water a pond if it is less than two acres in surface area and is more or less circular. Sloughs are similar in size but are narrower—long, still waters that were once channels in a stream but now stand alone after the live channel has moved because of flood or other alteration. Small lakes usually are over two acres in surface size up to several hundred acres. Large lakes are a mile or longer.

Trout lakes and ponds are formed by the trapping or damming of water flows from springs, by precipitation runoff, or by stream channels. Glaciers, earthquakes, landslides, storms, and floods are major causes of natural lakes. Man and beavers are responsible for dammed lakes. In the last fifty years, most new ponds and small and large lakes have been built by man. Stocking these new waters and many hundreds of barren natural lakes that have cold and relatively unpolluted water has greatly expanded trout fishing. In fact, although never as popular as streams, lakes are becoming more important and popular each year as good stream fishing becomes less available due to damming, pollution, closing, irrigation, and sharply increasing numbers of trout fishermen. A good working knowledge of trout lakes can lead to success and pleasure fishing them. I find lake fishing as challenging, rewarding, and enjoyable as most stream fishing I've done.

Lakes, much like streams, have specific natural foods, water sources, physical structures, and environmental influences; these determine their value as trout fisheries. Like streams, large, medium, or small lakes generally function the same, but the smaller ones are easier to read and find fish in. The larger and deeper they are, the more unpredictable they become as to where the trout are and what their behavior is. This is actually a blessing in disguise, for width and depth give trout decent sanctuary from fishermen. Such sanctuaries usually provide better numbers and larger sizes of trout than small lakes and streams. The small and large streams that flow into these large lakes often receive feeding runs and spawning runs of these better lake fish—which of course vastly improves them compared to those trout streams not emptying into such lakes.

Resident lake fish of a given age are normally larger than resident stream fish of the same age. This is due to a somewhat easier lifestyle. Food gathering is simpler, there are fewer land and water predators, and lakes suffer less from environmental extremes such as flood, drought, and temperature excess. An average four-pound stream trout would probably weigh seven to eight pounds in a lake of equal fertility.

To pick and fish lakes successfully here are some important facts you need to know:

Water source. The fresh water that fills most lakes comes from one or a combination of springs, direct snow or rain runoff, ground seepage, or inflowing streams. Generally, the lake is richer in growth potential for plants and animals if the water source is from subterranean springs or seepages. Water from such underground inflows is usually clear and does not "shock" the fishery with fast fluctuations in level or water temperature. This water is usually much richer in dissolved carbonates and other important mineral salts that maintain an ideal water pH of 7 or greater. Such rich water will support a fine trout fishery.

Water from rain or snow runoff—often acid from the capture in the atmosphere and dissolving of carbonic acid—is usually softer; it also carries the acid leechings of surface-decaying organic compounds that are also much more acid in chemical nature. This runoff water is more apt to carry larger amounts of silt, clay, and other organic wastes that affect the water's clarity and purity. It is also much more prone to excess levels and temperature fluctuations. Such natural acidity inhibits most aquatic plant and animal growth, thus limiting trout growth.

The fertility of streams that flow into a lake greatly influences the lake's fertility. The degree of agriculture and animal raising along the lake's water-drainage source will also greatly determine its potential to support a trout fishery; the degree and nature of such activity can either enhance or inhibit a lake's potential.

Water depth. Trout lakes vary much more in depth than do streams. If year-round water temperature does not allow winter-kill freezing, the shallower lakes generally provide the best trout fishing. Shallow, clear, spring-fed lakes, such as Henrys Lake in Idaho, consistently support the best trout fisheries; the water's content, temperature, oxygen, and sunlight penetration enables the plants and animals to develop abundant populations. Trout living there enjoy the best of this environment and grow fast and strong.

Deeper lakes are usually less productive since excellent levels of light, heat, and oxygen are confined to the shallower perimeters of the lake. Deep lakes are more prone to stratify in warm weather, thus exiling trout to a deep, cold, narrow area called the thermocline. This area is usually twenty to forty-five feet deep, out of the practical range for fly-fishing.

Since most trout foods—such as aquatic insects, crustaceans, leeches, snails, and minnows—are born and live in water from one to six feet deep, trout must use these areas to find food. Areas such as inlets, flats, points, islands, shallow bays, jetties, shorelines, moss beds, lily pads, terrestrial vegetation (such as flooded or fallen trees), and channels adjacent to shallows are all prime trout-feeding areas.

In these areas, trout must feed by cruising to intercept, collect, or catch various foods. In streams, most of their foods are moved to them or made vulnerable by the water flowing to their holding and feeding stations. Occasionally, trout living in lakes have food delivered to them at stream inlets or during windy periods. Some trout foods, such as damselflies, scuds, leeches, and minnows, will move or migrate en masse to cer-

Overhead view and vertical cross-section of a typical shallow trout lake

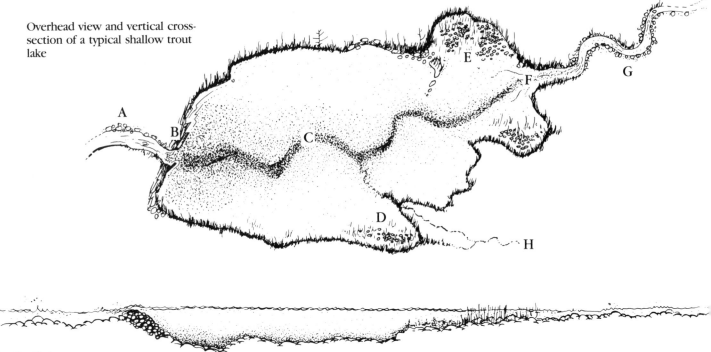

A. Outlet

B. Dam

C. Channel (Main)

D. Arm or Cove

E. Weedy Shallows

F. Inlet

G. Feeder Stream

H. Tributary Feeder Stream

tain lake areas to hatch, feed, or spawn. Trout hold in these areas and easily intercept the incoming foods.

Reading the lake's surface. The lake surface, its intermediate area, and its bottom can be read or studied like a stream to recognize the most important factors needed to identify, match, and fish trout foods effectively where and when the trout are feeding.

The water's surface shape in a lake does not tell nearly as

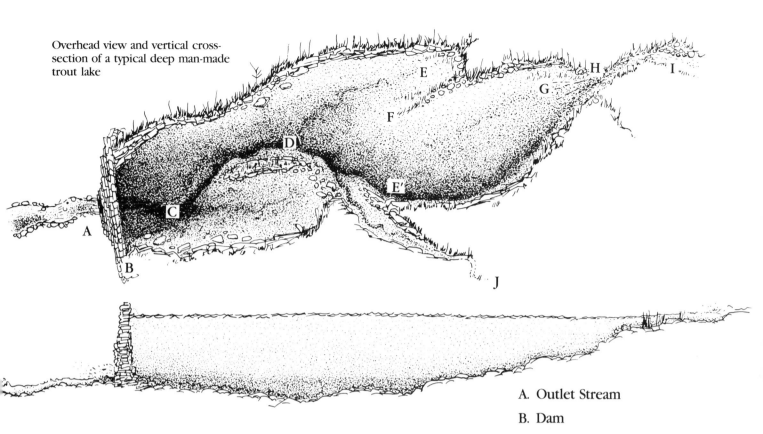

Overhead view and vertical cross-section of a typical deep man-made trout lake

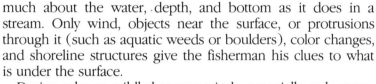

much about the water, depth, and bottom as it does in a stream. Only wind, objects near the surface, or protrusions through it (such as aquatic weeds or boulders), color changes, and shoreline structures give the fisherman his clues to what is under the surface.

During calm or mildly breezy periods, especially early morning and at sundown, fish feeding just below or on the surface make surface splashes, swirls, or rings that usually reveal concentrations of trout . . . and their cruise direction and feeding pattern.

If the water is quite clear, you will be able to read the structure and even see the fish at some depth. Manual bottom-sounding or electronic "fish finders" are useful in this respect. When trout are looking for particular foods or are holding at certain comfortable depths, they will choose bottom structures that best support their needs. Gravel, rubble, sand, silt, weed,

A. Outlet Stream

B. Dam

C. Main Channel

D. Reef along Channel

E. Shallow Neck or Arm

E'. Deep Neck or Arm

F. Shallow Point

G. Upper Shallows

H. Stream Inlet

I. Main Feeder Stream

J. Tributary

Trout feeding near a lake's surface on aquatic food

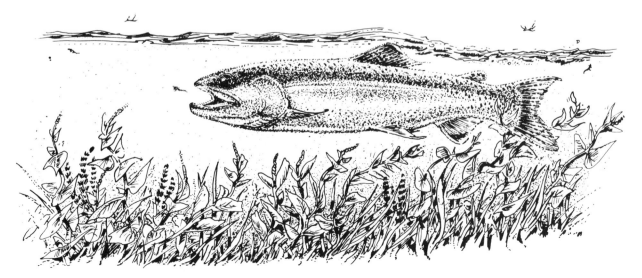

moss, and the like are significant and must be recognized in reading lake water, for they create the "landscape" of a lake bottom.

Random fly-fishing in stillwaters, especially the larger lakes, has seldom been popular—and is rarely productive. Yet, purposeful study of trout foods, matching their physical properties and action as well as reading the water can provide challenging trout fishing. And the chance to catch *very* large trout on a fly is many times greater in these waters than in most streams.

The Seasons of Water

In most trout streams and lakes the water is directly affected by the seasons. Typical trout waters are seasonally altered most by changes in water volume and temperature. Tailwaters below some southern dammed lakes and large spring-fed waters are exceptions since the temperatures of these waters are not so much affected by weather. Sunlight variations also accompany seasonal changes.

Trout, like all fish, are cold-blooded and will assume approximately the same temperature as the water. A slightly increased temperature comes to them through digestion, metabolism, and absorbed radiant energy from the sun. But for practical purposes, trout activity is governed by water temperature.

There is a general temperature range in which trout best function. This range is approximately forty to seventy degrees Fahrenheit, with fifty-five to seventy degrees being ideal for their metabolism—or active feeding and growing periods. Brook and lake trout (true char) prefer lower ideal ranges—forty-five to fifty-five degrees. Rainbow, cutthroat, and golden trout prefer an intermediate range of fifty to sixty degrees. Browns and domesticated rainbows prefer the highest range, fifty-five to sixty-eight degrees. Most trout can adapt in two or three generations to shifts by these optimum metabolic ranges of five to ten degrees.

Other cold-blooded creatures—including the natural foods trout eat—react similarly to these temperature ranges in natural trout waters. So not only does water temperature affect the fish but it also affects their foods' activity and availability. Seasonal water temperature is the base or foundation of a river's physical properties.

Throughout the year, trout will seek the ideal temperature, or, if there is no such choice for them, they will locate themselves where they can best cope with less-than-ideal conditions. Within the structure of a stream or lake, this means they can be predictably located if we know the general water temperature, its variations in specific places, and even the general air temperature.

Here is a general outline of where trout will be during seasonal and temperature ranges in a stream and the trout's responses.

PERIOD	WATER TEMPERATURE RANGE	TROUT LOCATION	FEEDING ACTIVITY
January–February	33–38°F	Deepest, slowest pool, water, or deep spring holes	Very limited in amount and duration—early afternoon usually best
March–April*	38–45°F	Upper and lower portions of pool, spring mouths, or deep in runs	Midday—much more responsive to natural food activity
May*–June	45–55°F	Shallows of pools, upper portions of runs, and deep riffles and flats	All-day feeding activity
July–August	55–70°F	Riffles, spring mouths, tails of pools, shade line of runs and pools—at night, tails, flats, upper runs, and riffles	Best at twilight and night hours
September–October*	50–60°F	Throughout all areas	Mornings and afternoons
November*–December	38–45°F	Deep runs and heads of pools	Midday and afternoon to evening best

These periods are spawning times for mature wild fish. Rainbows, cutthroats, and goldens are generally spring spawners. Some domesticated rainbows and hybrid rainbows spawn in the fall. Brown trout, Dollys, brook and lake trout (char) are fall spawners. In each case, mature fish will spend from one to three weeks in upstream movements and spawning activities before resuming normal activities and feeding. During spawning some feeding occurs in the staging (mating) and spawning locations.

Water Color

Water clarity and color in both streams and lakes can be major keys to the existence and abundance of trout foods. Water color comes from the dissolved inorganic and organic chemicals, suspended particles, plus the color of the sky light and stream or lake bottom. By looking at the water I can usually tell many things about the condition of a stream or lake. Having the water's temperature and being able to evaluate its color condition will enhance your ability to read water. Here are a few useful observations on water color:

1. **Transparent with almost no color, clean pure water, very stable and level conditions:** flies, leaders, and tackle must be exacting; approach and presentation of flies must be careful.

2. **Clear with slight milky greenish-blue tint:** water is probably from limestone springs and probably very hard. Excellent fertility and growth rate of fish and foods. Probably lots of aquatic vegetation present. Excellent conditions for most fly-fishing.

3. **Clear with hazy-bright pea-green cast:** water is receiving agricultural runoff and is high in nitrates, phosphates, and organic compounds. Color comes from abundance of simple plants thriving on pollutants, and bottom rocks will be coated and slick from this algae growth. If not excessively polluted, water will remain fresh and cold and fishing will be fair to good.

4. **Transparent with a distinct amber (brown) cast:** color usually comes from decomposition of plant matters. However, this tannic acid could cause water to be infertile if pH is less than 7 (or on the acid side of the scale). This chemical evaluation of color can be inaccurate if ground waters contribute enough hardness to neutralize the acid or if the color source is from iron deposits. If aquatic vegetation is present, water will probably offer good fishing.

5. **Transparent with deep reddish-brown cast:** water is receiving large amounts of tannic acid or mineral iron. Trout and trout foods will be scarce.

6. **Milky grey-green:** common to areas that have excessive glacial runoff. Color is due to glacial silt and water is usually harmful or discouraging to trout and trout food due to excessive siltation.

7. **Milky brown:**
   a. if level is rising, color is due to erosion from snow, rain, or irrigation water; at such times, fishing is usually good with bait but poor with flies unless they emit noise or odor.
   b. if level is stable, then water is saturated with silt, probably from a regular source of pollution; it will most likely be poor habitat for trout and trout foods.
   c. if level is falling, then color is due to excessive erosion as a result of water fluctuation. If it seems to be clearing, fishing can be excellent, especially with large nymphs and streamers: trout usually are very unselective in low-visibility water to these larger, more vulnerable aquatic foods.

Even transparent or clear water always has *some* color because only distilled water is truly colorless. You can use this color to read the water's depth. By being aware of the water color at known depths as you fish—such as along the shoreline, knee deep, and waist deep—you can accurately determine the depth of all the water. Such trout-holding areas as pockets, ledge drop-offs, channels, depressions behind boulders, undercut banks, bars, and the like can be identified in size and shape just by the water-color changes they show.

Water color also helps me locate other sources of water such as springs or feeder streams. Where such waters meet the stream or lake they usually produce a ribbon of color change before they are completely mixed and diluted with the main body of water.

Very clear water requires more exacting flies, tackle, and methods because trout here use their sense of sight mostly. As water increases in color, trout use their eyesight less and their hearing and smelling sensors more. Methods and tackle can be more liberal, but your flies need to be large or noise-producing or even scented. Also, slow-fished flies are better in muddy, deep, or nighttime waters to give trout more time to find and strike them.

Overhead view of a trout stream. The increasing depth shades out the trout and bottom structures.

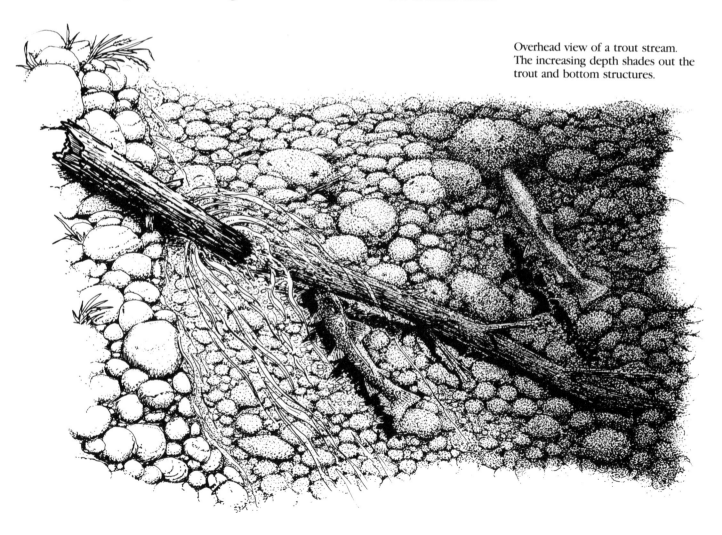

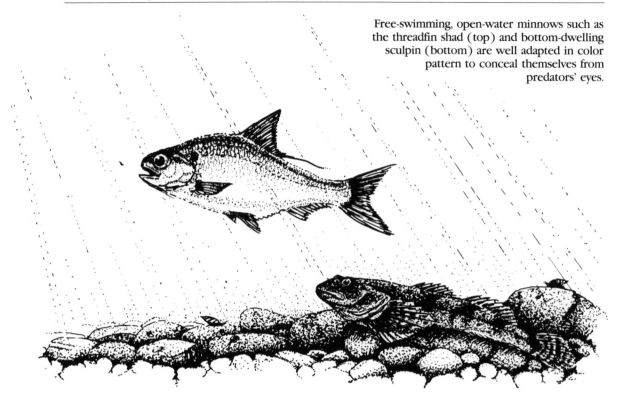

Free-swimming, open-water minnows such as the threadfin shad (top) and bottom-dwelling sculpin (bottom) are well adapted in color pattern to conceal themselves from predators' eyes.

In clear or transparent streams or lakes, the bottom structures have their own color plus that caused by such plant growth as green, red, and brown algae, or by mineral-deposit staining. Angles of the sun and shadows also tint or shade the water, creating strong contrasts. The trout and their foods camouflage themselves by assuming colors and patterns of colors to blend with this natural scheme. Suspended minnows and trout will be colored on their backs similar to the bottom color and water color. Their sides will reflect the water color and their undersides will be very light colored to blend with the lighted surface.

Other bottom creatures, such as aquatic insects, sculpins, and leeches, will take on more intricate bottom-color camouflage patterns. So, by looking at the water's color and the bottom, you have an absolute key to how your trout-food imitations should be colored.

In fly-tying, the use of colors exotic to the natural color schemes is common, but you should not confuse what they suggest. Most of the bright colors that naturally appear on spawning minnows, fish eggs, or on insects and crustaceans during certain metamorphic changes will be discussed in later chapters. Some colors are thus natural attractors and some will be entirely unnatural attractors. I've observed trout being put off by the use of the wrong colors on food imitations they are familiar with. A live scud, for example, is grey with either tan or olive casts; bright pink or orange, colors scud imitations are commonly tied and sold in, are its colors after it has been eaten by a trout and is dead and affected by the trout's digestive juices. If such an unnatural color works, it is because it serves as an attractor—not an imitation. Fish are extremely sensitive to natural colors and color patterns, and they react to high-contrast light-absorbent and light-reflective surfaces.

Water as an environment is as foreign to us as air is to trout. Yet a good angler must be able to relate to life beneath the surface almost as well as he relates to his own environment. Perhaps it is this mystical difference that makes fishing so interesting to so many people everywhere in the world.

I urge you to become a student of all water mechanisms in the streams and lakes you fish, for water is the most important primary element of the environment in which fish live.

3
HOW TROUT FEED

Trout, char, grayling, and landlocked salmon living in freshwater lakes or streams have specific physical characteristics that govern their feeding behavior. The fly tier and the fly fisherman must understand these in order to succeed in catching these fish with aquatic-food imitations. Trout live in an environment that few if any anglers understand completely; water drastically alters and handicaps our senses when we swim beneath the surface. How trout—whose senses are keyed for them to survive in water—

swim, see, smell, taste, hear, and feel relates directly to how they eat natural aquatic foods or accept artificial imitations. It is a great learning experience for trout fishermen to spend a few hours swimming underwater in both clear and murky trout lakes and streams. Such an adventure greatly heightens one's ability to understand trout and their unique environment.

Trout are not capable of mystical, magical, or highly intellectual reactions. They simply use their well-adapted senses in combinations that give them the best results for any given water and food situation. In murky water, for instance, their sight is greatly handicapped but they then exploit their acute senses of smell and hearing to locate food or escape danger.

Trout see, hear, feel, smell, and taste very well. Their bodies and senses are well designed to function efficiently within the limits of their environment. But one must not compare water with our far less restrictive air environment. Water is many times denser, thus greatly altering what can be sensed. Movement is also greatly affected due to increased density and the effect of water turbulence or motion.

Trout are well adapted to live in stillwaters and flowing waters with currents up to ten miles per hour. They can swim up to twenty miles per hour for short periods and maintain a five-mile-per-hour speed for many hours. Their compact shape and soft-rayed fins and tail enable them to move through the water efficiently. Even as they inhale the water through their mouth and expel it through their gill openings, they produce a jet action that moves them through the water. Their entire body and fins have mucous glands whose secretions greatly reduce water drag and guard against injury or infection.

A trout uses its dorsal fin and anal fin as vertical body stabilizers (or keels), as rudders, and to brake themselves. The pair of pectoral fins assists in ups-and-downs or planing movements, braking, backing up, and turning slightly. The paired pelvic fins are used to some extent as secondary planers, but they more consistently serve for balance and protection against the bottom when resting on or near it. The tail (caudal fin) is used mostly for propulsion but also as a rudder, for protection, and for digging. The entire body length behind the head is a series of muscles whose strength is directed into the tail. Being predators, trout have perfect body-fin-eye coordination with their well-developed and efficient mouths.

A trout can achieve a high peak of efficiency by becoming nearly weightless through use of its internal swim bladder (or air bladder). By adjusting its air pressure, a trout can float, reach neutral buoyancy, or, by becoming heavier than water, sink. Trout can make these minor adjustments as they swim, feed, rest, or even sleep. A trout sleeps by relaxing itself into a semiconscious state,

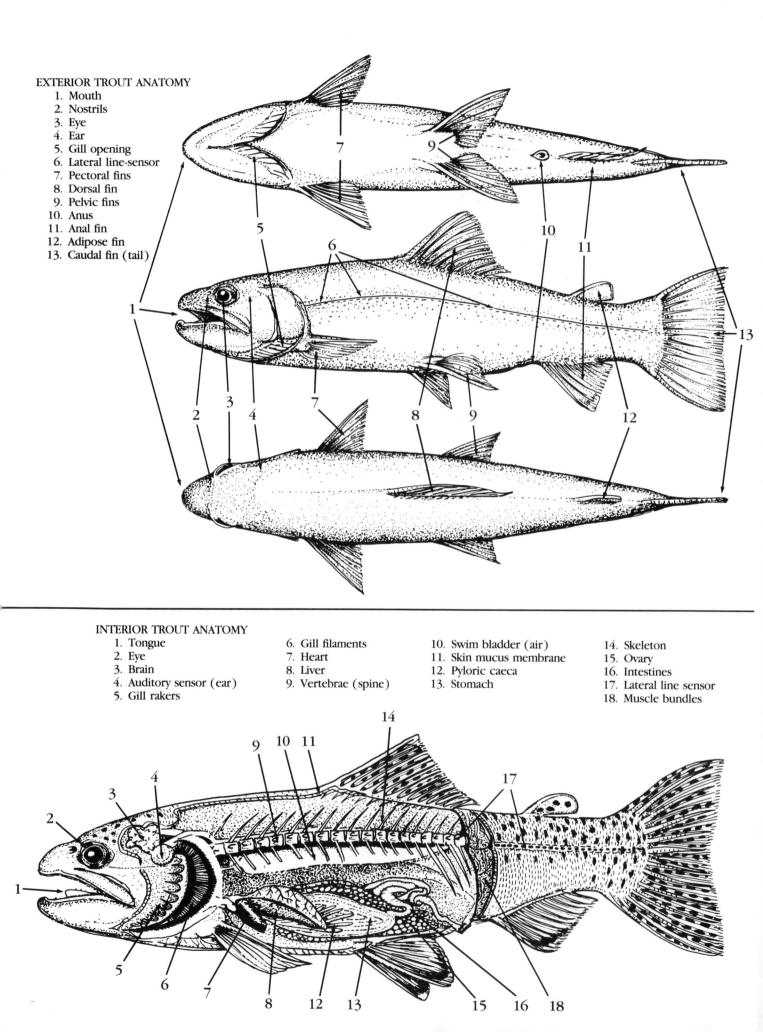

EXTERIOR TROUT ANATOMY
1. Mouth
2. Nostrils
3. Eye
4. Ear
5. Gill opening
6. Lateral line-sensor
7. Pectoral fins
8. Dorsal fin
9. Pelvic fins
10. Anus
11. Anal fin
12. Adipose fin
13. Caudal fin (tail)

INTERIOR TROUT ANATOMY

1. Tongue
2. Eye
3. Brain
4. Auditory sensor (ear)
5. Gill rakers

6. Gill filaments
7. Heart
8. Liver
9. Vertebrae (spine)

10. Swim bladder (air)
11. Skin mucus membrane
12. Pyloric caeca
13. Stomach

14. Skeleton
15. Ovary
16. Intestines
17. Lateral line sensor
18. Muscle bundles

still alert to external stimuli as well as maintaining its holding position with involuntary fin and body movement. Its eyes have no lids, so it does not appear to be asleep. Sleep periods can last just a few minutes to several hours.

In flowing waters, trout move up, down, or sideways by using the current's energy against their body and the attitude of their fins, just as you would control a glider in moving air. Minimal energy need be used. Study the diagram and movement vectors. It is easy to see the hydrodynamics of the trout's body.

In calmer waters such as sloughs, deep pools, ponds, and lakes, trout must provide most of their movement with muscular flexes of their fins and tail. However, it is well to remember that though they use a little more energy foraging and capturing food in calm waters, they do not use as much total energy as trout holding position against a constant flow. Trout of equal age and nutritional intake in lakes will consistently be heavier bodied than their stream counterparts; but a stream trout is usually a bit faster and has greater endurance.

Trout, like most other predator fish, are generally considered sight feeders, using their other senses to a lesser degree to capture their foods. They have excellent eyes with which to see their environment. The round lens of their eyes has a very short focal length; it can only be refocused by muscular movement closer to the retina. Trout cannot flatten the lens as we can on our eyes to obtain greatest total focal length; but they seldom need to see more than ten to fifteen feet away as water clarity in most places becomes greatly restricted past those distances. Water supports large amounts of dissolved minerals, chemicals, and particles and is a poor transmitter of light. So a trout's near-sighted vision is best adapted to its watery environment.

Trout have binocular (or stereo) vision directly in front of their heads at an approximate forty-five-degree angle, and monocular vision on each side of their head and body. Trout use binocular vision to see an object best with depth perception; monocular vision is best for detecting movement peripherally.

If the fly is on or in the water's surface a trout has a distorted view of it; this is caused by surface movement, refraction, reflection, and similar phenomena. If the fly is immediately beneath the surface film it comes *into full, clear, undistorted view of the trout's eyes* . . . a fact many anglers seldom realize as they view the same fly through the surface (which is highly distorted and reflective).

Trout see colors quite well but adapt slowly to drastic light changes or intensities. This is because the trout eye has a fixed iris that cannot adjust amounts of light the way the human eye can. The trout eye adjusts to light intensity by extending or with-

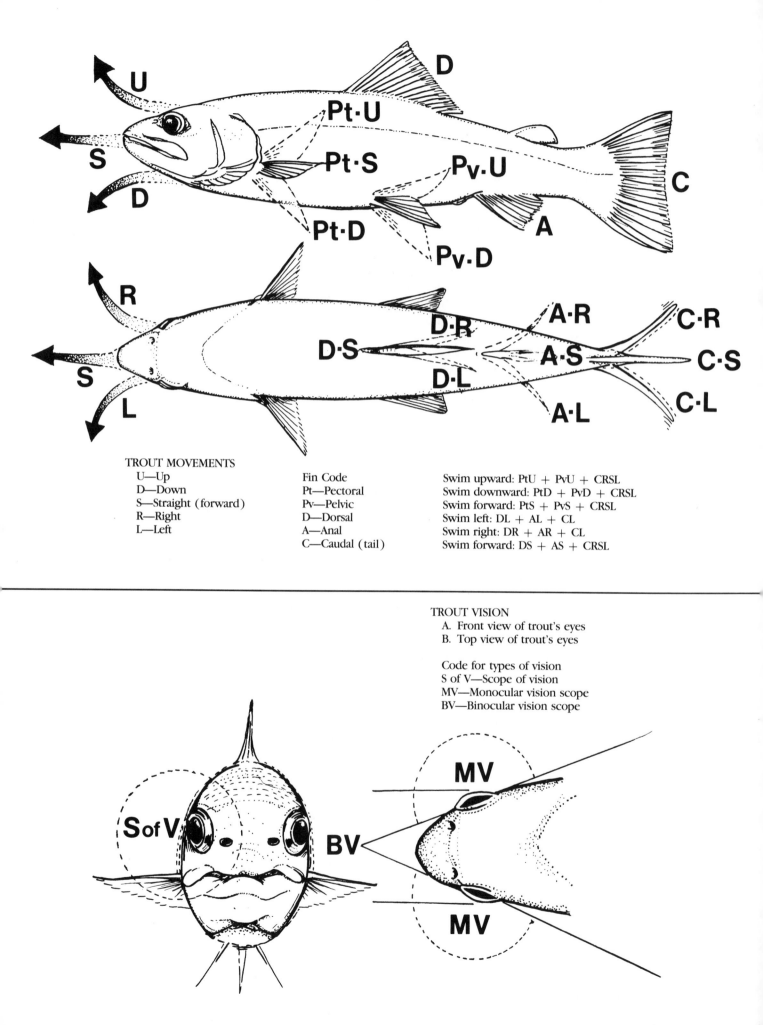

TROUT MOVEMENTS
U—Up
D—Down
S—Straight (forward)
R—Right
L—Left

Fin Code
Pt—Pectoral
Pv—Pelvic
D—Dorsal
A—Anal
C—Caudal (tail)

Swim upward: PtU + PvU + CRSL
Swim downward: PtD + PvD + CRSL
Swim forward: PtS + PvS + CRSL
Swim left: DL + AL + CL
Swim right: DR + AR + CL
Swim forward: DS + AS + CRSL

TROUT VISION
A. Front view of trout's eyes
B. Top view of trout's eyes

Code for types of vision
S of V—Scope of vision
MV—Monocular vision scope
BV—Binocular vision scope

drawing the rods and cones on the retina; this is a slow process. Bright lights, then, are least preferred. Trout will hold in deep water or in heavily shadowed areas when such light is present. It can take as long as two hours for them to become comfortable after a drastic light change has taken place.

In deep water or on the darkest nights, trout see poorly—both colors and low-contrast objects. In such situations they shift to their other senses to locate food.

A trout hears by two methods: two ears inside its head and its lateral-line sensors. Water, due to its greater density, transmits sound or pressure waves much faster and more efficiently than air. The inner ear is used to hear high-frequency vibrations (sounds). The lateral line senses low-frequency, close vibrations (pressure waves) most efficiently; it is more a true pressure sensor than a modified ear. Trout can usually tell the size, direction, and speed of a moving object up to twenty feet away with their lateral-line sensors. Beyond twenty to thirty feet, trout depend on their ears to hear with. Of course most of these high- or low-frequency sounds are identifiable by the trout and it reacts accordingly to what it detects . . . food or foe.

If an angler wades toward a trout, the trout hears the splashing of the water and the grinding of the boot soles against the bottom. It detects the pressure wave of water movement, the angler's size, speed, and direction beneath the water with its lateral-line sensor. An insect, minnow, mink, watersnake, or other creature is also sensed, identified, and reacted to in this way. A sleeping trout depends almost entirely on its lateral-line sensor; this is its first line of alarm detection. Danger or fleeing aquatic creatures can be quickly detected by the snoozing trout and it will awaken at

HEARING AND FEELING OF TROUT
LF—Low frequency sound waves (pressure) are picked up by trout's lateral line sensor
HF—High frequency sound waves (noise) are picked up by trout's ear

Movement of leg transmits LF through water; movement of shoe on rocks transmits HF through water.

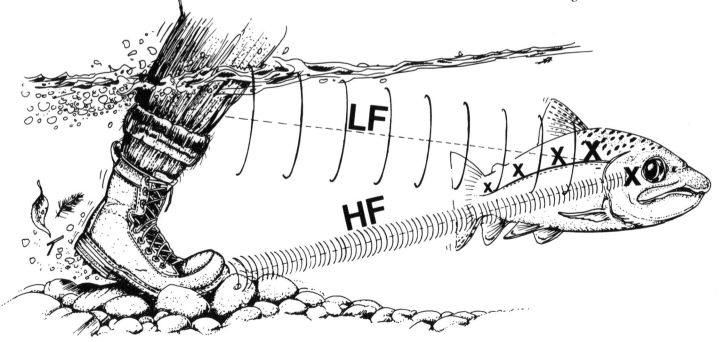

once. Trout can be aroused by noisy foods or lures, as well. The sounds of aquatic trout foods or other feeding trout often triggers a trout into feeding.

Trout have a highly developed double-nostril olfactory system. They can detect a wide range of smells in very low parts-per-million concentrations. The physical nature of water transports smell extremely well. Odor becomes crucial when a trout's sight is limited in detecting desired aquatic foods. I am convinced that odor is a close second to sight in determining trout-food choice.

Trout rely heavily on their sense of smell to confirm the edibility of any food object. All natural foods emit great amounts of odor. Dead or alive or artificial, the odor can be identified by a trout. Wild trout also recognize the unique scents put out by panic-stricken minnows, injured live foods, insects and crustaceans going through metamorphic skin changes, or by freshly laid eggs. Young or foolish trout or those under stress from food scarcity or high competition with other trout will abandon their smell sense, but most large wild trout use it religiously. I've seen many big browns and rainbows refuse a fly after smelling or tasting its tail. Cutthroat and brook trout have reputations for great gullibility; this may be due to their lack of concern for food odor.

It is well documented that all salmonids are put off by human or organic chemical odors that are foreign to their environment. A new fly reeking with head cement, Pliobond, varnish, paint, detergent, or dyes, as well as human hand scents might well cause trout to sneeze or cough and look elsewhere for a good mouthful. I'm sure the smell of a mink, snake, or heron has an equally traumatic effect on a wild trout.

The fly tier and fly fisher should give careful consideration to how his flies smell to a trout. Limiting offensive odors, washing flies carefully, masking such odors, or adding natural food odors will help you achieve optimum results. For example, when I fish subsurface imitations of aquatic food forms, I'll rub the fly with the bottom of a rock or a piece of vegetation taken from the stream. This not only helps eliminate offensive odors, but it also wets the fly to help it sink. There is no doubt that a fly so treated performs better than one that carries human or chemical scents.

A trout can taste and feel sensitively with its mouth as it strikes, inhales, and closes its mouth down on its food. I've often watched a trout mouth and expel an artificial fly unencumbered by leader or drag. I tossed the fly in the water to study the trout's reaction to its taste and feel. Hard flies, and those made of plastic or enameled materials, are ejected immediately. Flies constructed of soft materials, especially natural furs, feathers, or soft synthetics, are retained longer or sometimes swallowed. The texture of a natural food or artificial is critical in the flash of time the trout retains the captured food; this is especially true for the underwater, slow-fishing techniques such as nymphing.

As trout grow and mature they become greater masters of their physical abilities and senses, at least until old age overtakes them (usually between seven and nine years). From their earliest days, most trout prefer to collect or intercept their foods. If the supply of aquatic insects or other small, slow-swimming natural aquatic food is plentiful, they will continue to feed largely on them throughout their lives. However, these smaller foods usually become less practical for large adult fish to gather in adequate quantities. So they commonly turn to larger, more available foods, such as minnows, crayfish, amphibians, and small trout. But these live foods require much more active foraging than do the smaller food forms. Adult trout can swim faster; and they usually develop stronger and more heavily toothed jaws for seizing and killing their prey.

There is usually a practical order of large-food preferences after wild adult trout abandon the insects, scuds, and smaller creatures. This is predicated on food value versus ease of gathering. Such foods as leeches, tadpoles, crayfish, sculpin, school minnows, individual free-swimming minnows (chubs, whitefish, shiners, and others), and small trout are preferred in that general order. Bottom or deep-swimming large foods are greatly preferred over shallow-water or shallow-swimming foods, again because they are easier to find, flush, chase, and then kill and eat. The leech, crayfish, and sculpin are all extremely practical big-fish foods as each has little defense against the predator trout and dwells on or near the bottom.

The various species of trout, char, grayling, and salmon exhibit individual characteristics. The differences between wild-born trout, trout stocked as fry, and domesticated hatchery trout can be drastic also. Tame trout live by different conditioned reflexes and standards than do wild-born or stocked-as-fry fish. Knowledge of this can be of great value to the angler. For instance, brown trout and to a slightly lesser extent brook trout are twilight and night-time feeders. Both commonly "hole up" in the daytime under objects, in beds of aquatic vegetation, or on the bottoms of deep pools, pockets, or holes. They often sleep all day and stir only as the sun begins to set. Though this is not always so, it occurs commonly across their range during the warmer months.

Rainbows and cutthroats are classic daytime feeders. They prefer to suspend themselves off the bottom adjacent to cover but not beneath or in it unless danger is present. Often they flee from their enemies rather than hide from them. Even sleeping or resting they suspend off the bottom in relatively open areas and seldom allow any major objects to pass by unnoticed.

Thus it is easy to see why a rainbow would be considered easier to take on a fly than a brown on most days. It is swimming, wide awake, and ready when most of us are on the water. The brown isn't caught because it is deep, asleep, or waiting for darkness to feed. If you fished only at night you might well think browns more gullible or plentiful than the light-loving rainbows present in perhaps equal numbers in the same waters.

A domesticated or manmade "plastic" hatchery trout of either species is probably motivated to a frenzy of feeding by a man-set clock time and the sound of thousands of pea-sized pellets striking the water. This continues for *as long as a year* after these trout have been dumped in the water. I've taken a handful of small bits of gravel and cast it over the surface of a pool that contained stocked trout. In seconds, thirty or forty eight- to ten-inch, pellet-begging, grey-spotted forms would appear at the surface around my feet.

Such unusual environmental conditions as tailwater releases, snow runoffs, rains, droughts, storms, and temperature extremes can drastically alter trout feeding cycles. Major hatches or aquatic-food migrations can also throw normal cycles off. An alert fly fisher quickly recognizes these key changes and uses them to his advantage.

With these physical and sensory characteristics in mind let's look at several hypothetical situations to relate how a trout locates and takes its food.

Nymphing. There is a classic mayfly hatch on a clear trout stream. A nice wild rainbow trout is holding in two feet of water just below the riffle. It has adjusted its weight so it can suspend about eight inches off the bottom and is eagerly intercepting the rising nymphs. A weighted, soft-fur nymph is cast about fifteen feet above the working trout and sinks about

Nymphing rainbow

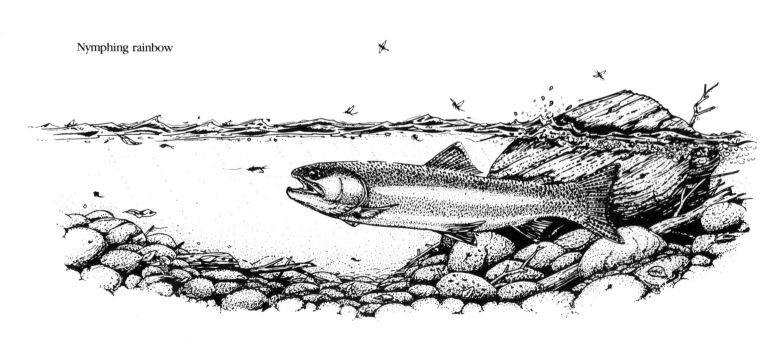

a foot before it drifts more or less straight downstream toward the waiting trout. The noise level of the dancing riffle masks its splashdown entry from the rainbow's ears. The trout senses the nymph's movement about four feet upstream and to its left with its sensitive peripheral vision. It turns toward the nymph using its dorsal and pelvic fins so it can see the nymph more clearly as it approaches. Interested now, it cocks its pectoral fins up and begins to drift back while rising upward to meet the nymph. As it intercepts the fly it watches, sniffs, and then opens its mouth to enhale the nymph. Once the nymph is captured, the pectoral-fin edges bend down and the trout begins a drifting dive back toward the bottom. Now it planes down and swims leisurely back to its holding position as it attempts to swallow the fake nymph.

In this case, the trout principally used its vision, smell, and touch senses and bodily movement to locate and capture the nymph.

A night-minnow-feeding brown trout. It is two hours after dark and there is no moon. A large brown trout is cruising around a big pool searching for its nightly prey of sculpins, crayfish, and large surface insects. The fly, a large, dark, deer-hair-head sculpin is cast across the tail of the pool. The brown hears the big streamer plop down and it stops, tenses, and becomes silent. Next the streamer is slowly stripped deep across the bottom, sometimes swimming, sometimes bouncing off rocks, aquatic vegetation, and sunken tree limbs. The brown detects from these movements the pressure waves and noises.

Night-feeding brown trout feeding on sculpin

Slowly at first, it begins to swim toward the fly. The closer it gets the more it accurately interprets the fly's distance, size, and speed with its lateral-line sensor. About two feet away, the brown sees the fly's outline and surges to it for the kill. The sense of touch is next used as the brown strikes the sculpin with stunning closed-jaw blows. Something is drastically wrong! It does not give off a characteristic panic odor, blood smell, or injured vibrations. It has a horrible unnatural odor. So the brown follows the streamer, smelling its wake for several yards, then turns and swims away, seeking another, more realistic prey.

In this case, darkness restricted the trout's distance vision so it used its ears and lateral-line sensor to detect and locate its prey. But its senses of sight and touch and smell were all used in the final decision to strike but not to eat the object.

A murky, cold, rain-swollen brook-trout stream. The thirty-foot-wide stream has risen a foot only a few hours after a cold, early-spring rain. Its water temperature has risen from forty-six to fifty degrees and has put a fine brook trout on the feed. The brook can barely see six inches clearly, so it holds deep in a pocket under a steep, rooty cutbank just below the riffle of its home pool, listening and sniffing the stream's flow.

The fly fisherman casts a very large, black, marabou-winged, weighted Muddler on a short leader and a High-Density sinking-tip line twenty feet above the brook's lair. The big fly splats down on the water, and the trout is alerted as it picks up the entry sound with its ear. The fly sinks rapidly, dragging as it begins to swing across the stream and approach the trout. The Muddler's blunt, bulky deer-hair head and wiggling marabou wing sets up a series of low-frequency pressure waves as it moves across the current.

The brook trout picks up this movement with its lateral-line sensor, identifies its general size and speed, and moves to its left to intercept the still unseen object. The waving black wing suddenly comes into view as a silhouette and its Mylar body glints, presenting a form of vulnerable life. The brook charges with a strong tail thrust to seize the fleeing form. The scent trail of the wet, well-used streamer is that of natural origin, given to it by several previous catches of chub and trout; this masks the initial man-given odors of tying, finishing, and handling. The strike is sure and violent and the streamer crushes under the trout's bite, further confirming its reality.

In this case, the trout stationed itself safely and quietly in a deep, calm, protected area and turned on its ears and nose. The

Brook trout feeding in a murky
rising stream

streamer was heard, felt, seen, and smelled in that order before
the strike came. If the fly had been slender, small, light-colored,
and dead-drifting, it would have gone unnoticed.

As you can see in these three simple examples, trout use various combinations of their body attributes and senses to find,
identify, and take or reject possible food. A consistently productive fly fisher will understand these things and choose his fly designs and fish them accordingly. Knowledge of a trout's senses,
the water's environmental condition, and reading the water are,
therefore, the three keys to fishing the right artificial.

With all the keenly honed natural instincts and senses a wild
trout possesses, you might feel catching them on imitations is an
almost impossible task. Actually, the opposite is true. Wild trout
are not difficult to catch on flies if your flies, tackle, and methods
are chosen with proper understanding of the situation. Realize
your mistakes as you observe a trout's reaction to your attempts
to catch them: are they not biting, is it too hot or cold, not there,
frightened, selective, or just not interested in your offering for another reason? Fly refusal or acceptance is explainable if you understand the fish. Ignorance of basic facts can handicap you for
years, while knowledge of them can and will accelerate your success and pleasure as a fisherman.

4
MAYFLIES
Ephemeroptera

Mayflies are the best known and most popular of all trout foods. These graceful, lovely, highly visible, harmless insects create the very essence of fly-fishing's image: to match with delicate floating flies the hatch to which trout are rising. The beautiful, sail-winged, slender, curving-bodied insects float by the angler or rise in flight to reach a nearby willow bough.

Since the beginnings of the sport of fly-fishing for trout, these aquatic insects have received more attention in fly-fishing literature, lectures, art, films, photography, and fly-tying than all the rest of the trout foods imitated by the artificial fly. Few of us challenge the mayfly's role as the cornerstone of modern fly-fishing for trout, even though its place and importance today compared to other trout foods is not as significant as it once was. Yet over the last decade, when information about the mayfly must surely have doubled all past attention, I have found that far less than ten percent of all trout fly fishers have enough working knowledge of this insect to identify, match, and fish it successfully when trout are feeding on its various life stages.

This is because all aspects of fly-fishing have traditionally suffered from far too much complication spawned by "experts" using their hard-earned knowledge to bewilder and discourage (if not consciously) the newcomer. Unpronounceable Latin nomenclature, confusing biological terms, and irrelevant facts from chemistry and biology turned me and many other fly fishers off to the simple, beautiful, interesting, and important *basic* facts about playing fly-fishing's finest game: to recognize, match, and fish trout foods as close to nature as our artificial means and personal abilities allow.

Because the arts of fly-fishing are my profession, I forced myself to learn these subjects. But I have decided to do my best to see that others will not have to endure the pain to know the pleasure of the sport.

The aquatic-insect order we commonly call mayflies is scientifically termed Ephemeroptera, which simply means it is a "short-lived, winged insect, enduring but a day." Adult mayflies seldom live more than twenty-four to forty-eight hours, depending upon species and weather. However, mayflies have four life stages—the egg, aquatic-nymph, and air-breathing adult stages of subimago (dun) and imago (spinner); the cycle takes one year for most mayfly species.

The egg stage, which lasts days to a couple of weeks, is unimportant to fish and fishermen. Regardless of whether the life cycle is composed of several generations per year or a generation once every year or two, the nymphal period is the most significant for both the trout and the fly fisher.

In the nymph stage, the insect is aquatic—breathing, dwelling, and feeding below the water's surface. During most of this period, the nymph's importance to the trout we are interested in catching is nominal; nymphs will at this time be too small to interest such fish and too small for us to imitate their size and action effectively. As the nymphs feed on live and dead simple plants, they develop body structure and grow. Because their rigid outer skin, which serves as their structural skeleton, limits inner growth and the development of shape, they must shed these hard skin-skeletons periodically. The nymph accomplishes this molting by first splitting its skin down the top of its body. It then frees itself from the skin by pushing itself out—thorax first, with head, abdomen and legs following. The nymph is very soft, feeble, vulnerable, almost colorless for several hours to a day before the new exoskeleton (or skin-skeleton) forms and pigments. The times between skin molts are called "instars."

Instar periods are common to other aquatic insects and to the crustaceans. The process by which these organisms accomplish growth in the immature stages is fascinating. After the organism sheds its exoskeleton, it ingests water and swells its body. A new exoskeleton is secreted from its epidermal cuticular membrane, which hardens over the entire body and appendages of the swollen insect or crustacean. Once the hardening takes place, the organism dehydrates, thus becomes smaller, and gives itself room to grow within its new exoskeleton. When this space is filled, a new instar period begins with another shedding of the exoskeleton. During the period of time which the organism is without a hard, protective, camouflaged exoskeleton it is quite vulnerable to trout, and the fly tier can imitate this instar by choosing the appropriate materials and colors for his patterns. Trout often prefer the fresh instar over the forms with hard skins.

As the nymphs grow to one-eighth inch (3-3.4mm), they become increasingly important as trout food and begin to "fit" our means of tying and fishing their imitations. At this age-size stage, the mayfly nymph's body structure gives it a characteristic appearance that can be used to identify the insect; and in turn, we can now imitate it with an artificial nymph design. These exterior anatomical structures are used to identify the order as well as the different families that are uniquely shaped and live in specific areas of streams and lakes. These important basic structures are:

1. three major body regions—head, thorax (midsection), and abdomen
2. six legs with one sharp claw on each foot
3. three tails (in most)
4. two short antennae on front of head
5. one visible pair of wingpads on top of thorax
6. gills on top and sides of abdomen
7. abdomens have ten segments

Four major body designs reflect the adaptation these insects

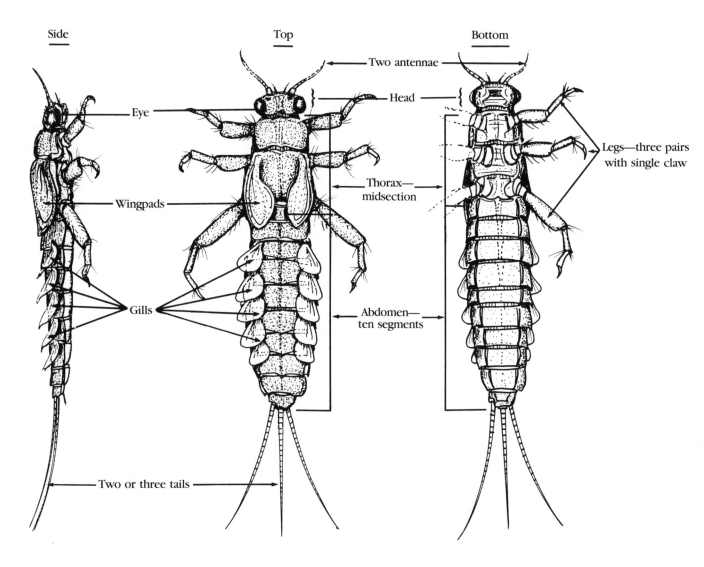

Side   Top   Bottom

Two antennae

Eye

Head

Wingpads

Thorax—
midsection

Gills

Legs—three pairs
with single claw

Abdomen—
ten segments

Two or three tails

ANATOMY OF MAYFLY NYMPH

have undergone to best fit the areas in which they live. There are
crawlers, clingers, burrowers, and swimmers. These nymph types
have made it possible for nymphs to breathe, feed, and reside in
the particular areas of streams and lakes we have discussed in the
chapter on water. The study of these types is extremely interesting; each serves as an important guide for shaping appropriate artificial nymphs and where and how they should be fished. As the
mayfly nymph grows and matures in its preferred water environment, it uses its shape, coloration, particular mobility, and bottom

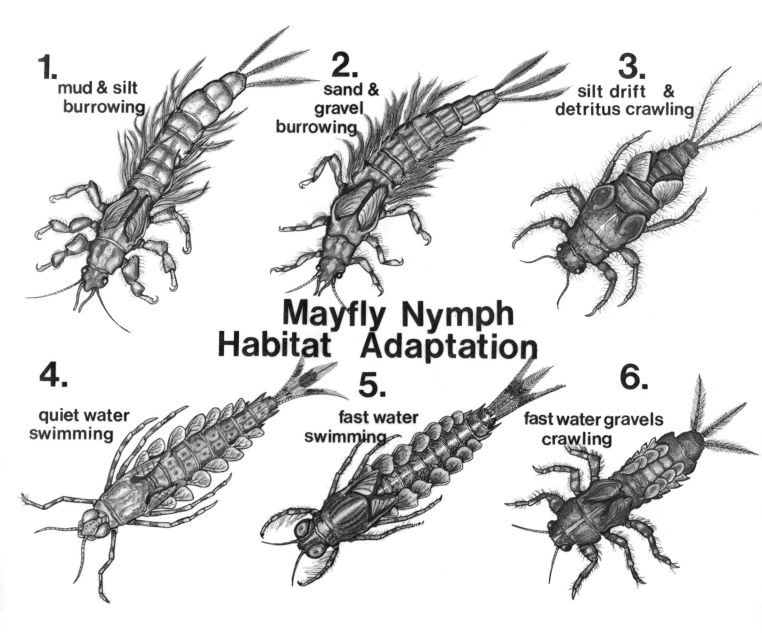

1. mud & silt burrowing

2. sand & gravel burrowing

3. silt drift & detritus crawling

Mayfly Nymph
Habitat Adaptation

4. quiet water swimming

5. fast water swimming

6. fast water gravels crawling

covers to avoid or escape such predators as trout.

When I began to try to learn about mayfly nymphs I was totally confused and discouraged by the seemingly endless shapes, sizes, colors, actions, and species names—common or Latin. After years of hot and cold study, I finally developed a simple perspective on these nymphs that serves me exceedingly well. This system is based on suggestion (or simulation), not the impossible exact-imitation method.

I use three major body shapes to span the full range of mayfly nymphs, a few natural color patterns, a hook-size range bracketing the maturing nymph's length, and body textures that simulate

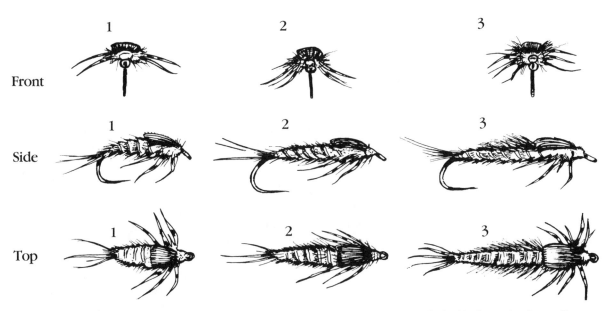

Front

1 2 3

Side

1 2 3

Top

1 2 3

those of live nymphs. I fish these to act like particular resident mayfly nymphs to complete this system.

My system works extremely well because all the imperfections are accounted for. That is, no two natural nymphs are exactly alike and no two trout react the same way; so these special artificial nymphs, fished imperfectly to near perfection by us, allows for error, which is important because we never know exactly what is in the mind or seen by the eye or smelled by the nose of the trout. This approach works as well or better than any other I know of today, and it is beautifully simple and easy for all of us to use despite our experience, knowledge, or skill at the tying vise or at fishing the nymph. Then, as our experience and fishing success builds, we learn more specifics about species and their exact habits, life cycles, emerger actions, and anatomy. I now enjoy learning about a specie if it is important to the stream or lake I will be fishing. But this has come only after development of a general working knowledge of each order of aquatic insects.

The third and most dramatic stage of the mayfly life cycle begins when the aquatic nymph reaches its maximum growth and age. The nymph has now developed all the body mechanisms it needs to transfer it from aquatic to terrestrial life, or from a water-breathing nymph to an air-breathing dun. I still class this process as a natural miracle.

The mature nymph exposes itself from its natural cover and begins to swim toward the surface. This upward movement is seldom completed on the first tries, and appears almost to be a ritual dancelike swim. When the time is right, the angular rise movement causes the nymph to reach the surface film almost without effort and, as in other nymphal skin molts, it leaves aquatic life by crawling out of the nymphal skin and unfolding into a delicate, upright-winged, surface-floating, air-breathing insect. It uses a back-arching motion to push up through and out of the nymphal

Whitlock's three simple mayfly nymph shapes
1. Short (1X to 4X short hook)
2. Medium (1X to 2X long hook)
3. Long (3X to 6X long hook)

skin. The wings, prothorax, and head break free first. Initially, the wings appear to swell into a light-colored clump or bubble, which the insect then rapidly unfolds in an accordionlike expansion, using internal gases or fluids to inflate an intricate system of hollow vein-like tubes within each wing. Once this is accomplished they air harden or dry, becoming rigid supports for the delicate wing membrane. The nymph then uses its legs to push on the surface film, which holds the nymphal skin, to pull and push itself free much like a person would extract himself from a sleeping bag. The newly emerged dun is water repellent and sits on the surface as if the surface were a thick shiny film of vinyl plastic. Its gills are now replaced by a tracheal tube diffusion network in its abdomen. As its skin and wings dry and harden in the air, it begins to flutter over the surface, escaping the last vestige of its aquatic life—the nymphal skin. It is now a dun, or subimago. Within seconds, or perhaps as long as a minute or two, the dun begins to flutter off the surface, soon obtaining flight. It then heads for the nearest waterside trees or weeds. The dun lights there, secluding itself as best it can in these foliage covers. If such cover is not available, it will hide in the streamside grass or rocks, or continue to fly until a suitable hiding place is found; which may be as much as a quarter of a mile or farther from its emergence point.

Once this transformation takes place, the dun flies off the water and is of little or no consequence to the trout and fly fisher until the last phase of the next, or fourth stage, of the mayfly's life cycle. But during the nymphal emergence and surface transformation, the mayfly is most attractive and vulnerable to the trout. It is this hatch period that sets up the most dramatic situation and classic opportunity to enjoy catching trout with subsurface and surface aquatic-insect imitations.

From the moment that the mature mayfly nymph makes its practice swims toward the surface until the dun's flight, the trout assume classic feeding positions to seize these delectable live morsels; they collect dozens to hundreds during the progression of a single hatch period. But there are key situations to which the fly-fishing hatch matcher should relate his fly designs and methods if he is to enjoy the full opportunity of each rise.

It has finally been established and accepted by most fly fishers that fishing the nymph in several fly designs and methods is the best method for hooking the greatest number of the largest and most selective of the hatch-feeding trout. Traditional fly-fishing snobbery put subsurface flies on the same plane as bait. Such is not the case. Fishing the nymph is as much if not more sophisticated and complex a technique as the floating-fly techniques once touted by the dry-fly purists.

Mayfly dun, side and front views

The deep-fished nymph, the rising or swimming nymph, and finally the surface-film, floating, nymph-emerger present the most challenging and deadliest methods of fishing the hatch. On most hatches I've fished, ten to fifteen nymphs are usually consumed to every winged dun. Trout stomach samples verified this.

Yet I do not want to downplay or ignore the dun. Fishing the visible, floating dun to rising trout is certainly the most classic and exciting experience in fly-fishing for trout. Trout often follow the nymphs to the surface and suck them in out of the surface film just before or during transformation to the free dun. Such visible surface-feeding easily misleads us into thinking the trout are concentrating on duns. If one uses dun imitations at such times the trouts' response may be so poor one is further misled that there is something wrong with the pattern, size, or technique. Wasted time and frustration will follow, accompanied by mediocre, if any, catches.

There are times when trout will show less preference for nymphs over the duns, but these occasions are usually characterized by smaller fish or occur at the last stages of the hatch when only the crippled or imperfect duns are trapped on the surface and there is little else for the trout to choose from.

Fishing the dun should be considered a "calculated-handicap" game and you should understand the game and be willing to play it against the fish. You must be ready to handle more rejection than acceptance when working over selective trout. There are times when I love to play this game, picking a good fish and using all my knowledge, ability, and wit to trick it into accepting my dun imitation over the live duns and juicy, wiggling subsurface nymphs. When a true surface rise and bubbles replace my upright dun, there is a sweet feeling that has no rival for me in fly-fishing—each time it is repeated the thrill is as satisfying and more exciting than the time before.

The fourth stage of the mayfly's life cycle is commonly known among fly fishers as the spinner; biologically, it is the imago stage. It usually begins shortly after the dun retires to the protective covers adjacent to the hatching site. Within a few hours or as long as twenty-four to forty-eight hours, the final development of reproductive organs, eggs, and sperm products takes place.

Like the nymphal molt, the dun—holding firmly to a rigid surface—splits its skin and the spinner escapes the final restrictive skin sheath of body, legs, and wings. This seldom-seen and intricate process is another miracle. In fact, the mayfly is said to be the only insect that molts its skin after development of functional adult wings.

The spinner retains the general shape and proportions of the dun, but the male and female display more exaggerated sex char-

Adult mayfly spinners
   A. Adult at rest
   B. Male in flight
   C. Female laying eggs

acteristics. Their saillike wings elongate and become more hya-line, usually glassy, and nearly colorless except for supporting vein structures. The spinner's body is usually more vividly colored and clearly marked than that of the dun. Males and females of the same species will often have different color patterns. Males are usually one-half to one full hook size smaller than the females. The male's abdomen will be somewhat thinner than the egg-laden female's. His legs, especially the front pair, will be much longer and his compound eyes larger. Tails of the male will be almost twice as long as they were in the dun stage.

Once the dun-to-spinner transformation is complete and suitable conditions of light, temperature, and time occur (usually within twenty-four hours of the time the dun hatched) the male spinners fly boldly from their hiding covers. They assemble in numbers adjacent to or over the water. Here they engage in a prenuptial dancing flight; this dance has a fascinating rhythm—frantic, disorganized, up and down. The egg-laden females join them a short time later and each is soon caught, held, and mated in midair by a male. When the female is released, she quickly begins to lay her eggs on or below the water's surface. Females of some species dip and skip, some light, and some actually dive into or below the surface to deposit their eggs.

This mating and egg-laying exhausts both sexes and they soon light on or fall to the water's surface or land to die. This is called a spinner fall and it gives trout their third major opportunity to prey upon mayflies. As the spinners flutter low over the surface, dip in or below it, light or fall onto it, and finally in death are trapped on or sink below the surface, the trout respond accordingly. This gives the alert spinner-fall fly fisher a rewarding opportunity to match the mayflies in these positions with surface, surface-film, and subsurface spinner imitations.

Spinner-fall fishing is perhaps the most exacting and least predictable or dependable fishing of the mayfly's life cycle. This is because even with the most reliable daytime spinner mating swarms and falls, nature is extremely fickle in how, where, and when she brings the flies down. Even the trout seem at times perplexed with this timing and will let a good fall of flies float past without seriously rising to the occasion!

Before I began to understand spinner falls and trout feeding to them, I regularly misinterpreted what was going on and would use flies and techniques that did not work. I put fish down or only caught a few subpar trout on my nymphs, duns, or adult caddis. Now, with a better understanding of spinner falls and the trout's responses to them, I can interpret and enjoy this fourth stage of fishing the mayfly.

Nymph, dun, spinner—each may play an important role in providing trout food. These three stages naturally vary in size, shape, color, action, and age for each specie or family. Studying the differences between the three or four hundred species is impractical and unnecessary to the fly fisher who simply wants to fish mayfly imitations for trout. Each year on the same or different waters there are only a few significant species that are important to imitate and fish.

I was pleasantly surprised and relieved to learn that many mayfly species overlap each other in their size, color pattern, shape, action, and life cycles. If one *objectively observes* the mayflies present in the water where he fishes he need *not* identify one specie as to its name—though once you are familiar with particular unknown species you will see reason and interest in their names.

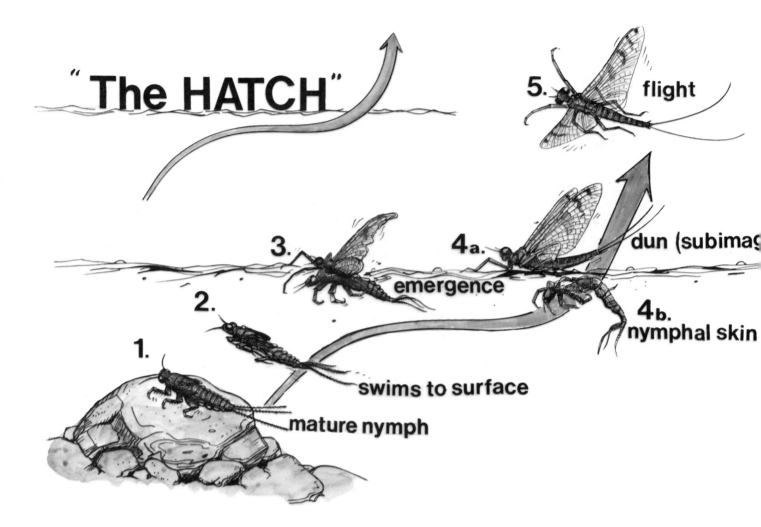

"The HATCH"

1. mature nymph

2. swims to surface

3. emergence

4a. dun (subimag[o]

4b. nymphal skin

5. flight

Identifying, Matching, and Fishing the Mayfly

The nymph. Mayfly nymphs have efficient gill-breathing systems that enable them to live in streams or lakes in which trout reside. The insect displays quite a wide range of habitat adaptation, and this is clearly reflected in its body, leg, and gill anatomy. Using bare hands and a small aquarium hand net or seine, it is a rather simple, pleasant, and interesting task to catch mayfly-nymph specimens as well as many other trout foods. In fact, the capture and study of all trout foods can be as much fun as catching trout on the imitations—and a lot easier to do! In lakes or streams at normal levels you will find most specimens near, on, or in the bottom in relatively shallow water. Mayfly nymphs are the most adaptable of the major aquatic insects trout feed upon. Therefore, you will find various species in rubble, gravel, sand, mud, silt, aquatic plant beds, and swimming freely.

Simple observation of specimens will tell you their size, color, shape, living mode, and location in the stream. Closer observation with 4X magnification can help identify them as to family and species if you wish to go that far. Many times I will carefully release individually captured nymphs and watch to see if and how they return to the bottom. This can tell you a great deal about how to fish the imitation nymph correctly.

The dun. The dun stage of the mayfly is first observed floating in or on top of the water's surface film. The upright, saillike wings are a dead giveaway. Use a small, nylon-mesh net and dip up these floating specimens. Bare hands or closed-end containers such as cups or cans won't work since surface film and movement will force the insect away from you. A small, plastic box with the bottom replaced with screen wire and the lid removed works beautifully to capture and cage a lively insect off the water.

To capture the nymph before or as it hatches into the dun, you must hold the small or large aquarium net (two-by-three or six-by-ten inch) below the surface for several minutes in the same area you see the duns floating. Usually within a reasonable time

Mayfly dun on surface just after "hatching" from nymphal skin

several emergers will be trapped. Fast observation or quickly chilling the emergers in ice will allow you to see this stage before the dun pops its wings and body from the nymphal skin.

When you catch these insects, *objectively observe* and *measure their body lengths and wing, tail, and leg proportions. This is the size information that is undoubtedly the most important factor to matching the nymph, dun, or spinner. Don't trust your eye; it is seldom objective or accurate enough. Write the measurements down in a small notebook. Consult these size, shape, and color charts when choosing or tying imitations.*

Once the dun flies off the water it can be captured with an aquarium hand net or butterfly net, but this is a bit more difficult. The duns usually light and hide in the shoreline foliage and can be shaken out and captured in midair or on the water with the same net. Sometimes they can be observed or caught at night around or near the water with an electric light or gasoline lantern used to attract them. Even spider webs will provide an opportunity to see what is hatching.

The spinner. Before they come to the water to lay eggs or fall, spinners are strong, fast, wild insects and it takes a butterfly net to capture them effectively from the mating swarms. A simple fly swatter will work to knock them to the water or ground if you aren't concerned with study of the live insect. Before and during this period, spinners are also attracted to strong night lights or captured in spiderwebs like the dun. Once the flies are on the water an aquarium net is adequate for dipping them up for observation and identification.

As you try to catch on-the-water spinners, watch them first to see their activity and position. Then relate this to the feeding ac-

Adult mayfly—imitations
proportions
   N—Natural
   I—Imitation
   B—Body length
   Ww—Wing width
   Wh—Wing height
   T—Tail length
   BN=BI, WwN=WwI, etc.

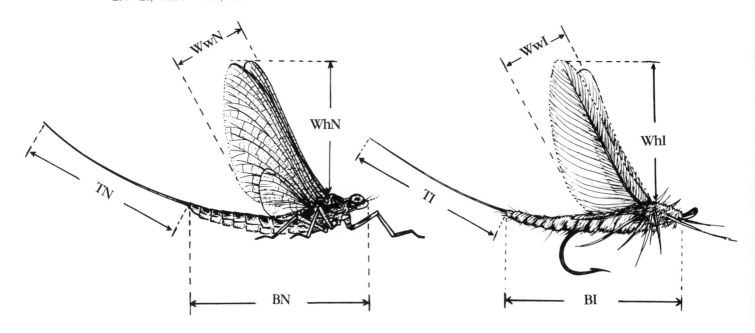

tivity of the trout that are rising to eat them. If the rises are splashy or leaping, the spinners are probably fluttering on the water, either egg-laying or just beginning to fall. Head-and-tail rises that leave a bubble behind indicate the spinners have begun to weaken and flatten on the surface. Slow back-fin and tail rises or just small rings indicate the spinners are well down, dead, or even beginning to sink into or below the surface film. Very large trout feeding on daylight spinner falls usually only respond to the last stages described and make very small, quiet, visible riseforms, if any. Some large spinner eaters I've encountered suspend themselves and just suck down the insects with almost none of the head-and-body motion we commonly call "rising."

The spinners will be upright, fluttering, spent and live, or spent and dead. Try to identify if they are males or females and the percentage of each. Trout will feed selectively according to the percentage, size, and color of these male-female differences. It sounds complicated but it's not—just as long as you deal in the general terms of size, shape, and color.

A Typical Mayfly Life Cycle

1. The mayfly spinner (imago) female deposits eggs on or below the surface.

2. Mayfly eggs sink and stick to lake or stream bottom structures. They will hatch into tiny nymphs within a few days to two weeks.

3. Nymphs distribute and locate themselves according to the particular water and bottom environment they are best adapted for. Feeding on various live and dead plants, the nymphs spend the major portion of their life cycle in these areas. The nymphs are only displaced from these areas by such water fluctuations as flood, drought, or such poor environmental water quality as low oxygen content and high temperature. During their metamorphic skin changes the nymphs might also be subject to dislocation until their skins are again hardened.
   a. The crawlers, clingers, and swimmers live in areas of rock, rubble, coarse gravel, and aquatic vegetation of stream and lake bottoms.
   b. Crawlers also live in slow or sluggish areas of lakes and streams that have small gravel, accumulations of dead aquatic and terrestrial vegetation, and silty areas.
   c. Burrowers dig into the lake and stream bottoms, where U-shaped burrows in sand, silt, and mud areas are their homes until the hatch begins.

4. The first stage of the hatch begins when the fully mature nymph exposes itself to swim or float to the surface for conversion into the dun. Nymphs are most vulnerable to the trout when they rise from the bottom to the surface film.

5. The second stage of emergence occurs when the nymph moves up to the surface film and splits its nymphal skin down its back. Just before or when it reaches the surface film the dun begins to leave its nymphal body and emerges into the air-breathing winged dun. Wings, thorax, head, legs, and abdomen usually come free in that order as the nymphal shuck serves as a final platform stuck in the surface film to launch the new dun into its airborne life. This process takes only seconds to a long minute or so to complete unless the mature nymph is deformed or injured. Then it may well struggle endlessly to escape the nymphal husk and hold of the surface film. Such dilemmas usually result in incomplete emergence. (Carl Richards recognized and first called these defectives "stillborn duns;" and he also recognized this moment as a major feeding opportunity for the trout and an overlooked area for new fly-pattern design.)

   Most mayfly species hatch over a one-to-three-week period once a year. Some of the smaller mayflies, especially on such near-constant-temperature waters as spring creeks, may have multiple generations that hatch almost every ideal day throughout a general season.

6. After the floating surface dun (subimago) escapes its nymphal skin, air quickly hardens its body skin and wing membranes. It often flutters its wings and begins a skipping, fluttering sequence prior to takeoff. Surface crosswinds also affect its action by moving the mayfly like a small sailboat. Very cold air will chill newborn duns and delay their takeoff for extended lengths of time. Some become so cold they do not obtain flight, and eventually drown or wash ashore. When the dun's first flight is accomplished it is directly to such shoreline foliage as weeds, bushes, and overhanging trees.

7. The dun conceals itself on branches or beneath leaves and sits quietly for twelve to twenty-four hours awaiting the right weather conditions and temperature to begin its final transformation.

8. The dun, like the adult nymph, sheds its skin and also the wing's outer membrane to emerge into its final stage as the spinner (imago). This transformation in most species usually takes place where the dun first concealed itself. However, a few of the smaller mayflies transform from duns into spinners on the first initial flight from the water.

Mayfly life cycle

9. The sexually developed male spinners form a mating swarm near or above the water that harbors the mature nymphs. Females join them and are caught and mated by the males in midair. This spinner flight and mating usually extends over a one-to-three-hour period and is typically timed twenty to twenty-four hours after the duns hatch.

10. The female spinners deposit their eggs on or below the surface. This takes several minutes to half an hour. Some light on or dive beneath the water, but most quickly dip and skip

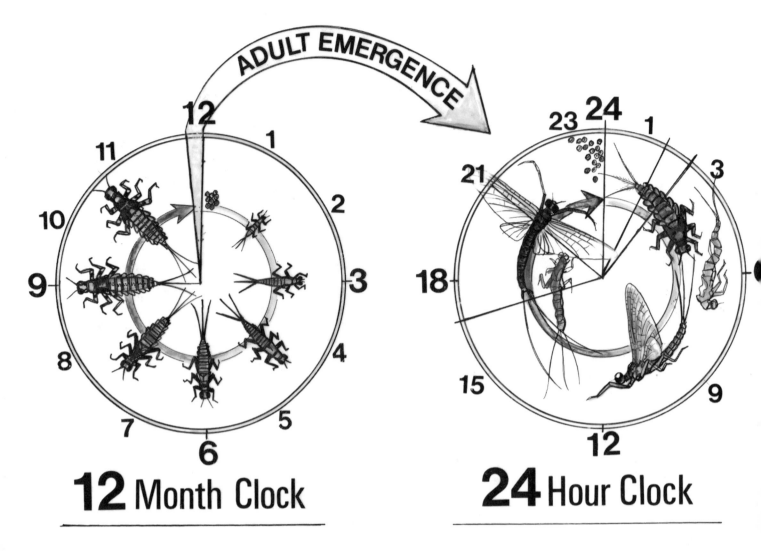

ADULT EMERGENCE

12 Month Clock

24 Hour Clock

over the surface to distribute their eggs and to avoid capture by fish and airborne predators.

11. Once the females and males accomplish mating and egg-laying, they quickly become exhausted and fall over the water or the adjacent shoreline. Soon they die.

12. The mayfly eggs sink and incubate in areas that the mature nymph emerged from just hours before. Eventually they will hatch into the next generation of mayflies. Thus they complete the four-stage life cycle of egg to nymph to dun to spinner.

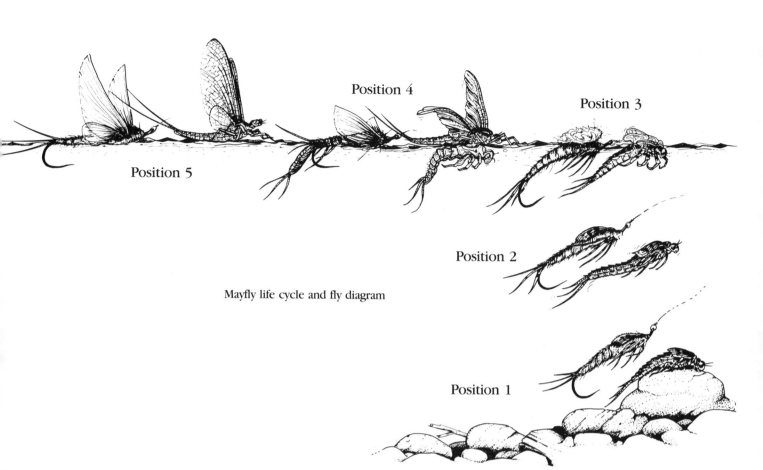

Mayfly life cycle and fly diagram

Position 5

Position 4

Position 3

Position 2

Position 1

1. Mature mayfly nymph

2. Mature emerging nymph

3. Floating-hatching nymph

4. Advanced emerger or stillborn dun

5. The dun

My Favorite Mayfly Fly Designs

All my nymph designs reflect my suggestive imitation philosophy. All are tied with soft, water-absorbent materials that have as much action and natural nymph texture as possible. I cannot stress the importance of this too much. These designs are to be tied *simply;* they are *suggestive,* with much more consideration given to size, texture, and action than to exacting appendages and color perfection. A simple nymph made merely of a grey muskrat-fur body, with no other detail, is ten times more effective than the more sophisticated "eyeball, elbow, and arsehole" museum works of art some fly tiers endorse!

The Nymph

I use four basic nymph designs to imitate the different stages of the mayfly nymph's development: the mature nymph, the mature emerging nymph, the floating-hatching nymph, and the advanced emerging nymph.

MATURE MAYFLY NYMPH (NO. 1 POSITION)

This fly is to be fished as a nymph in the pre-emergent stage and not as one in the final emergence sequence. I try either to match the general color scheme and tone or make the nymph one or two tones lighter in color to suggest the more succulent, soft, helpless nymph during the molt period.

1. **HOOK:** regular or extra-fine wire, turned-up or ring eye preferable
   a. shank weighted on one-third its length with turns of lead wire; lead wire should be equal in diameter to hook wire
   b. clinger: 1XS or regular-length shank
   c. crawler: 1XL shank
   d. swimmer: 3XL shank
   e. burrower: 4XL shank
2. **TYING THREAD:** nylon Herb Howard Flymaster same color as nymph body
3. **CEMENT:** thinned Pliobond for underbody; thin clear cement for head. If Pliobond is unavailable, Goop is a substitute.
4. **TAILS:** three soft hackle fibers of partridge, emu, pheasant, or similar bird to match general length, color, and shape of natural's tails
5. **ABDOMEN:** soft blends of natural-fur or synthetic-wool dubbing to match abdominal area of nymph
   a. rib: fine gold or copper wire
   b. gills: dubbing picked out on top sides of thorax to simulate gill filaments

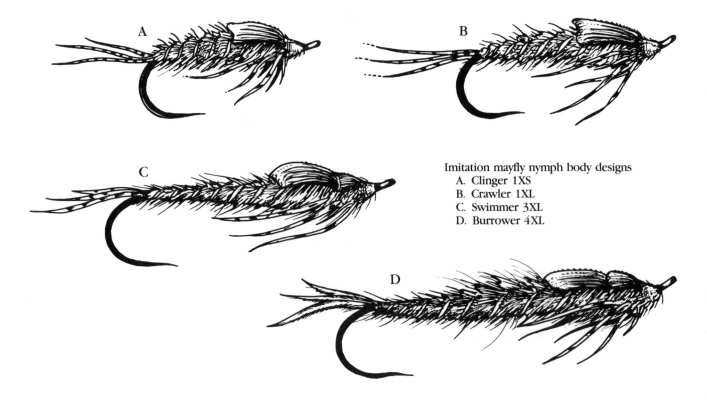

Imitation mayfly nymph body designs
A. Clinger 1XS
B. Crawler 1XL
C. Swimmer 3XL
D. Burrower 4XL

6. THORAX: use the same dubbing as on abdomen, but make it slightly larger; note relative thorax-abdomen proportions on all four types of nymphs

7. WINGPADS: Swiss or poly-rayon or hobby straw; this material is tough yet easy to work with, and it softens in water—wet or dry it looks exactly like the live nymph's wingpad. If it is not available in the colors you need, simply dye it or color it with a waterproof felt marking pen. Latex, soft hair or soft feather fibers can be substituted. I tie the wingpad aft and fore of the thorax on most simple nymphs. On large, more complicated nymphs, such as the *Hexagenia limbata*, I use this material for burrower-nymph wingpads as well as the top of abdomen, top of prothorax, and top of head—this better simulates the dark back and light underside that is the natural coloration of the nymph

8. LEGS: soft, webby feathers such as those found on the bodies of grouse, pheasant, partridge, and hen chicken. Keep legs simple and few to accelerate the sinking rate and to simulate the swimming-crawling action of the natural nymph. The DeFeo style of legging nymphs provides a simple yet neat method of tying in swimming-nymph legs. Remember: no mayfly nymph has more than *six* legs! When mayfly nymphs swim they press their legs close into the side and bottom of the thorax to reduce drag and wiggle the abdomen to swim, usually in an up-and-down motion. On the small and fast swimming nymph, legs on the imitation are completely unnecessary.

9. HEAD: I prefer to finish the heads of these nymphs off with dubbing material also, since their heads are of the same texture and color as their bodies. Traditional hard-laquered, thread heads are unrealistic and detract from the overall effect that I want in my nymphs—the soft natural effect

These nymph designs are to be fished on or near the bottom. Do not exaggerate their movement in lakes or streams. *One of the biggest mistakes new nymph fishers make is to move their nymphs too fast and at impossible directions for the real nymphs to accomplish.* Study the natural's action and speed whenever possible.

These nymphs are best fished in a natural drift or with just a small twitch or drag swim against the current. In lakes, cast them out and let them sink completely to the bottom; wait a few seconds to a minute and then begin a very slow erratic hand-twist or short-strip retrieve . . . keeping the fly as deep as possible.

I prefer to use a full floating fly line with a nine- to twelve-foot knotless leader and a thirty- to forty-inch tippet of very soft, fine nylon for best sinking rate and most natural water action. In most cases I use an open Duncan loop knot to give the nymph maximum action in the water. This knot also allows the nymph to sink at the fastest possible rate.

Sinking lines, sinking-tip lines, and lead-weighted leaders offer many alternate methods for fishing these mayfly nymphs. I opt for the line and leader type dictated by the specific water conditions. However, in most of the places I've fished these nymphs, the floating line, long leader tippet, and weighted-nymph system (plus a strike indicator) works best for me.

MATURE EMERGING NYMPH (NO. 2 POSITION)

This nymph is to be fished in an emerging-nymph situation either in the preliminary up-and-down, off-the-bottom false rise or the rise from mid-depth to the surface film. Use the same tying specifications as for No. 1, with these exceptions:

1a. Less lead wire or completely omitted
6. *Thorax:* build the thorax a little large and increase the wing size by one-third. Wingpads enlarge and darken a few days before emerging nymphs swim up to hatch into the winged dun

I use the No. 2 emerger nymph from an hour to four hours prior to the expected hatch and during the hatch, especially its early stages. With a floating line and long, light leader, I cast the undressed, wet, emerger nymph a yard or two above the area I wish to swim it through. Cast angle is either up and across or *downstream.* I use a *slack leader* presentation so that the nymph sinks quickly and drifts without drag. As the nymph nears the feeding trout I begin to lift or swim the nymph to the surface by slowly raising my rod and allowing drag to develop. I take considerable care to prevent the emerger from swinging across the current as this is totally unnatural. This is why I prefer to use a *slack-line downstream* cast—it affords more ideal *downstream drift* line and fly control. Usually the take of the emerging nymph is only a few inches below the surface or right at the surface. It is quite visible. I set the hook slowly and deliberately so that the hook is not pulled upstream out of the trout's still open mouth. The slow set allows the trout to close and the pull of the water engages the nymph in the side of the trout's mouth. If the trout seems to strike short or just flash at the emerger, it is moving too fast or swinging out of the natural downstream line of drift. Adjust the presentation to a more natural line and speed.

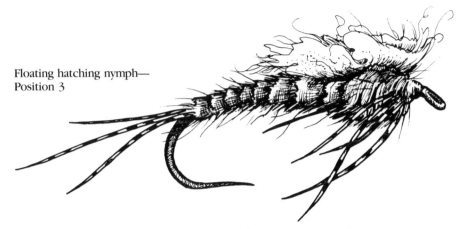

Floating hatching nymph—
Position 3

FLOATING-HATCHING NYMPH (NO. 3 POSITION)

Just as the emerging nymph reaches the surface film it begins to hatch by splitting its skin, starting on top from between its wingpads and extending to its abdomen. It then begins to push itself out of the skin on the surface film.

Use the same tying specifications as No. 1 with these exceptions:

1. HOOK: extra-fine wire, turned-up or turned-down eye
   a. no extra weight
7. WINGPADS: standard Fly Rite, Poly XXX, or Poly Wing tied into a clump equal to thorax's size or slightly larger. Light grey, cream, or light tan to match natural's unfolding wings also provides good visibility for the fly fisher
8. LEGS: same as No. 1 Position, step 8, or one or two turns of cock hackle clipped off at top and bottom. Hackle assists in flotation, but does not look as natural as do a few soft feather legs

The floating-hatching nymph is extremely effective during the hatch of the duns. Grease the *wingpad only* with paste fly flotant or a similar fly flotant. Fish the nymph *in the surface film* with a floating line and a seven- to nine-foot leader with a thirty-inch tippet. The fly should be fished dead or natural drift, using either a downstream slack-line or up-and-across cast to the areas in which trout are rising for the nymphs and duns. Of all the match-the-mayfly-hatch fishing, I most prefer the floating nymph for it has the effectiveness of nymphing and the charm of the visual rise.

ADVANCED EMERGER-STILLBORN (NO. 4 POSITION)

This design either imitates the dun as it first frees its head, thorax, legs, and wings from the nymphal skin or a helpless dun that has either experienced imperfect hatching or has died before freeing itself.

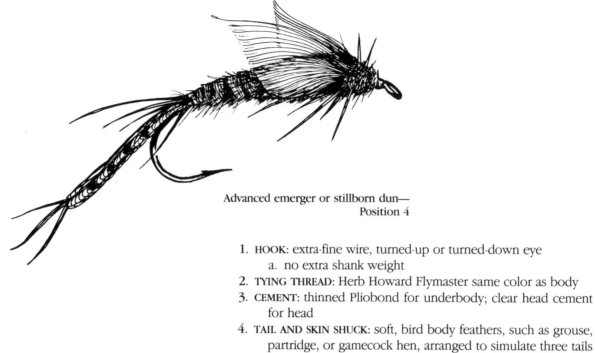

Advanced emerger or stillborn dun—
Position 4

1. HOOK: extra-fine wire, turned-up or turned-down eye
   a. no extra shank weight
2. TYING THREAD: Herb Howard Flymaster same color as body
3. CEMENT: thinned Pliobond for underbody; clear head cement
   for head
4. TAIL AND SKIN SHUCK: soft, bird body feathers, such as grouse,
   partridge, or gamecock hen, arranged to simulate three tails
   and nymphal skin *tied on to hooks' bend* and angled down
   and equal to hook-shank length
5. ABDOMEN: dub compactly with fine-textured synthetic blend
   such as Fly Rite or Spectrum; I try to match the underside
   color of the newly hatched dun
   a. rib: if the abdomen of natural appears very segmented, rib
   over dubbing with contrasting nylon floss
6. THORAX: with same dubbing as abdomen, build thorax one-
   third length of hook shank and a slightly larger diameter
7. WINGS: with two sections of a pair of primary duck-wing quills,
   tie upright Sidewinder-style wings approximately equal to
   length of body and one-half width of body. One or both
   wing tips can also be tied down at the hook bend to further
   simulate incomplete emergence from nymphal skin
8. LEGS: one or two turns of cock hackle, thorax style. Trim any
   hackle fibers from bottom of fly
9. HEAD: sparsely dub up to hook eye and whip-finish

This design, pioneered by my friends Carl Richards and Doug Swisher, is well detailed in their books *Fly Fishing Strategy* and *Tying the Swisher/Richards Flies.* I fish this pattern as a dry fly, dead drift, with a long leader and floating line. It is cast to rising trout or fished carefully along eddies, deadfalls, and sweepers where trout often station themselves after the hatch is over to pick up the scraps. It also works nicely fished undressed or wet in riffles.

The Dun (Position No. 5)

There are dozens of successful dun designs that enable us to fish almost any water's surface correctly. Also, some mayfly duns are so large or so small that tying, flotation, and durability present special problems. But here are the two designs I use most consistently.

DAVE'S DUN

This is a variation of the Swisher/Richards No-Hackle Sidewinder.

1. HOOK: extra-fine wire, 1XL, turned-up or turned-down eye
2. TYING THREAD: Herb Howard Flymaster, color to match fly's body
3. CEMENT: thin clear head cement; Tuffilm for spraying wings; Scotchgard for waterproofing and increased durability
4. TAILS: three very stiff hackle barbules or mink-tail guardhairs, one to one and one-half times the length of hook shank
5. BODY: dubbed with a fine-textured synthetic blend such as Fly Rite or Spectrum. Taper it from tails to just behind the hook eye
   a. rib: only if natural's abdomen segments contrast sharply
   b. color: I try to match the color of the dun's underbody
   c. do not enlarge thorax area until wings are tied on, but do tie wings down over dubbing to give them a better base than the bare hook shank allows

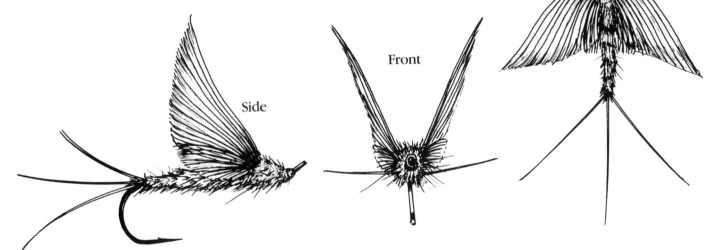

Dave's dun—Position 5

Side

Front

Top

6. WINGS: from the wings of a small and large duck—for example, a mallard and a teal—select two pairs of primary wing quills. Spray each with Tuffilm. Cut pairs of wings from each type. *Width* of large-feather wings should be one-half the *length* of the body. This pair matches the forewings of a mayfly dun. Second pair, from small feathers, should be one-third the length of the body in width
   a. tie each pair on at midthorax, No-Hackle Sidewinder style; tie on large pair first, and then beside them the smaller pair
   b. trim forewings to one and one-half the length of body, and hindwings to one-third the length of forewings
   c. forewings should slant slightly back; hindwings should be almost horizontal to the body
   d. these wings give a very realistic silhouette and greatly enhance the Sidewinder outrigger flotation
7. BODY: carefully dub thorax around, behind, and in front of wings to enhance the wing position and build up the thorax
8. HEAD: when cement dries, lightly spray entire fly with Scotchgard. Additional waterproofing, with flotants such as Mucilin, Dilly Wax, or Gink, is also necessary under most fishing conditions. Scotchgard as an undercoat greatly improves any dry fly's durability

I fish Dave's Dun or the similar but simpler No-Hackle Sidewinder for most hatches in hook sizes 10 to 18, particularly when trout are most selective. When the size and color are the same, it is hard to tell them apart from the naturals. For sizes 18 to 22, the No-Hackle Sidewinder is much easier to tie and I can see no difference in effectiveness.

Either design should be fished to duplicate the natural dun's float pattern and action. For calm-surfaced water, I prefer the downstream slack presentation; but for fish rising along banks, the right or left reach cast is also quite good. Fast, choppy water or pocket water fishes best with the up-and-across curve cast.

S & R PARADUN

1. HOOK: extra-fine wire, regular or 1XS, turned-down or turned-up eye for extended body; 2XL for regular body
2. TYING THREAD: CSE (Creative Sports Enterprises) or Danville single-strand or flat-waxed nylon floss to match the natural's body color
3. TAIL: three wild-boar bristles, fine hackle stems, or moose hairs the length of body
4. BODY: coarse elk or deer rump hair dyed the color of natural dun's underbody

   a. rib: strand of CSE nylon floss the color of the abdomen
      segments
   b. body is tied either extended (for large sizes) or regular
      (for small sizes)
   c. the coarse elk or deer rump hair is extremely durable for
      easy tying of extended bodies
5. WINGS: deer body hair the color of natural's wings
   a. wing length is equal to body length
   b. wing width is equal to one-third of body length
6. HACKLE: one long grizzly dry-fly saddle
   a. dyed or bleached to match legs
   b. hackle is wrapped parachute-style around base of wings,
      or thorax-style and trimmed off at bottom.
7. HEAD: the elk or deer rump hair is extended past thorax, tied
   off, trimmed, and whip-finished
8. FINISH: clear head cement on head; body undercoated with
   well-thinned Pliobond or clear Head Cement; after drying,
   spray fly with Scotchgard

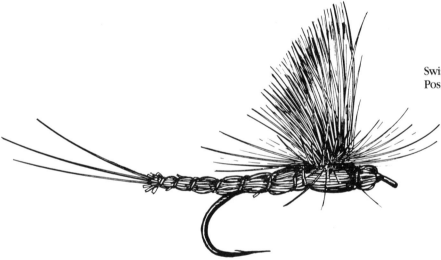

Swisher and Richards paradun—
Position 5

I use this design for most large mayfly duns in hook sizes 6 to
14—green drake, brown drake, and *Hexagenia limbata,* for example. This design is also excellent in rough, fast rivers. The same
fly tied on a light-wire, 2XL hook without extended body makes
a very durable design for matching smaller hatches and fishing in
rough water.

Other dun patterns I like are: Dollings XT Dun, L & L Dun, Kips
Inverta Dun, Cut-Wing Extended One-Feather Body Dun, and
Swisher's Clumper Dun.

The Spinner

I use three fly designs to match the spinners returning to lay eggs and fall.

FLUTTERING EGG-LAYING SPINNER

1. **HOOK:** extra-fine wire, regular to 2XL shank, turned-up or turned-down eye
2. **TYING THREAD:** Herb Howard Flymaster to match spinner's body color
3. **TAILS:** two or three stiff hackle barbules or mink-tail guardhairs one and one-half times the length of the body
4. **BODY:** fine-textured synthetic dubbing and stripped hackle stem or peacock quill
   a. form tight underbody with dubbing
   b. overwrap dubbing with stripped quill or stem to form abdomen
   c. match natural spinner's body coloration with materials. Egg cluster can be included if appropriate, using a small ball of dubbing.
5. **WING:** barred flank feather from wood duck or mallard, rolled and split into a pair
   a. wings are tied upright and split
   b. wings should be one to one and one-half times the length of hook shank
   c. match wing color of spinner
6. **HACKLE:** two dry-fly quality cock-neck hackles or one long saddle hackle
   a. size: use one hook size larger than usual hackle length for hook size
   b. color should match wings, not legs
   c. for fluttering egg-laying fly, leave hackle collar wide and full
   d. for surface-riding spinner, trim off all of the lower hackle so that fly lies flat on water—study diagrams for 6c. and 6d.
7. **HEAD:** tie off with a small, neat head and whip-finish
8. **FINISH:** coat thread-head wraps with head cement; spray entire fly with Scotchgard and allow to dry. Next, overcoat lightly with Mucilin, Dilly Wax, or Dave's Bugflote for the high flotation this design requires

I fish this fly like a live, active spinner, either slightly twitching or dragging it during the egg-laying or early stages of the spinner fall.

1. Natural mayfly dun
2. Dolling XT dun
3. L & L dun
4. Kips inverta dun
5. Cutwing one-feather body dun
6. S & R clumper dun

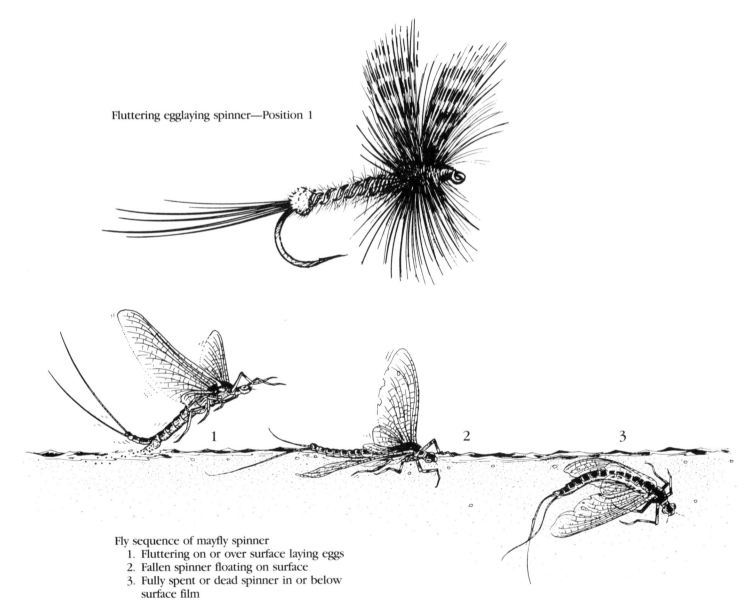

Fluttering egglaying spinner—Position 1

Fly sequence of mayfly spinner
1. Fluttering on or over surface laying eggs
2. Fallen spinner floating on surface
3. Fully spent or dead spinner in or below surface film

DAVE'S FALLEN SPINNER

This improved design is a classic spinner tie combined with some new ideas to simulate the dying spinner's shape; it is durable and floats extremely well.

1. HOOK: extra-fine wire, regular to 2XL shank, turned-up or turned-down eye
2. TYING THREAD: Herb Howard Flymaster, color of fly's body
3. TAILS: three extra-stiff hackle barbules, mink-tail guardchairs, or small stripped hackle stems
4. ABDOMEN: small stripped hackle stem and a fine-textured synthetic dubbing
   a. wrap abdomen with a thin layer of dubbing
   b. overwrap (rib) with the hackle stem (tip first) to form a tight, tapered, segmented body
   c. rib with fine gold wire or fine monfilament nylon in an opposite direction over hackle-stem rib
   d. abdomen should be two-thirds the length of shank and colored to match naturals
   e. if adults have noticeable egg sac at tip of abdomen, imitate it with a small ball of dubbing of appropriate color and size placed behind tails around hook bend
5. THORAX: fine-textured synthetic dubbing
   a. make thorax about two times the diameter of abdomen and one-third hook shank long
   b. match natural's color
6. WINGS: hackle—two very stiff dry-fly neck hackles or one extra-long saddle hackle
   a. sized so that barbules are one to one and one-half times the length of fly's body
   b. tie to hook shank reverse style before thorax is dubbed
   c. wrap hackle over thorax
   d. after fly is finished, trim off all barbules on bottom of thorax and about one-half of them off top of thorax. Hackle barbules suggest clear wings of spinners, not legs
   e. option: to suggest fully spent (or dead) spinners, I trim off all but a few hackle barbules on sides of thorax and all off bottom and top

Dave's fallen spinner—Position 2

This design is highly effective and extremely durable. It is my favorite spinner fly. The hackle-barbule wings last very well and simulate the clear wings better than feathers or polypropylene.

FULL SPENT-DEAD HEN SPINNER

This Swisher/Richards pattern is my favorite surface-film or drowned-spinner design. When fished wet, it also imitates the diving egg-laying spinner of some species.

1. HOOK: Extra-fine wire, regular to 2XL shank
2. TYING THREAD: Herb Howard Flymaster, color to match fly's body
3. TAILS: three hackle barbules
   a. stiff ones for dry fly
   b. soft ones for wet version
   c. make tails one to one and one-half times the length of body
4. BODY: same as Dave's Fallen Spinner, or make body of all synthetic dubbing; same color as natural
5. WINGS: two hen-chicken-neck hackles or chicken-body feathers
   a. wing feather width at least one-half the length of hook shank
   b. color should be same as insect's wing color
   c. wings should be tied full spent at right angles to body
   d. reinforce wing base with thorax dubbing
6. HEAD: dub just past thorax-wing area and whip-finish head
7. FINISH: apply a small amount of head cement to head. Pick out a few dubbing fibers on sides of thorax. For dry version, spray with Scotchgard. After drying, overcoat with Mucilin, Dave's Bugflote or Dilly Wax. For wet pattern, do not spray or overcoat with any water repllent

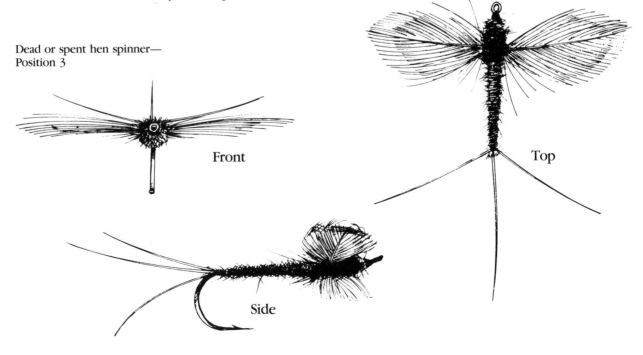

Dead or spent hen spinner—
Position 3

Front

Top

Side

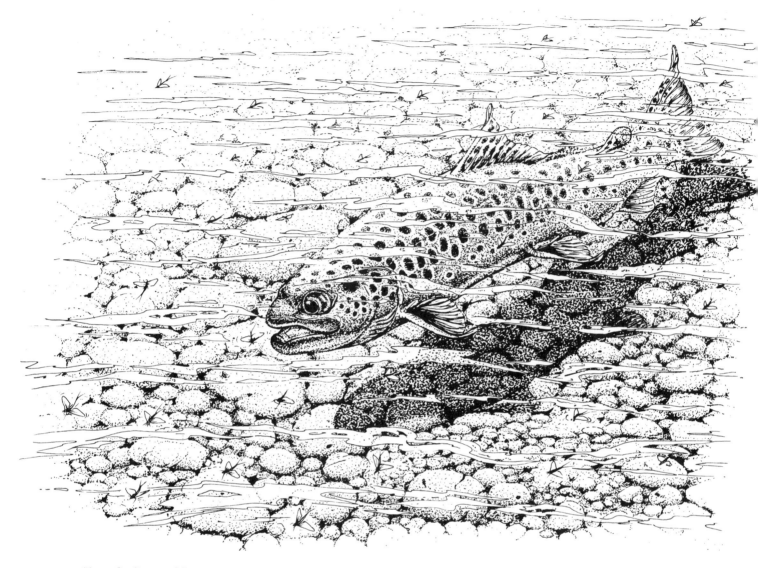

Trout feeding on fallen spinner

I fish this spinner when the spinner fall is well on or after all the spinners are gone. It must be fished *dead drift* and is best fished to a specific fish. I fish the wet spinner like an emerger or "flymph" if the mayfly spinners are *known* to dive and lay eggs.

For very large mayflies, the Paradun extended elk-hair-bodied design can also be used for imitating the largest spinners. Just vary the wing color and use the spent-wing position as well as matching the body colors of the spinner.

5
STONEFLIES
Plecoptera

Stonefly adult and nymph

Stoneflies are a special and important group of aquatic insects that all trout fishermen and fly tiers should understand. They and two other groups of aquatic insects rank just behind the mayfly in importance to trout and anglers; the other two groups are the caddisflies and midges, both of which are discussed in later chapters.

The stonefly's life cycle, habitat, and size make it highly compatible to fly-fishing and fly-tying ... maybe even more so than the mayfly. Trout waters where large populations of stoneflies exist, particularly in the Rocky Mountain and Northwest Coast streams, support some incredible numbers of large trout—and have become legendary fly-fishing meccas. Excellent examples of these super stonefly hatches are those experienced each June or early July on the Madison, Gunnison, and Deschutes rivers.

As their name implies, stoneflies generally thrive best in aquatic environments that have small-to-large rock-aggregate (rubble) bottoms. Their Latin name, Plecoptera, is a clue to their adult physical characteristics: *pleco* means "folded" and *ptera* means "wings." The adult stonefly has long, heavily veined wings that are folded and fitted back around the top and sides of the abdomen when at rest.

Stoneflies generally require clear, unpolluted, fast-flowing water with a high oxygen content. They actually require a higher overall water quality than most trout. Their aquatic breathing mechanisms, gills, and cuticular diffusions are not nearly as efficient or well adapted as those of the other three major groups of aquatic insects. So they seldom are found in sluggish streams or lakes in numbers significant enough to be important to fly fishermen. Thus the stoneflies' significant range is not as broad as that of other major aquatic insects trout eat. Due to the altering of their water systems, the number of stoneflies has been declining.

Stoneflies are physically distinctive. They are large aquatic insects that also have longer average life cycles in their aquatic forms than the other three groups. Most species that I've observed are weak or poor swimmers at best and usually crawl on the surface and side of a bottom object to move about. These behavioral and physical facts make the nymph form quite vulnerable year-round to foraging trout. Certainly they offer a regular bonus food to the alert trout even when conditions favor other aquatic-insect nymph activity. This is particularly true if the level, clarity, velocity, and temperature of the water are undergoing drastic changes because of snow runoff, rains, drought, or the like.

Stoneflies have a similar but longer average life cycle than mayflies. They have three major stages—the egg, nymph, and adult. The life cycle for most species that concern the fly fisher is between two and four years per generation. As with the mayfly, the major portion of this time is spent as an aquatic nymph.

The egg clusters that are deposited on the water's surface or just below it by the adult female stonefly separate, sink, and hatch over a wide time span according to specie. Some hatch within a few days; others take weeks, months, or almost a year. Though trout may catch the egg-layers, the eggs themselves are not important to the fly fisher. When the eggs hatch, almost microscopic nymphs emerge.

Stonefly nymphs, which are totally aquatic, establish a general residence in the most suitable areas at a very young age. Initially they are far too small to interest foraging trout. They are either predacious or herbivorous, depending on which family they belong to. However, they are strong food and territorial competitors, often at the expense of other aquatic insects. Predacious stonefly nymphs will eat other nymphs as well as small fish fry and other aquatic creatures.

As the stonefly nymph grows, it must periodically shed and renew its rigid skeletonlike skin to accommodate further growth. Each growth period is determined by water temperature, food consumption, and age.

Trout do not start to feed significantly on the nymphs until they reach one-half inch (14 to 16mm). As the nymphs increase in size beyond this point, trout like them even more.

Stonefly nymphs are usually easy to identify since they have quite visible and unique body structures and coloration patterns. Once you become familiar with the look of a stonefly nymph you

Three general stonefly nymph shapes, top and front views
A. Slender
B. Medium
C. Wide

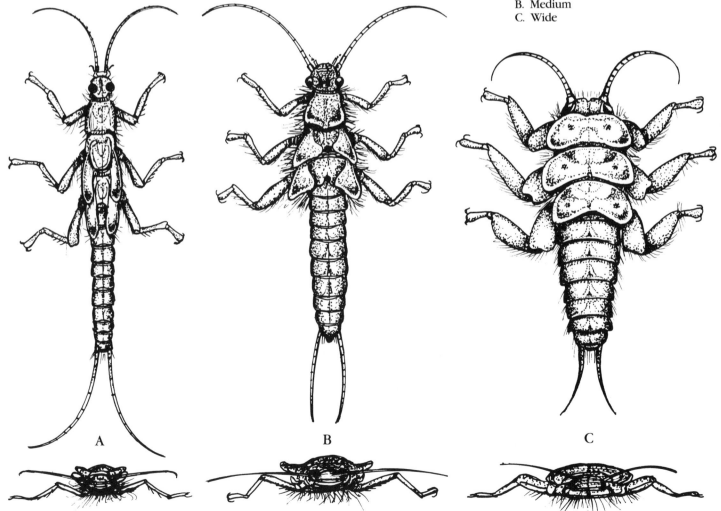

A   B   C

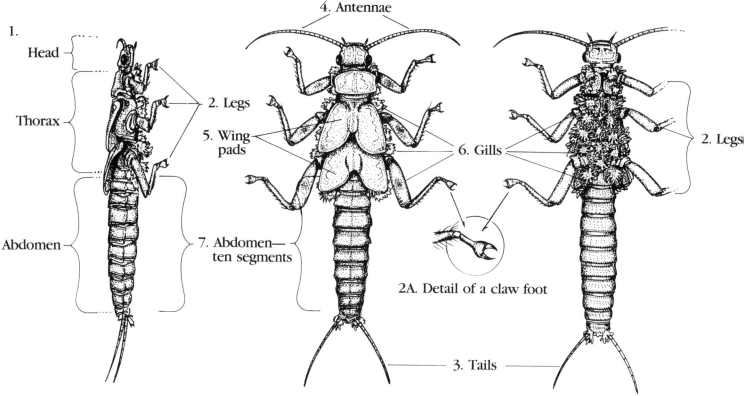

1.
Head
Thorax
Abdomen

4. Antennae

2. Legs

5. Wing pads

6. Gills

7. Abdomen— ten segments

2A. Detail of a claw foot

2. Legs

3. Tails

Three views of stonefly nymph structure

will seldom confuse it with other aquatic nymphs. The important physical characteristics common to all stonefly nymphs are:

1. three distinctive major body regions: head, thorax (midsection), and abdomen
2. six legs with two sharp claws on each foot
3. two well-defined and separated, almost bristlelike tails on the last abdominal segment
4. two long, well-defined, bristlelike antennae
5. two well-defined and enlarged wingpads on top of thorax
6. short, fuzzy, plumelike gills on the bottom of the thorax and between the legs or gills may be entirely absent (smaller species).
7. abdomen has ten well-defined gill-less segments and is evenly cylindrical

Stonefly nymphs are not nearly as adaptable to various environments as mayfly nymphs, so they exhibit less variation in shape. Some are more compact or compressed but generally size and color pattern offer better visual clues to the particular kind. The recognition of stonefly nymphs is much simpler than mayfly nymphs. By counting tails, wingpads, and checking gill location these two nymphs can be differentiated easily. Foot claws are another excellent key to identification and distinguishing the stonefly nymph from the mayfly nymph.

Because stonefly nymphs are generally large and well defined anatomically—with wingcases, large heavy legs, distinctive long tails and antennae, well-defined and marked abdominal segments, and so forth—fly tiers have had a field day tying exact imitations. Such sculptures in plastic, quills, latex, nylon, magnetic tape, lacquered feathers, and woven hair have idolized the stonefly. These artistic creations impress the users and creators but not always the trout. Compared to the suggestive, soft-bodied stonefly nymphs, they are inferior in depicting the living insects as trout see them.

I strongly advise the suggestive-impressionistic approach to tying stonefly nymphs. It is important to capture the color, texture, shape, and anatomical proportions of the living stonefly nymph. Chiefly, such nymphs must look "buggy" and simulate the action as well as conformation of the naturals.

For example, a size 4 hook just wrapped with black and/or brown chenille and fished properly will imitate the stonefly and catch some nice trout. But it has little class and doesn't excite my imagination either for fishing or tying.

Yet on the same hook, if I fashion a soft, brown or black, fur-bodied nymph with a ribbed abdomen, wingcase, tails, antennae, and soft feather legs, it looks more like a stonefly nymph and fishes even better. So with just a little more imagination and skill I can create a simple, effective nymph that the trout and I can both live with.

The more I learn about various orders and individual species of nymphs the more my tying and fishing becomes refined . . . but I never compromise texture, size, and action for detailed duplication. If that is done, the nymph attracts fishermen more, perhaps, but trout less.

I have made the following observations regarding live stonefly nymphs free of the bottom:

1. the swimming stonefly nymph arches its back with head and tail up and folds its legs to the side
2. the nonswimmers bend their backs to form a C shape, or fetal position, and enclose their legs and lock them beneath their thorax like a dead nymph would do
3. those crawling on the bottom present a long, straight outline with legs extended and tails and antennae extended horizontally

Stoneflies transform directly from the aquatic nymph into the winged air-breathing adult. This transformation occurs during the last few hours or days of the stonefly's long life cycle and is chiefly for the purpose of reproduction.

The emergence of a particular specie is dependent on a seasonal timetable and temperature. Once the stonefly nymph

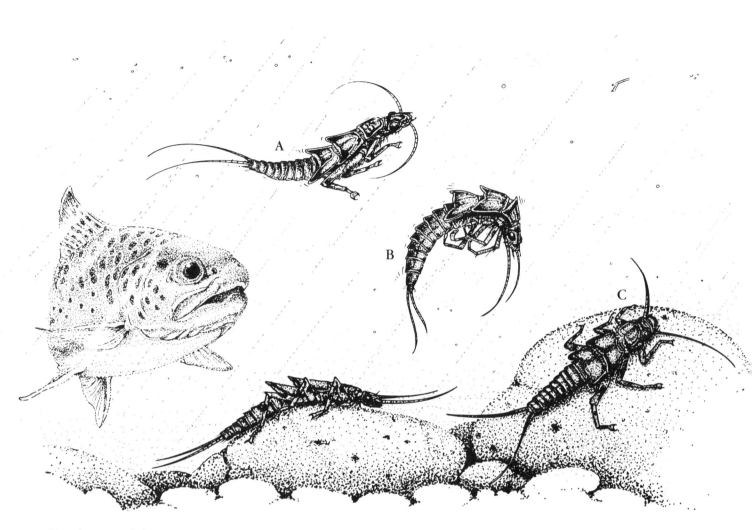

Nymphs suspended in water
  A. Swimming
  B. Nonswimmers adrift
  C. Crawling on surfaces

reaches maturity it can only await the right environmental condition, which is naturally reached with the progression of the season—that is, the ratio of daylight to darkness and the warming of
the water to a particular temperature.

Stoneflies have two basic methods of emergence. The most
common, particularly in the larger species, is to crawl to the perimeters of the stream and out of the water onto such objects as
exposed rocks, logs, roots, and banks. This streambed exodus is
normally begun at night and may continue into the day. Once out
of the water the air will dry the nymph skin. The nymph, holding
tightly to a surface with its legs, begins to split open its skin on
the dorsal line between the neck and abdomen, including the
wingcases. The nymph then emerges from the casing as an adult
stonefly. For most of the larger species, adult emergence is somewhat slower than the mayfly's transformation from nymph to dun.
However, for the smaller stonefly species, particularly those that

emerge off the water, the process is as rapid as the mayfly's. Water emergence is the second basic method of emergence.

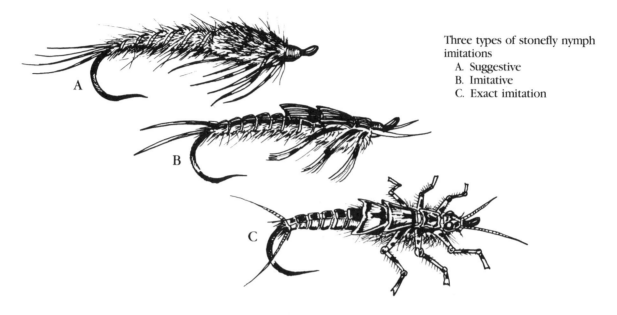

Three types of stonefly nymph imitations
  A. Suggestive
  B. Imitative
  C. Exact imitation

The new land-emergent adults usually allow their wings and body skin to air dry and harden as they continue to crawl higher up on the areas surrounding them. If they cannot find concealment immediately, they continue to crawl and search or fly up and back over the land until they find seclusion in willows, weeds, roots, or other objects.

On prime stonefly streams such as the Big Hole in Montana, Gunnison in Colorado, and Deschutes in Oregon, at certain times of the year this emergence is an awesome spectacle to witness. The banks and shoreline rocks and exposed roots will be encrusted with millions of dried nymphal shucks. The streamside trees will droop with the weight of hundreds of thousands of emerging and mating adults. I've seen a single yard-long willow stem with a hundred or more two and one-half-inch-long adult stoneflies clinging to it and each other. I've shaken alder and willow bushes over the water and blanketed the surface with fallen adults. It is almost a ghastly sight to anyone but those who fish the stoneflies—or the gorging legion of trout that enjoy them.

Trout often will feed so excessively that the flies will be passed half-digested from their swollen and extended intestines. However, the unobservant fly fisher will fail to notice moderate hatches because they begin at night and the stoneflies quietly crawl out, emerge, and conceal themselves with as much secrecy as possible.

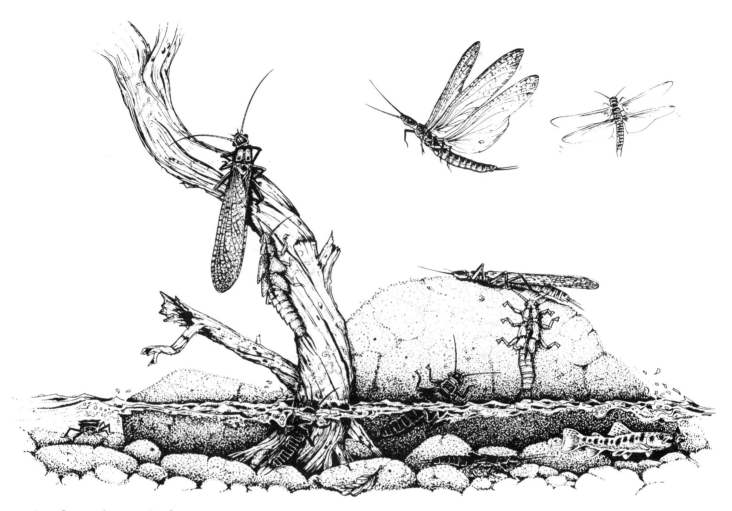

Stonefly nymphs emerging from nymphal skins on tree limbs and stones exposed above the surface of the water

A number of smaller-sized stonefly emergences occur on the stream's surface, particularly early and late in the season. These stonefly nymphs swim or rise to the surface even at midstream, especially in the riffles and runs below riffles. Much like emerging mayfly nymphs, these stonefly nymphs use the surface film to lever themselves out of the nymphal shucks and emerge as adult stoneflies. They seem to accomplish this much faster than the larger stones do when crawling out.

They rest *low and flat* on the surface, almost invisible to the casual fly fisher's eye. Some of the small, pale-yellow, sulfur, and light-green species can be seen—but the slates, olives, and blacks are tough to detect. You can see them as they begin to rise off the surface, flying to the shoreline to seek concealment. Then they suddenly *appear* and often trick me into thinking they are caddis or even mayflies. Once you learn to recognize the characteristically clumsy, slow wing beats of the adult stonefly, however, it only takes your close attention to know what they are. The adults also beat their four long wings above (or over) their bodies rather than above and below like the mayfly or caddis.

Many fine surface-emergent hatches of the smaller stoneflies go

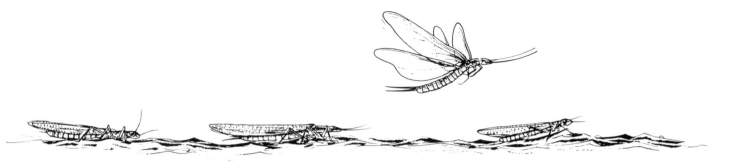

Small adult stoneflies resting and flying after emergence

unnoticed or masked by caddis or mayflies that may also be active at the same period. I've been particularly guilty of this mistake since I'm always thinking mayfly or caddis when I see midstream surface feeding. Significantly, unless the other flies are very abundant, trout will prefer the typically larger and easier-to-catch emerging stonefly nymphs.

The adult stonefly is somewhat more durable than the adult mayfly, and during the mating and egg-laying period it may survive for several days up to a week. But most of this time it is out of the reach of trout—along the streamside covers, especially in bushes and tree foliage. Concealed here and there, the adults mate, seldom flying unless stimulated by wind, birds, or the urge to seek greener pastures.

When the female has mated she flies back and forth to the water, each time depositing part of her egg mass. The females often appear to crash-land or clumsily skitter and skate across the surface . . . resembling in action and form a helicopter flown by a very intoxicated pilot. Such flight trips will occur for a few hours on up to periods of several days.

At this stage the stonefly adult becomes an incredible sound and sight attractor to the waiting trout. Trout of all sizes and ages wildly surface to grab and gulp this juicy bonanza. As the egg-laying flights reach their peak of intensity, the trout become more

Adult female stonefly laying eggs on water's surface

satiated and slow down to a more selective feeding pace. I've noticed that on big daylight egg-laying flights a sudden breeze or hot wind will stimulate the greatest flight activity. The stimuli of moving foliage and fresh, warm air puts the flies up and out over the water. On dark, cool, cloudy days, many of the nocturnal stonefly adults will jump the gun and carry out limited egg-laying flights to the water . . . a bonus to trout and daytime anglers. I've observed this phenomenon much more on the eastern and midwestern low-altitude streams than on the higher western mountain rivers.

Eventually, as most of the eggs are deposited, the females and the males become less active and the adult stoneflies soon fail to clear the water's surface. They float along until they are eaten or drowned. Emergences and egg-laying flights vary, of course, by specie, but usually are rather short-termed, peaking rapidly and usually falling off within five to ten days.

Most stonefly hatches begin on the lower miles of a river or stream and progress upstream a few miles per day. This is due to water temperature; flowing water typically warms more rapidly

Large trout feeding on adult egglaying stoneflies

at lower elevations. Progressive warming at higher altitudes moves the hatch up with it.

The stonefly emergence and egg-laying can occur anytime during a twenty-four-hour period. Even for similar or identical species, this will be during the day in the Rockies but mostly at night in Michigan, Ontario, or Pennsylvania. Generally, most of the late-winter and spring stonefly emergences will be midday events. As spring warms into early summer, there are more sunrise and sunset events, particularly at the lower elevations of twelve hundred to fourteen hundred feet; summer emergences change to nighttime at these elevations. Higher or colder regions in the North have daytime hatches.

Generally, too, the small, dark stones hatch early; the medium to largest come during late spring to midsummer; and the small, pale-colored stones are the last to emerge in late summer and early fall. There are exceptions, of course, usually caused by exceptional water-system conditions. But the above is a good basic emergence sequence for a typical freestone trout stream.

Identifying, Matching, and Fishing the Stonefly

Stoneflies have two major stages with which trout, fly tiers, and trout fishermen need to be most concerned—nymph and adult. In addition, the adult stage is best subdivided into the adult emerger and the adult egg-layer. We can now see the stonefly as the trout sees it and eats it—as nymph, emerger, and egg-layer.

You can learn about the forms, colors, and actions of these three stages of the stonefly's life cycle from this book and from your own experience where you fish for trout. It is no more complicated than that. You will not need to consult an entomological encyclopedia, a microscope, or an entomology professor to tie or fish stonefly imitations for trout successfully.

By keeping a few mental or written notes on the waters you fish each season as well as listening to the experiences of other anglers, you will quickly have a well-condensed and practical knowledge of the significant stoneflies trout feed upon in your waters—there may be a dozen or so species present but actually only three or four important ones for you to know. From these, by using my impressionistic-suggestive method of matching the naturals, you will also get good overlap into the lesser flies—if the trout happen to be thinking that way on a particular day.

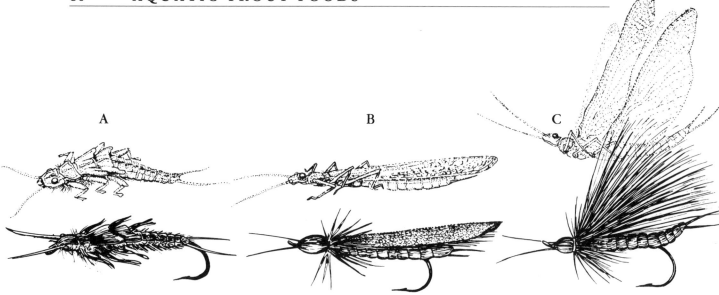

A

B

C

Three suggestive stonefly imitations
  A. Nymph
  B. Adult resting on surface
  C. Fluttering egglaying adult

The nymph. Stonefly nymphs, because of their somewhat inefficient breathing system, will by necessity be in water that offers them the best amount of oxygen and the highest degree of water circulation of it to and away from them. A mayfly nymph can easily circulate water to and from its filaments. The stonefly nymph does not have this gill filament exposure and movement. Stoneflies live best where ideal water flows by under their bodies. At times when you are observing a captured stonefly nymph in a small container of still water, don't be surprised if it starts doing six-leg push-ups. Actually, it is going into its emergency response to a lack of oxygen. The up-and-down leg motion temporarily circulates water and more oxygen over its gill filaments. However, it will soon exhaust itself and die if the water condition does not improve.

Second to ideal water flows, the nymphs search out gravel, rock, and rubble bottom—or substitutes such as sunken tree roots and logs or coarse aquatic plant stems—for cover protection. Their foods, both plant and animal, are usually abundant in most of these areas.

Knee-deep, turbulent riffles, and the edges of deeper runs are the best areas in which to capture stonefly-nymph specimens. I use the same methods described to capture mayfly nymphs. In fact, this system works well for all important aquatic trout-food insects. When collecting specimens, you will seldom capture just one insect order or one species. Usually you will come up with a smorgasbord of aquatic insects, worms, leeches, snails, scuds, and so forth.

As you capture, identify, and observe stonefly nymphs, note their size, shape, color, and action. Most photographs or illustrations published show top views of stoneflies, but the nymphs also have front, side, and bottom profiles—study them closely in the live nymph. Also note each different one's relative abundance; this is an important key to their true significance as a resident trout food. Put each carefully back into the stream or into a clear jar of stream water and closely watch their behavior a full minute or two.

Some will immediately react, crawling or swimming to the bottom. Others will act more dead than alive, almost seeming to play possum. These observations will tell you how to tie and fish the nymph imitations you decide upon.

I'm firmly convinced that the stonefly nymph is one of the aquatic nymphs most regularly picked off the bottom and eaten by trout when there is not a significant emergence of other nymphs in progress. They regularly move about over the streambed surface, especially at night. Their size and generally sluggish crawling speed make them easy pickings for the sharp-eyed bottom-nymphing trout.

In studying aquatic life underwater and in a stream aquarium, stonefly nymphs are among the few aquatic insects usually visible. I've often mused at how wrong most speculation by tiers and fly fishers is regarding the accessibility or visibility of other aquatic nymphs to trout in the water and on the streambed. If they were that visible few would survive. I think the sudden appearance of a vulnerable imitation is a grand event and attracts the trout more than it matches what the trout see of the naturals.

The adult emerger. The surface-emergent stonefly adult is often difficult to capture, while the crawler-emerger is easy to check out. A large aquarium or sturdy butterfly net works well to catch the swimming and flying emergers. You can usually just pick off the crawlers.

The most significant physical feature of the adult is its long, folded, or rolled, heavily veined wings that extend well past the abdomen and twin tails. The whole fly at rest has a flat, compressed, sticklike look. Usually the two antennae will be longer than the two tails.

Unfold the wings and you will see that the front wings, or forewings, are somewhat more slender than the back wings. In flight, the insect appears to be overwinged. This is because it flutters or beats its large wings slowly and mostly vertically to its body.

The adult stonefly is a harmless insect; if one bites you, then you have made the wrong identification. Some fishflies, dobsonflies, and dragonflies resemble large, dark stoneflies but have large jaws and will attempt to bite if restrained by your fingers.

Nighttime emergers are best identified by capturing with a butterfly net stoneflies you have attracted to a bright streamside light. For daytime emergers, look low on the water and low along the shoreline for nymphs, nymph shucks, and freshly hatched adults.

Certainly use the same *objective observations* that I have

stressed for mayflies. Note carefully and measure body length and width. Wing size and shape must be studied. *Look both at the color of the top and bottom;* for the adult the *wing color and bottom color* are most significant. For the nymph the *top and side color* are the most important to match.

The adult egg layer. The mature, mated adults will be active along the perimeters of the water through the most pleasant part of a twenty-four-hour period. The egg-laying or return flight to the water is a much greater event for the large, crawling emergent species than the surface emergers. It is important to capture and observe these larger stoneflies and to study their egg-laying flight because trout really respond to them. Shaking a tree limb over the water, air-netting, and bright-light capture all work well to collect the large egg-laden adults. Again I stress that there is no need to classify each bug you catch—just observe them closely. This will provide you with good basic fly-tying information.

The egg-laying females and males usually appear to be the same shape and color. But there is a size difference between the sexes; females are one-half to two hook sizes larger than the males. Since the females are most likely to be back on the water, they are the size the trout will key on . . . not the smaller, less available males.

As the females lay their eggs, note if they initially strike or light on the water. Do they flutter or keep their wings unfolded? Or do they fold their wings and rest quietly or actively on the surface? *Whenever possible, note which flies seem to be drawing the rises . . . and most important, watch which ones the larger trout chase!* An active egg layer may only be attracting small, noisy, young trout while back under the willow limbs that hooked mouth and heavy dorsal fin slipping up and down through the surface film may be vacuuming the surface for flush-floating, exhausted flies.

I've observed that once the active adults begin to move with or against the current, rather than at right or left angles to it, they interest feeding trout much more. Stoneflies that have some twitching movement trigger interest from trout more than dead or very active flip-floppers.

A Typical Stonefly Life Cycle

1. Adult female stonefly deposits eggs on or just below the water's surface.
2. Eggs drift, sinking and scattering while they incubate. Hatching occurs within a few days to weeks.

3. Stonefly nymphs emerge from eggs and search out suitable environments along shallow bottoms of streams or lakes. Some types are herbivorous and others predacious.
4. Stonefly nymphs living on the sides and bottoms of stream-bottom structures feed and grow, developing to maturity in two to four years, depending on the specie.
5. Once the nymph reaches maturity it awaits the right seasonal water condition and temperature, then crawls to streambanks or swims to the surface to emerge into the adult stonefly by splitting its nymphal skin and leaving via flight to dry land.

Stonefly life cycle

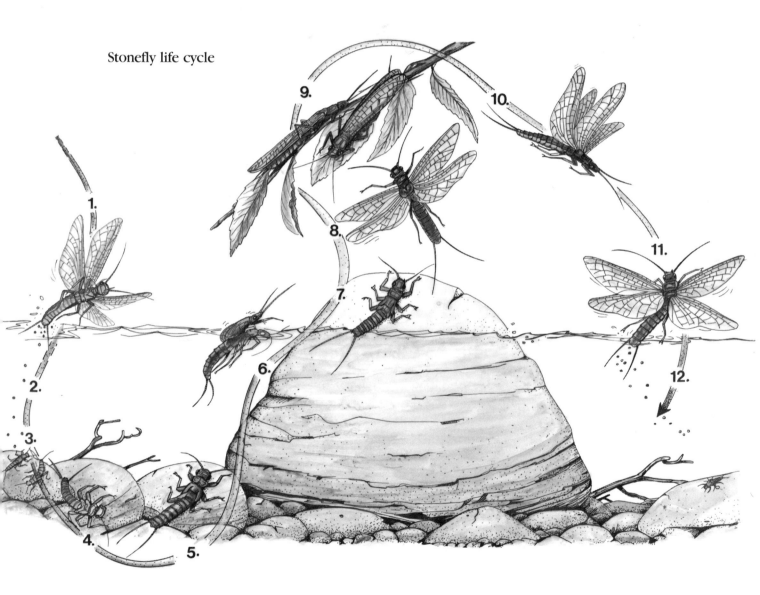

6. Surface emergence: some stoneflies are swimming surface emergers and undergo emergence at the water's surface.
7. Crawling emergence: other stoneflies crawl to the surface, using protruding rocks, streambanks, tree roots, and so forth to leave the water and emerge into air-breathing adults. Once out of the water the nymph's skin dries and splits open down its back. The adult then emerges from the nymphal skin case.
8. The emergent adult flies or crawls directly to protective terrestrial cover once its wings and body skin air harden.
9. Adults rest in protective concealment where mating occurs. They remain in this area until egg-laying conditions are right—usually within twelve to forty-eight hours.
10. Females return to the water in flight to lay their eggs.
11. Egg-laying females either flutter across or light on the water's surface to lay eggs. Several trips are made back and forth until all the eggs are laid. Adult males and females soon perish from mating and egg-laying exhaustion.
12. The deposited eggs complete the life cycle and begin another generation.

My Favorite Stonefly Fly Designs

The most effective stonefly imitations should simulate the insects in significant periods of the insects' lifecycle—that is, the periods when they are attractive and vulnerable to trout. My philosophy of suggestive-impressionistic imitations of both adults and nymphs applies to the stoneflies as much as to any other form of trout food.

The Nymph

The stonefly nymph is basically a stream-bottom dweller. My three-phase design is tied to simulate the nymph in the three actions or forms in which it is taken by the trout. Just as with mayfly nymphs, metamorphic changes make stonefly nymphs temporarily softer in texture and lighter in color at different times during the nymph stage.

For several years I was puzzled why several light-tan and grey Whitstone nymphs were generally more effective than similar ones in black, dark brown, and dark gold. These darker flies more closely imitated the stonefly nymphs of the Madison, Big Hole, Missouri, and Yellowstone rivers in Montana. I finally dis-

The stonefly life cycle and its imitations
  A. Crawling stonefly nymph
  B. Tumbling stonefly nymph
  C. Swimming or surface-emerging stonefly
     nymph
  D. Spent or resting stonefly adult
  E. Fluttering egglaying stonefly adult

covered the answer when questioning the strong color variations in some identical stonefly nymphs I caught alive and found in the stomachs of cutthroat trout in the Yellowstone River. Such imitations in lighter colors, fished dead drift and helplessly rolling along the bottom, really created the impression of the soft, helpless nymphs that had lost their hold and control during this stage. A few questions linked with a biological fact, simple observation, and experience solved the riddle for me.

This stonefly-nymph design can be either long and slender or wide and compressed, according to the natural insect you are imitating. I do not generally use both shapes, opting instead for an average shape somewhere between the two. You may consult the color and size charts for colors, but stonefly nymphs generally vary from an earthy black (with highlights of olive, brown, and burnt orange), dark brown, dark olive brown, gold, golden yellow, to light yellow green. The underside is somewhat lighter than the back and sides of the nymph.

The corresponding colors of the stonefly nymphs when they are in the new metamorphic stage—when they have shed their confining exoskeleton and are soft, light colored, and vulnerable to trout—are:

black: reddish brown to copper
dark brown: light brown to yellowish brown
dark olive brown: light yellow to yellowish brown
dark gold: light golden olive to dirty yellow
dark yellow: light dirty yellow to cream
olive yellow: light yellow to cream

Long and wide stonefly nymph naturals and average Whitstone nymph imitation

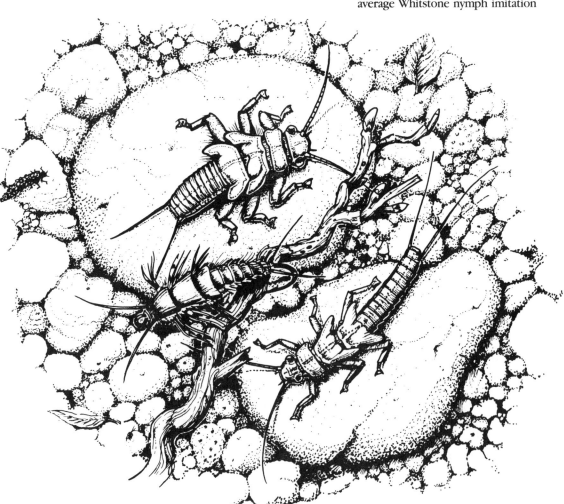

STONEFLY NYMPH NO. 1—A, B, C

1. **HOOK:** 1A (bottom-crawling stone nymph): standard wire, ring or turned-up eye, 1XL to 3XL shank. The low-water Partridge Atlantic salmon hook is ideal for all three styles. 1B (swimming stone nymph): standard wire, turned-up eye, 1XL to 3XL shank, hook shank bent up. 1C (tumbling stone nymph): standard wire, turned-down eye, 1XL to 3XL shank, hook shank bent down. Remember that the stonefly nymph arches back-up when swimming and back-down when tumbling loose and out of control. The hook is bent after the fly is finished, which facilitates tying procedure. Certainly 1A is the best all-around choice

   a. hook weighting: I use a lead-wire loop tied to the sides of the hook shank; the lead wire is approximately the same diameter as the hook wire. This lateral looping gives the nymph body both width and weight

2. **TYING THREAD:** Danville's single-strand nylon floss, color to match the nymph's general underbody color

3. **CEMENT:** thinned Pliobond for underbody; clear head cement for head

4. **TAILS:** two leading-edge fibers from a pair of turkey primary-wing quills or lengths of soft monofilament dyed to match general color of natural nymph's tails

5. **ANTENNAE:** same as tails, except that they are generally not the same size and length as tails

6. **BODY:** the stonefly nymph has three major body sections; check the diagrams for general proportions. The tops of the nymphs are darker than the sides and bottom. To simulate this color variation, the body is wrapped with dubbing to match the lighter sides and the bottom is then overlaid with a darker material to match the darker back

   a. the underbody is made of blends of Orlon and Kodel polyester yarns and natural furs such as beaver, muskrat, African goat, and seal

   b. back, head, prothorax, wingcases, and top of abdomen: Rayon ribbon (Swiss Straw), turkey quill, or latex sheeting. I much prefer Swiss Straw for ease of tying, effect, and because water softens it to enhance the nymph's soft, likelike texture. One four-inch strip of Swiss Straw will make the thorax, wingcases, prothorax, and heads in most nymph sizes

   c. abdomen rib: because the abdomen is distinctively segmented, use an overwrap of oval tinsel, small-diameter wire, or single-strand nylon floss to match the lighter rings on the natural's back. This ribbing also reinforces the Swiss Straw for durability

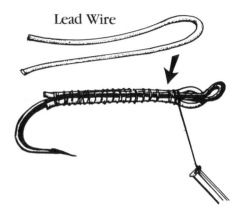

Lead Wire

Lead wire loop method of weighting the stonefly nymph hook

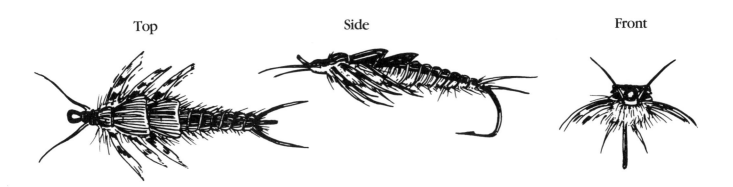

Top   Side   Front

Detail of crawling whitstonefly nymph

7. GILLS: the stonefly nymph's gills are often much lighter in color than the underbody. Large ostrich herl—cream, light yellow, or white—makes ideal gills when wrapped over thorax underbody before the legs and wingcases are tied down

8. LEGS: soft cock- or hen-pheasant body feathers, natural feather color or dyed to match the natural nymph's leg color. Legs come out from sides. Do not "overleg" the nymph—no legs are better than too many. The naturals only have six legs. The swimming and tumbling stonefly nymphs draw their legs in close to their bodies

9. HEAD: the head is tied and finished off like the other body parts—not merely shaped with hard tying thread as so many patterns call for. The antennae are put in place, then the area is dubbed over and Swiss Straw pulled down and tied off. Excess Swiss Straw is cut away, and a whip-finish and cementing completes the tying

These stonefly nymphs are to be fished near or on the bottom to match the activities and circumstances of the live stonefly nymphs.

The crawler is generally used deep, with a downstream dead-drift method to suggest normal behavior before any emergence occurs—crawling about, washed loose, or during metamorphic change. *An extremely deadly time to fish the deep crawler is just after a very muddy, silty spell has occurred.* This silting causes many stoneflies to crawl on top of the bottom rocks to breathe better. They will often wash loose in the swift water. I recall having such an opportunity late in September on the Big Hole River after a heavy two-day rain. Every trout in the river seemed to be gobbling stone nymphs as the water started to clear. I've never had such outstanding stonefly nymphing. Each riffle produced browns and rainbows from fourteen to twenty-two inches. After the water cleared completely, fishing returned to normal as the stones went back into hiding.

Swimming stonefly nymph

Tumbling stonefly nymph

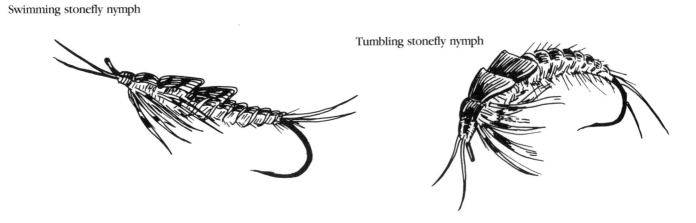

Fish the nymph down and across to suggest the nymph crawling out to hatch. An even better method is to short cast straight across to midstream and slowly pull the fly back to the rod. It can also suggest the swimming stone, even to the extent of surface emergence, if not allowed to sink or if raised to the top with line pull.

The swimming version can be effective when fished just off the bottom with some drag or as an emerger.

The tumbling version seems best when fished in very high or turbulent water, especially in rough riffles, below waterfalls, and in fast pocket water. I fish it deep, dead drift, and straight downstream. I generally prefer to fish stonefly nymphs with as much fly and line control as possible to keep the nymph looking natural and to detect the trout's subtle pickup of these usually helpless nymphs deep in the river. For this I like the light-colored floating line, orange strike indicator, long leader setup. With a long rod (eight and one-half to ten feet), these nymphs can be fished very well where they will be most effective. With this setup I usually present the three types of stone nymphs upstream on a very slack leader. The nymph sinks deep under the slack leader. I mend the line and watch the floating one-inch indicator for a telegraphed response that indicates the nymph has stopped or slowed down. When it comes I immediately strike.

As with most of my nymph designs, I greatly prefer to tie it to the tippet with a small, open Duncan loop knot to enhance the nymph's sinking and natural action.

Occasionally, especially in the larger western rivers, the riffles and runs will be strong and deep, and getting a stone nymph down before it goes very far calls for lead on the leader or very-fast-sinking lines. With such lead and lines it is really difficult to control the fly's downstream line and drag movement or detect the strike. But it is a trade off that one has to live with on such waters to fish these nymphs effectively.

The sinking-tip lines with ten- and twenty-foot, high-density sinking portions are usually much better to deep-nymph with in these waters than full, fast-sinking lines. They allow some line-and-fly control, mending, visible strike detection, and easier pickups. With such fly lines I use a sight-sense-feel system to detect a pickup by the trout. It basically involves immediate recognition of an unnatural line action, feel, or response. Concentrate so that you will strike as this *begins* to occur—not after it happens. A rather stiff graphite rod is a big advantage in this type of strike sensing.

Often in nymphing, the taking trout feels you long before you feel him, especially in slower water or on longer casts. Trout usually spit or blow out the fake that is pulling them sideways or backward. With the sinking lines and in very fast water most trout

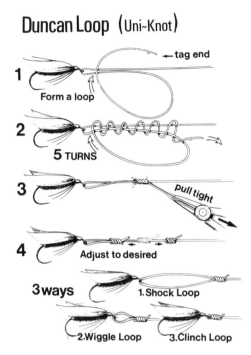

Duncan Loop (Uni-Knot)

1 Form a loop — tag end

2 **5 TURNS**

3 pull tight

4 Adjust to desired

3 ways
1. Shock Loop
2. Wiggle Loop
3. Clinch Loop

are self-hooked. If you doubt this, look where they are hooked—most will be hooked in the deep corner end of the mouth. When you sight strike, as you do with dry flies, trout are usually hooked in the front parts of the upper or lower jaw.

Stonefly nymphing is deep, bottom fishing in most circumstances. It is not easy unless you do it right and try to have as much going for you and the fly as the trout has going for him.

The deep, unseen, stone nymph should have a needle-sharp hook, a soft body, and natural action and attitude. It should act like a normal stonefly nymph, not a jet-propelled one, and be attached to a tackle system that will most enable you to sense the trout's mouth take hold of it. I'll emphasize again the value of a long, stiff graphite rod in feeling the nymph's situation.

The Adult

Following are two fly designs that imitate the stonefly adult stages that interest trout: the surface-emerging adult stone and the egg-laying adult stone.

FLOATING-HATCHING OR STILLBORN STONE

This design, which is usually fished in the surface film or just below the surface in very rough, swift water, simulates the stonefly that has come to the surface and is practically out of its nymphal skin. At such a time, some nymphs hatch into adults, some are trapped, and some die while hatching. This pattern will actually have the outline of a nymph with some part of the adult sticking out of its top or back. Since most stonefly surface emergers are size 8 or smaller, this pattern is seldom used for the larger stoneflies.

The surface emerger is tied much like 1A of the preceding stone nymph design as to proportion and tying technique. No weight is used, however, on the hook shank. The other exceptions are:

Stillborn surface-emerger stonefly nymph

1. HOOK: light-wire, XL shank (such as salmon low-water Mustad 94240 or Mustad 94831)
5. BACK: between the wingcases form with Fly Rite poly dubbing a loop or ball to simulate the unfolding wings and back of the emerging adult from the nymphal case

I prefer to bend the hook shank down slightly *after* the fly is completed to simulate the arching of the nymph as the adult emerges.

This surface nymph is superb when the surface-emerging stoneflies seem to be popping off the water. It should be cast upstream on a floating line and long leader, then allowed to float downstream with the current. The expanded wingcase is rubbed with some paste flotant such as Mucilin, Dave's Bugflote, Dilly Wax, or Gink so that it holds the fly in the surface film and the wing is visible to the angler's eye. This fly works best when fished to a working fish in calm waters; in turbulent water, however, it can be fished like an unseen nymph, using the floating line and strike indicator. I like to fish this design during the early, small, dark-slate stone emergences and later when the little yellow and pale-olive stones are popping off. It should be fished to risers (surface swirls and/or porpoiselike rises) for best results. Remember: there are times when trout don't come up for the surface emergers well.

This is also a useful design up to several hours after the hatch has occurred. Then I think the trout are taking it as a stillborn or as just an opportune tidbit. I normally feel when I'm fishing any suggestive floating-nymph pattern that the trout see it as one of any number of food items—from a mayfly, stone, or caddis emerger to a hapless terrestrial insect stuck in the surface film. Surface emergers by any name are almost as much fun to sight-fish as the higher-riding adult imitations we call dry flies and usually several times more effective for interesting good trout when fished by the average fly fisher.

ADULT EGG-LAYING STONE

The adult female stonefly will fly back to the water once her eggs are fertilized and ripe. Usually such purposeful flights will occur within a twenty-four hour period following mating when temperature and humidity best favor the particular specie. Another major stimulus is wind. If sudden or long, hard gusts of wind occur while the stoneflies are in the trees, many will dislodge or excite into flight and flutter out over and down onto the water. The same general dry-fly design will serve for both these situations.

Because adults fly across, skitter, or rest on the surface depending on conditions and specie, I use two types of wing design to depict them. For the flying or fluttering adult I use a high, full, hair wing and hackle; for the surface-resting adult, I prefer a low, neat downwing of Microweb and stiff elk hair.

1. **HOOK:** Mustad 90240 (low-water salmon), Mustad light-wire 94831, or Mustad 9672. The size should match the adult's body length

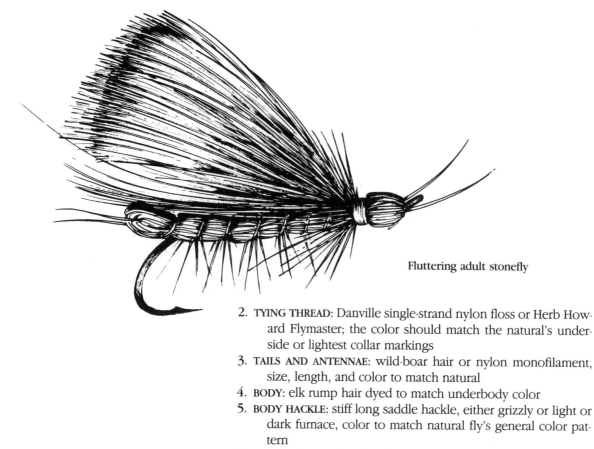

Fluttering adult stonefly

2. **TYING THREAD:** Danville single-strand nylon floss or Herb Howard Flymaster; the color should match the natural's underside or lightest collar markings

3. **TAILS AND ANTENNAE:** wild-boar hair or nylon monofilament, size, length, and color to match natural

4. **BODY:** elk rump hair dyed to match underbody color

5. **BODY HACKLE:** stiff long saddle hackle, either grizzly or light or dark furnace, color to match natural fly's general color pattern

6. **RIB:** single-strand nylon floss, same color as tying thread

7. **WING:** A (flying, fluttering design); stiff elk or northern white-tailed deer mane hair tied to flare back and up over and past body to simulate unfolded, moving wings of the adult. The color should match the natural's wing. Natural elk- or deer-hair color is a good compromise for most stonefly wings. B (at-rest design): underwing of stiff elk hair or squirrel-tail hair; overwing of a section of Microweb wing material cut and rolled to shape and colored with felt-tipped waterproof marking pen to match adult's wings. The underwing gives flotation as well as the bulk needed to properly form the overwing

8. **HEAD AND COLLAR:** well-tip-marked, stiff northern white-tailed deer or mule-deer body hair dyed to match natural's back and legs. Collar (legs) and head are formed by tying hair butts down and forward and making a hollow bullet head; tips form collar by doubling the hair butts back again. This type of head gives outstanding flotation, silhouette, and durability to the design, particularly in the rough waters in which stonefly adults normally prefer to lay their eggs

I extend the elk-hair body one-third the shank length past the hook bend to enhance the look and balance of the fly. The body is first ribbed with the tying floss and overribbed (or palmered)

Adult stonefly resting on surface

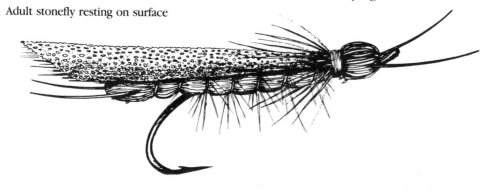

with the saddle hackle. For the fluttering adult, I leave the body fully palmered. For the resting adult, I trim off the top and bottom of the hackle as well as the deer-hair collar; this way the fly rests and silhouettes on the water like the real adult. Both patterns are sprayed with Scotchgard and overcoated with a paste flotant such as Mucilin, Dave's Bugflote, Dilly Wax, or Gink. Twitch or skitter the fluttering pattern well when fishing it.

I try to observe the active adults and how the trout are reacting to them instead of pounding away without an estimate of what is happening.

Usually the larger stoneflies that crawl out of the water to emerge will make direct flights out over the water from the streamside foliage. I cast toward the banks from midstream and skitter the fluttering-adult pattern a couple of times on the water, making foot-long twitches. I then let it rest and float, and then repeat the procedure. The fly can also be twitched or skittered up, down, or across the current if the naturals are doing the same. *But watch where and when the trout are taking these visible adults.* A good procedure is to pick out one or two larger risers and watch the action before you begin your presentation. Often my second guessing or overanxiousness has caused me to miss out on the best fishing.

I fish the resting adult with more or less standard dry-fly techniques: that is, up-and-across or down-and-across presentations. I usually let it ride drag free. On occasion, though, the adults will be twitching, twisting, or dipping to lay eggs or to take off from the water. At those times I impart some twitching. This is best accomplished with casts that angle down and across.

The resting adult is also appropriate when surface-emerging adults are riding the current before and during their initial take-off attempts.

Let's go back again to observation. *Try to see what is going on between the insects' actions and the trouts' response to them*—that is the key. It may even change every few minutes with the wind,

Spent adult stonefly

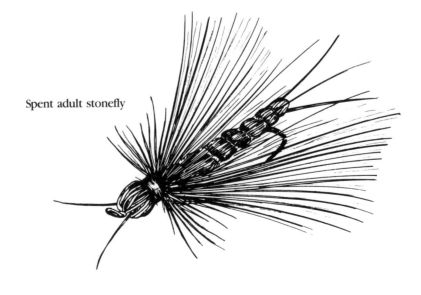

light, or adults' activities. Not all the trout will be concentrating on one opportunity or area. The larger fish will probably be working on the most helpless or vulnerable forms and will be hidden from most eyes as they feed. Look twice! Then stop and look hard and long again at any particular feeding situation. Binoculars are a great help when spying on surface activity. You will be surprised at how much you did not see or realize at first. Trout, especially older and larger ones, do not pick random feeding stations. They look for safety, overhead cover, slower current, and areas that seem to funnel food to them. The pecking order is usually such that the smaller or younger fish will be the most visible and easiest to cast to—so look, identify, and study the alternatives.

On occasion, particularly where the larger stonefly adults are very abundant, the dead surface adult will be eaten. These are insects that have died from age or exhaustion. Usually this situation becomes more significant after the peak activity of egg-laying has occurred for a few days or up to a week or so. In this situation I use the adult resting pattern without the Microweb wing. But when I tie this design I spread out the sparse elk-hair underwing. I do not dress the fly with flotant paste, so it rides in or just under the surface film like the dead and wet spent naturals do. They are fished dead drift to working trout or at random in heavy-water or pocket-water areas. Even if you don't see much feeding activity, there is a good chance that the trout will be expecting these last tidbits of the grand stonefly hatches.

6
CADDISFLIES
Trichoptera

C addisflies, which are also known as sedges, are the third major aquatic insect on which trout feed in most waters. These insects, which assume mothlike and grublike forms, have not traditionally been as popular with trout fishermen and fly tiers because of their looks, complex life cycle, and erratic behavior. Yet trout in both streams and lakes eagerly include the caddis in their feeding in numbers as significant as any aquatic insect available.

Caddis are much better adapted to a wider range of aquatic environments than the stonefly; and they equal or excell the mayfly in this respect. In fact, throughout the lakes, ponds, swamps, creeks, and rivers of North America, there are many more species of caddis than either mayflies or stoneflies. They seem able to cope with man's tampering with their water systems more successfully than most aquatic-insect orders. Their widespread availability, numbers, and size make them very attractive and important food for most wild and semiwild trout, especially the small and medium-size trout most often sought by the fly fisher.

Yet caddis are truly a fly fisher's paradox; most of us catch at least some trout that mistake our other fly patterns for caddis and when we do recognize a caddis hatch or egg-laying flight, we fish it rather unskillfully or even ignorantly. And if most of us see aquatic insects on or above the water, and rising trout in the area, we seldom go for our caddis imitations first. Yet knowing what I now know about the caddis, I think *it is the best aquatic insect for the average trout fisher to imitate successfully and fool trout with.*

I make this statement because most subsurface and surface aquatic-insect imitations are fished out of "natural-action" control. The caddis—including the emergent pupa and the surface egg-laying and diving egg-laying adult—are erratically active and forceful insects. So excessive fly drag and speed, or a fly moving counter to the current or buffeted by the wind—all common problems for the average fly fisher—actually suggest the caddis' normal life-cycle activities.

The caddis certainly have the most interesting life cycle of trout-stream insects. The insect has four major life-cycle stages, or what entomologists call a "complete metamorphosis:" egg, larva, pupa, and adult. Their life cycle, though aquatic, closely resembles that of most terrestrial moths and butterflies.

Trichoptera, which identifies this order of insects, means "hair wings." The four large wings of the adult caddis have a velvetlike carpet of hair over their surfaces. The true moths and butterflies, which closely resemble the caddis in shapes and life cycles, have scales on their wings instead of the hairlike wings of the adult caddis.

The four-stage caddis life cycle lasts an average of one year, with some species producing new generations every six months to two years. The various species display an ability to adapt to a wide range of aquatic habitats, flourishing in any successful trout habitat. The wormlike or grublike caddis larvae do not swim but are generally quite mobile. They can utilize many bottom types for food, concealment, and breathing. I never cease to be amazed at where I find caddis larvae living; like the common English sparrow, if need be they will adapt themselves to almost *any* situation. Of course the larvae in most caddis families do well because they construct cases or "suits of armor" that serve as portable homes as they seek suitable environments or forage for food.

Unlike the mayfly or stonefly, the individual caddis species differ greatly in life-cycle stages and physical appearance, especially in the immature stages. The eggs stick to the surface of various bottom structures after being deposited directly or indirectly by the ovipositing female. The eggs usually incubate for about two weeks before hatching. The tiny, grublike, six-legged larvae emerge and establish themselves in a nearby area.

Neither the eggs nor new larvae have any immediate significance to trout or trout fishers. The larvae feed aggressively on live and dead plants and animals. I've seen handfuls of cased larvae feeding on the bodies of dead salmon in Alaska.

The larvae grow rapidly. Those that make cases continue to enlarge them or build new ones as they grow. The outer-skin changes between instars are similar to those that the mayfly and stonefly nymphs undergo.

Most caddis larvae visible or accessible to trout are case-builders. Those that are most mobile are usually exposed foraging on the sides and tops of bottom structures such as rocks, ledges, aquatic vegetation, and dead wood. Though trout sometimes eat the case and larva, seldom does this cased-caddis foraging provide a significant need to imitate and fish such imitations.

The free-living caddis larvae—that is, those that do not build larval cases or homes—hide in crevices, cracks, or holes on the sides and undersides of water structures. I have some doubts as to how many of these larvae are available to trout. In my underwater observations I see few free-living larval specimens exposed or drifting in a way that would make them vulnerable to trout. Some angling writers create an image in the fly fisher's mind that stream and lake bottoms look like an aquatic-insect grand buffet—which trout leisurely pick and choose from. This is usually a distortion, for concealment and protection are absolutely necessary or the populations of insects would be immediately and seriously depleted by fish and other predators.

The important physical characteristics common to all caddis larvae are:

1. three major body sections—head, thorax, and abdomen: the head and thorax, which has three wingless segments, will be much darker and coarser skinned than the abdomen.
2. three pair of legs, one pair per thoracic segment: legs are positioned on lower side or under thorax.

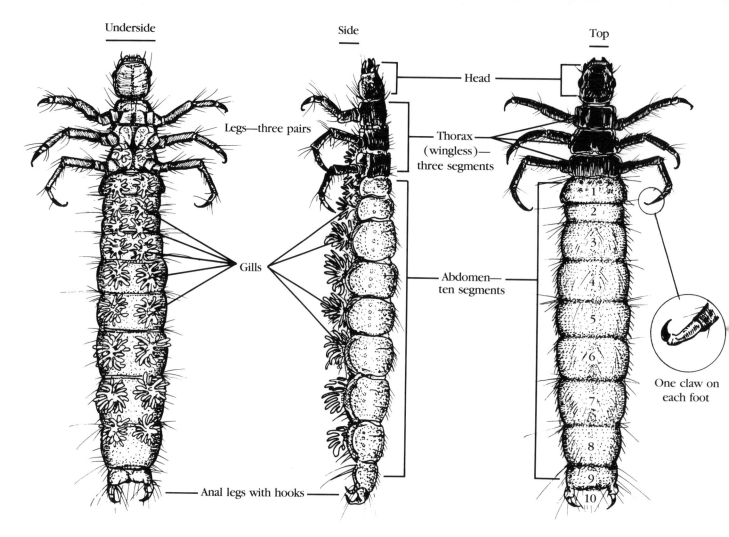

Underside

Side

Top

Head

Legs—three pairs

Thorax
(wingless)—
three segments

Gills

1
2
3
4
5
6
7
8
9
10

Abdomen—
ten segments

One claw on
each foot

Anal legs with hooks

A typical caddis larva

3. each foot has one large, sharp claw.
4. gills may appear as filaments on underside of abdomen and as hairs on sides and tops of head, thorax, legs, and abdomen.
5. there are no visible tails or antennae. The end of abdomen will have one or more "hooks" with which the caddis holds itself or its case in place.
6. larva has no wingcase and has a very definite grublike or wormlike appearance. Posterior end of abdomen will usually form a slight crook or hook when loose from the bottom or if you hold one to examine it

Caddis adapt easily and the larvae's living modes best illustrate this. The way they live also distinguishes them from other aquatic insects. Here is a summary of caddis-larvae living modes:

1. **Free livers.** Larvae do not build a case but utilize protective body-color camouflage and use bottom concealment for protection. They move about freely, foraging for food on sides and undersides of bottom structures. Possibly there are limited quantities available to bottom-foraging trout.
2. **Net spinners.** Larvae do not construct a case but reside in crevices, cracks, and holes and spin unique web nets on

which to collect food. Webs also serve as camouflage cover over the larvae's dens. They are seldom visible at this time to foraging trout.

3. **Tube makers.** Small species of caddis whose larvae burrow and construct tubelike homes in the bottom of lakes or streams, in mud, sand, and/or clay. Unavailable at this time to foraging trout.

4. **Saddle-case makers.** Larvae construct strong, sand, grain, or pebble cases which are relatively portable, on the sides of

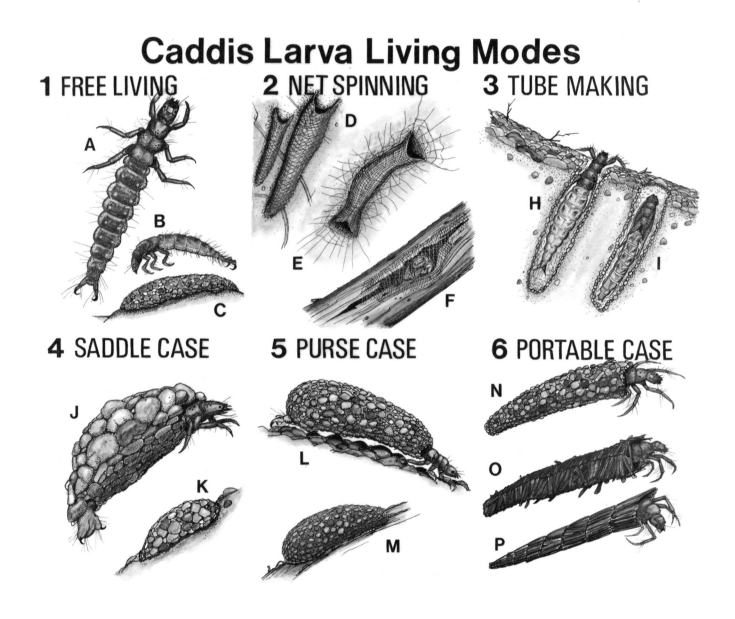

Caddis Larva Living Modes
1 FREE LIVING
2 NET SPINNING
3 TUBE MAKING
4 SADDLE CASE
5 PURSE CASE
6 PORTABLE CASE

bottom structures. Larvae and cases are visible to trout, but larvae are not actually available for trout to eat.

5. **Purse-case makers**. Larvae construct heavy, semiportable, bag-shaped cases of sand and pebbles. They move sluggishly about when food or environment is not suitable. Such cased larvae are not normally eaten by foraging trout.

6. **Portable-case makers**. Larvae construct cases that are tailored for portability and protection. Each species has a unique construction design of specific aquatic or terrestrial plant materials or various types of rock sizes—or combinations of both.

These are probably the most vulnerable regularly eaten caddis fly larvae, especially in colder seasons or when other free food forms are scarce.

Such larval cases are made by using a secreted mouth glue and a silk-like web material to hold various parts and particles of plants, stone, and even clam or snail shells together. The unusual glue is secreted from the larva's mouth glands, and it forms a strong waterproof bond with these construction materials—truly an amazing feat.

Caddis larvae tend to establish colonies. Sometimes these colonies completely encrust suitable bottom structures with cases. Such colonies would seem to tempt foraging trout into grazing on the encased larvae. This is true at times, particularly with the most vulnerable and accessible portable-case caddis. Trout digest the insect and pass out the indigestible portions of the case. However, imitating such larvae seems extremely impractical to me, for besides competing with hundreds of naturals, imitating and fishing such cased larvae is a feat I've not accomplished to any satisfaction. I believe the fish I have taken doing so, as well as other reports of same, are mostly trout responding to attractor stimuli of the unnatural look or action of the imitation, not to natural feeding patterns.

Caddis larvae, free-swimming or cased, rank second only to stonefly nymphs for prompting fly tiers into turning sculptors. Intricate designs have been made with latex rubbers, acetate floss, ostrich herl, quills, and even the real caddis cases soaked in head cement and epoxy fitted to weighted hooks. They are impressive wall or fly-box decorations, but I do not feel they are in the least impressive to a wild trout feeding on caddis.

I generally opt for much more suggestive or impressionistic caddis-larva imitations that are not cased—purely larval—in form and purpose. The larva and pupa can both be easily and practically and most effectively imitated by simple tying designs that reduce the number of patterns for most of us practical fly tiers and fishers. You will need to understand *both* larval and pupal stages to employ this system.

The third stage of the caddis, which is basically the period of transformation from wormlike larva to adult caddis, is a very important interlude for trout and fly fishers. The pupation period is a hibernationlike inactivity climaxing in an awakening of the fully developed pupa, its emergence journey to the surface, and its transformation into the air-breathing adult caddis.

Pupation begins when the larva reaches its maximum growth. Then it constructs a pupal case. The larvae use their living cases if they have such; if they don't, they build special pupal cases. In either event the case is strongly secured to the side or underside of the bottom structure. Once this is accomplished, the larva closes the exit end with a protective but porous seal. The larva then begins the pupation period, which lasts several weeks, inside the case.

Drastic anatomical changes take place during this period. The pupa forms its adult wings, appendages, air-breathing apparatus, and sex organs. Once the pupa is mature it only awaits the proper water conditions, which are usually light and temperature dependent, to emerge from its case to swim or crawl to the surface to transform into the air-breathing, winged adult.

During the pupation period, the insect is not generally available to foraging trout, nor is there any need to fish an imitation of this part of the pupa's life cycle—unless you want to glue the imitation to the side of a stream-bottom rock and trust your luck!

When the mature pupae free themselves from the case they are ready to emerge into adults upon reaching the surface. Unlike the clumsy, slow, crawling larvae, most are active, strong, graceful swimmers. With a natural buoyancy and leg-swimming action, the pupae head for the surface with haste. Most species swim and emerge on the surface, a few others—particularily some of the larger species—will crawl or swim to the perimeter of the water or onto an exposed object to emerge.

There are many complicated and contradicting descriptions of the emergence and transformation of caddis pupae. It does seem there is agreement that the pupae's outer skin swells or inflates and separates from the pupae and quickly splits once the surface is reached. The pupae normally escape quickly, transforming into the winged adults, which free themselves of the pupal skin.

The mature pupae, once out of the seclusion and protection of the pupal case, are extremely vulnerable and attractive to foraging trout. It is the direct or indirect journey to the water's surface that exposes pupae to their attack. The almost minnowlike, bottom-to-surface movement triggers trout into rapid responses to catch these emerging insects.

The important physical characteristics common to all mature caddis pupae are:

1. immature wings, one-third to one-half the length of body,

positioned on the lower side of thoracic region, appearing to be under pupa
2. six thin, long legs that are equal or longer than entire pupa
3. two very long antennae, often longer than entire body, pointing back over the top of thorax and abdomen
4. no well-developed, visible tails
5. round, tapering abdomen that is usually lighter and differently colored than thorax and head

I doubt if many fly fishers have ever captured live emerging pupae or retained them intact to study and identify them. Home aquariums can make such study practical. At streamside I usually just investigate various pupal cases I find glued to stream-bottom

Caddis pupa emerging from case

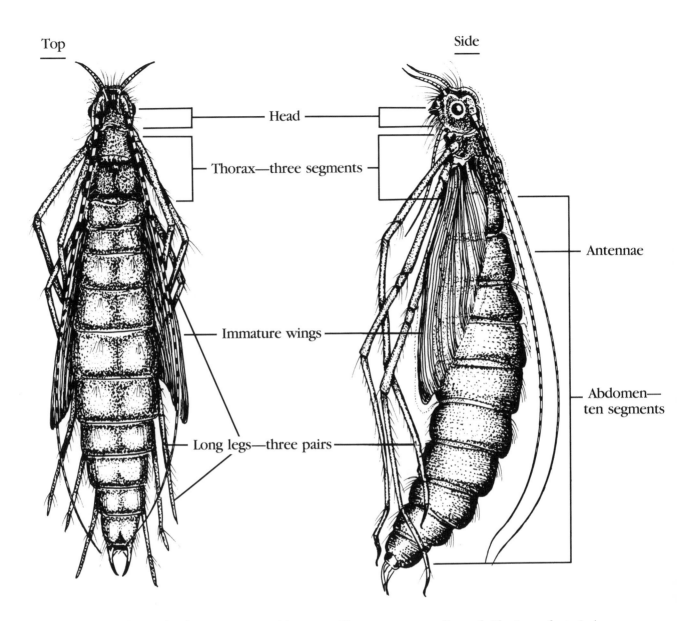

Top

Side

Head

Thorax—three segments

Antennae

Immature wings

Long legs—three pairs

Abdomen—
ten segments

structures, studying the live insects at this stage. You can get a very close idea of what the emergent caddis pupa will look like by carefully opening the cases and removing the live pupae.

Top and side views of a typical mature caddis pupa

When the pupa escapes its final aquatic jacket, it is born—or blooms—into the adult stage almost instantly. The emergence into adult flight has been likened to "the launching of a Polaris Missile." The caddis adult normally takes very little time unfolding and drying its wings, usually just a second or so, and then it takes off, leaving its pupal skin stuck on the surface. Unless the emergence is heavy, it is difficult to spot the caddis coming up before they launch into flight.

Few new healthy caddis adults are captured by trout or birds once they are able to fly. As with mayflies and stoneflies, they seek immediate terrestrial cover and seclusion. There they colonize with other adult caddis of their hatch or specie and begin a series of mating and egg-laying flights over a period of days or even weeks. This fast emergence and the length of adult life tends to mask the importance of caddis hatches when compared to the more apparent behavior of mayflies and stoneflies. Caddis are often more casually or routinely keyed upon than mayflies or stoneflies by resident feeding trout. Yet they may well be better insects for the fly fisher to imitate, since trout will be seeing and eating some almost every day of the season. This is especially true for visiting anglers unsure of local insect activity on a trout stream or lake.

The adult caddis, which is mothlike in shape, is a highly active, alert insect that is a rapid, strong, erratic flyier. It is also a quick runner on the dry and wet surfaces of its environment. Caddis females of many species, using their long, strong legs, even swim or crawl beneath the water to deposit their eggs directly on the bottom of a lake or stream.

Mating and egg-laying activities are usually keyed to the most pleasant time of day or night per season. During spring and sum-

Adult caddis at rest and in flight

mer, most caddis seem to prefer late afternoon to sundown or darkness to carry out their mating and ovipositing.

The adult caddis in flight and at rest is very easy to distinguish from the other major aquatic insects trout feed upon, particularily the mayfly and the stonefly.

At rest, the caddis from the side or top has a very distinctive wing outline, which is similar to the shape of a sloping pup tent. The fly appears fuzzy or soft colored, and usually its wings are mottled and have distinct horizontal venation. The abdomen is not visible from the top or sides. The body only extends back about two-thirds as far as the wings do. Its legs are long, and the long, hairlike antennae usually extend forward or are bent back over the top of the wings. If disturbed, the caddis runs or quickly launches into flight. The females are a little larger and heavier bodied than the males.

If you think it may be a moth, hold its wings between your fingers. If a silky and powderlike substance comes off the wings it is a moth. The substance is actually the moth's wing scales. Caddis have wing hair that does not show as such or as vividly on one's fingers.

In flight, where you are most likely to see the caddis adults, they appear to have large, wide, paddle-wheel-shaped wings— much like the moths you see near streetlights at nights. Their four large wings beat rapidly, windmilling and making a one-hundred-and-eighty-degree arc on each side. This beating almost completely obscures from sight the insects' small bodies. Now look at the front of the flying insect. If you see two very long, very visible antennae, it is surely an adult caddis. Some species have antennae one or two times longer than their body and wing lengths. It has no tail. The adult's flight is fast in very erratic, zigzagging patterns. The fly seems to be dodging unseen objects. The wing is a glowing blur in the open sunlight.

The three major stages in the caddisfly life cycle that are particularly significant to trout are larva, emerging pupa, and egg-laying adult. In certain situations during these stages they are most vulnerable and attractive to trout and thus are most practical to imitate and fish. These simple facts and your ability to observe and recognize the naturals and the trout's reactions to them will enable you to choose and fish the right imitation in the most effective manner.

Close and exact identification of the caddis species during these important stages is not necessary to angling success. Your own interest and objective observations will free you from the often boring and nearly impossible technical jobs of exact identification and dealing with unpronounceable scientific names. You will probably develop more interest in exact identification on

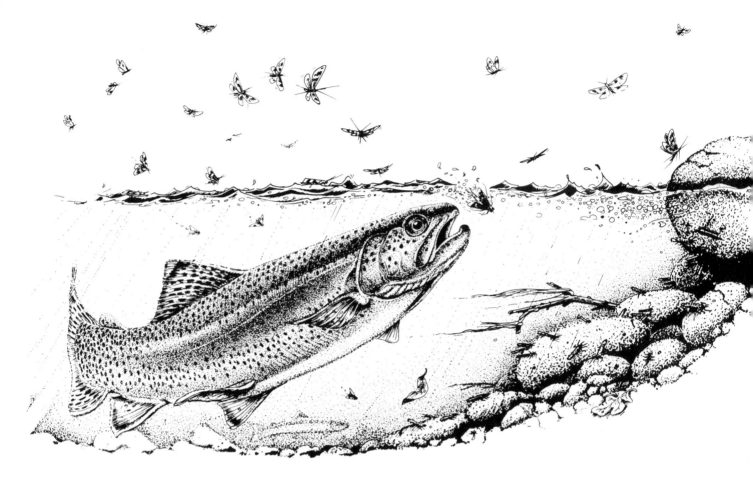

Trout feeding on returning caddis
adults, diving to lay eggs

your own, especially if you regularly or seasonally fish the same waters. Caddis species overlap in size, shape, color, and actions even more than do mayflies and stoneflies. An assortment of suggestive caddis imitations is a very practical method of matching various caddis species over the course of the season and in different waters.

I recommend the same philosophy of imitation for the caddis as for the aquatic insects previously discussed. Size, general shape or look, and lifelike action are the most critical factors in fly selection when fishing specific caddis species and stages. Soft-textured, impressionistic imitations normally create the illusion of living insects much better to the trout's eye than hard, exact sculptures.

Identifying, Matching, and Fishing the Caddisfly

The larva. Caddis larvae of various families will be widely distributed in most trout streams and lakes. However, they will of course be more abundant and significant in habitats where water quality, oxygen, food, and bottom habitat are optimum. This closely parallels those areas in which trout reside.

I don't ever recall sampling bottoms of trout water that haven't contained various free-living and cased caddis larvae. But it seems more larvae are present where the water depth is four feet or less and the bottom is very irregular, with rock, coarse gravel, rubble, aquatic plants, and large dead terrestrial plants and roots.

Some larger portable-cased caddis will be obvious on the tops and sides of large stones, but it takes a keen, concentrated look to spot many of the less mobile cased caddis, free-living caddis, and net-spinning caddis. I often remove various structures from the bottom and study their surfaces to better detect the larvae and cases. You can seine some specimens, but most are best captured by picking up bottom structures and removing specimens from the sides, undersides, cracks, and crevices. Some are very hard to see.

Imitating and fishing uncased or cased larvae seems to me not much more than attractor fishing. Few uncased caddis larvae are ever exposed and cased ones are nearly impossible to simulate with artificials. However, since the uncased caddis-larva imitations are so popular as nymphs and do catch trout for whatever reasons, I recommend that you understand the imitations and how to fish them best.

The uncased and cased larvae only crawl about—they are incapable of swimming. Some free-living, net-spinning larvae will thrash back and forth when removed from their bottom holds and dropped into open water until they settle on the bottom again. But all types naturally hold, hook, or otherwise adhere tightly to the bottom structure and move about at the rate just equal to an aquatic snail.

The freelivers and net spinners normally are much darker and better camouflaged than the cased varieties. Cased larvae plucked from their little body socks are usually very bright and lightly colored over the length of their abdomens, but few trout ever see such live, "nude" larvae unless the larva is impaled on a bait fisher's hook.

The emergent caddis pupa. The mature caddis pupa does not waste much time getting up and on to the important tasks above once it leaves its case. The sure, rapid pupal rise to the surface from the bottom is an absolute turn-on to wild or carry-over stocked trout. Their response must be sure and without hesitation or the opportunity is lost. The same goes for those fly fishers who wait to see and capture an emergent pupa. A subsurface aquarium net will capture some of the emergent pupae. One must look quick or emerse the catch into ice water to catch much sight of this quicksilver stage before the pupa hatches out.

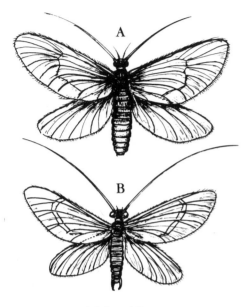

Adult caddis
A. Female
B. Male

If catching the emergent pupa is difficult, the next best option is to check for sealed pupal cases on the bottom. Look for the cases on the sides and undersides of exposed bottom structures. Remove the pupa by carefully cutting off the large end of the pupal case with your fishing scissors. With small tweezers or your fingernails, gingerly pull the pupa out. From several of the most abundant samples observe their size, shape, and coloration. If the pupa is removed carefully and is fairly near emergence, you can put it into a clear jar filled with water for further observation. Note the general body, wing, and leg attitude. Choose a fly design that best simulates its size, shape, posture, and coloration.

The adult. To capture, observe, and identify fast-flying adult caddis, a sizable aquarium or butterfly net is needed. I have found it best to remain still near the flying insects and let them move toward me, as they will avoid a large, aggressive, moving object.

The adult caddis is best captured with a net over the water or when attracted to a bright light at night. Since most caddis are active at night, light attraction near the water is best for sampling adults. Place them in a small, clear, capped jar for close observation and to avoid damage to or escape of the insect. You can use a fly swatter to kill or capture samples, but these dead or damaged specimens are not as desirable for examination and observation as the undamaged, live ones.

At times adults will fall victim to traps such as spider webs or car front ends. I often check out my camper's windshield or grill upon arriving at the fishing waters for freshly killed flying insects. Streamside spider webs stretched across dead willow limbs, bridges, and so on are ideal samplers to see quickly what is happening.

Once you have captured or observed and identified the insects as adult caddis and have a good idea of their *size, shape, and color,* then you can ask yourself "what action do the flies have that is attracting the trout to strike?" I'll stand or sit as close as I can, *without fishing,* and watch the rises and the surface. Once I begin to concentrate objectively I see where the flies are coming from—to the water, off the water, buzzing over or across the water, or caught in the surface film. You probably can't or won't do this if you try to fish during the observation.

When I get an idea of the feeding behavior of the trout, I begin trying to fish the fly like the naturals to which the trout are responding. This is, of course, one of the most interesting and challenging parts of fly-fishing for trout. Playing creator and puppeteer with these small morsels of hair, feather, and hook to simulate nature and fool the expert . . . a wild trout.

Sometimes the trout will be taking the freshly emerged adults that have just freed themselves from the pupal skin as they dry off and activate their adult legs and wings for takeoff. But there's a better chance it will be those female caddis that are coming down, across, and diving below the surface to lay their eggs that the trout are taking—a situation that makes the flies face the trout rather than escape from the trout's underwater advantage.

Adult caddis will also be accepted and eaten on occasion during heavy hatching or egg-laying activities when crippled or spent (dying) adults are trapped in the surface film. Abnormally severe weather will also cripple or kill adults and trap them on the surface.

Normally the splashy rise with a smacking or popping sound will mean the trout are rushing up to catch the pupa or newly hatched adult. Sometimes, if you look quickly, you will see the adult rise off the water in escape, missed by the trout. *Watch it closely. If it heads for the woods it is a new emerger, if it rises up and circles or buzzes over the water it probably is an egg layer.*

It may sound a little too complicated, but if possible try to identify the female caddis and tie or buy your imitations to match the lady. They are a bit larger than the males and more appropriate when the fish are after the egg layers. The female has a little fatter abdomen than the male and its eggs often show at the end as a different color than the underbody. The slimmer males have a more compact wing shape.

A Typical Caddisfly Life Cycle

1. The female caddis, over a period of several days, deposits eggs on or below the surface.
2. The eggs stick to surfaces of such bottom structures as rocks, gravel, weed, and wood. Then eggs incubate for several weeks and hatch into tiny, wormlike caddis larvae.
3. Caddis larvae distribute themselves, choosing suitable habitats to reside in depending upon their family and species adaptation.
4. The caddis larvae of many species build unique, portable, protective housing by gluing various natural materials together.
5. Some other species seek out seclusion on the sides and bottoms of various water structures, where they are free living or construct unique silklike capture nets over or near their lies.
6. In all circumstances, after the caddis have spent about a year in the larval stage, each cements a pupal case to the bottom

Caddisfly life cycle

and seals itself inside, much like caterpillars do. The larva then transforms in several weeks into a pupa.

7A. The mature pupa opens up its case and emerges. Note the drastic physical change from the larva to the pupa.

7. The pupa then swims rapidly up to the surface. As it does so, its outer skin separates or fills with a gas that assists its rise and escape from the pupal skin.

8. At the surface, the pupal skin quickly splits open and down the back and the adult emerges. This is a very rapid process.

9. The adult caddis quickly launches itself into flight, leaving the pupal skin stuck in the surface film. It is now an air-breathing insect.
10. The newly emerged adults fly directly to the seclusion of lakeside or streamside cover. For several days to weeks the adults congregate, flying over the water to mate or drink water.
11. Females fly back to the water's surface and lay their eggs on or below the surface. Each female may make several such flights until her eggs are all laid. The flies die after mating and egg laying.
12. The sticky caddis eggs adhere to bottom structures, beginning incubation and thus completing the four-stage life cycle of the caddisfly.

Phases of the caddisfly life cycle and their imitations
1. Larva—Position 1
2. Emergent pupa—Position 2, A and B
3. Pupa at surface—Position 3
4. Adult caddis at rest—Position 1
5. Adult caddis, surface, fluttering and egglaying—Position 2
6. Adult caddis, subsurface, swimming and egglaying—Position 4
(Note: Spent surface film adult, Position 3, omitted)

My Favorite Caddisfly Fly Designs

The caddis life-cycle stages that are important to imitate especially lend themselves to my suggestive-impressionistic philosophy of fly-tying.

Form, materials that suggest living action, and imitating the natural's movement are all keys to success when fishing caddis imitations to trout. Only the cased or uncased larvae pose a question as to the value of imitating them. I think there are a dozen more practical bottom-living trout foods to imitate that would bring the fly fisher better results. But for the sake of completeness, I include the uncased caddis larva here.

The Larva

The caddisfly larva, if available to trout in streams, would be *crawling over the bottom, adrift very near the bottom with no action against the current, or traveling downstream faster than the current.* In stillwaters it would never be off the bottom. Perhaps when the caddis molts its old skin, it would be out of its case or more apt to lose its grip on the bottom structure. In such instances, it would be considerably lighter in overall color than the cased larva. Extra weighting is also important to roll the larva fly along the bottom.

CADDISFLY LARVA (NO. 1 POSITION)

1. **HOOK:** regular or extra-fine wire, ring or turned-up eye (Mustad 94842 is excellent)
2. **WEIGHTING:** lead or copper wire over two-thirds of shank; wire should be approximately the same diameter as hook wire on all these designs
3. **TYING THREAD:** single-strand nylon floss approximating the color of natural's abdomen and thorax
4. **CEMENT:** thinned Pliobond on all these designs for underbody and lead; clear head cement for head
5. **TAIL:** tiny tuft of marabou, ostrich herl, or muskrat underfur, light cream color
6. **ABDOMEN:** Orlon sparkle knitting yarn, similar commercial nymph dubbing, or very soft natural underfur such as otter or beaver to match color of larva's abdomen
    a. rib: very fine gold or copper wire
    b. gills: after abdomen is dubbed and ribbed, pick out a few fibers on lower part to simulate gills; abdomen should be two-thirds total length of larva's body. Trim off any wild fibers on sides or top.
7. **THORAX:** squirrel, woodchuck, or muskrat body hair or synthetic dubbing to match natural's color. Usually caddis thoraxes are much darker and a different color than the abdomen, especially in the cased caddis larva

8. LEGS: the guardhair of the above natural furs will do very well to simulate legs, or one turn of soft, bird hackle can be used. In either case, trim "legs" off top and upper sides of thorax. There should be six legs, each about one-half to two-thirds the length of body.

9. HEAD: same as thorax, with a whip-finish and just a spot of head cement or another very thin, penetrating cement

When I fish such larvae imitations I always pick up a wet stone or piece of aquatic plant from the water and rub the imitation over it. This wets the fly and removes the unnatural man-made odors that may well be offensive to trout.

I would fish this type of larva in flowing water only. In lakes it could only imitate a pupa or attractor. It will fish best on a long, fine tippet. If the water is fast and pocketed, such as the water of the Roaring Fork in Colorado, use a small split-shot at the tippet-leader junction to assist in getting it to the bottom and controlling its downstream drift speed.

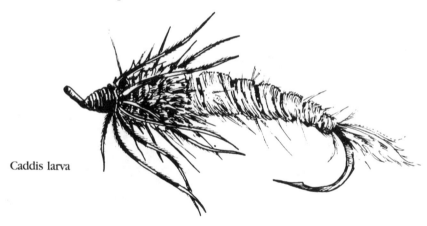

Caddis larva

Cast the larva up and across stream and let it drift and tumble in a *straight downstream drift path*. The distance across stream should be no more than can be easily mended to the line's tip with the fly rod for best drift control. *Larvae do not swim,* they crawl or tumble.

The long-leader, floating-line setup (described in the mayfly chapter) works best for fishing caddis larvae. The strike will be very soft if the trout mistakes it for a natural caddis larva. If it is dragging the strike will be more violent as the trout chases it thinking it is a fast-swimming pupa or just an attractor.

The uncased caddis larva tied and fished this way also is very suggestive of a number of trout foods, such as shrimp, scuds, sowbugs, midge larvae, and others. If it drags across, upstream, or downstream it becomes an attractor or is suggestive of the emerging pupa.

The Pupa

This pupa design suggests the stages of the caddis immediately after the pupa frees itself from the case. Positions 2A and 2B are weighted versions, while position 3 is tied without weighting so the pupa can hang in the surface film. This three-phase design is an extremely versatile and practical imitation for taking most pupa-feeding trout.

EMERGENT PUPA (NO. 2A, 2B, 3 POSITIONS)

1. **HOOK:** standard or light wire, regular-length shank, turned-up or ring eye best (Mustad 94842 is ideal)
2. **WEIGHTING:** lead or copper wire over one-half of shank length on 2A and B; no weight on 3

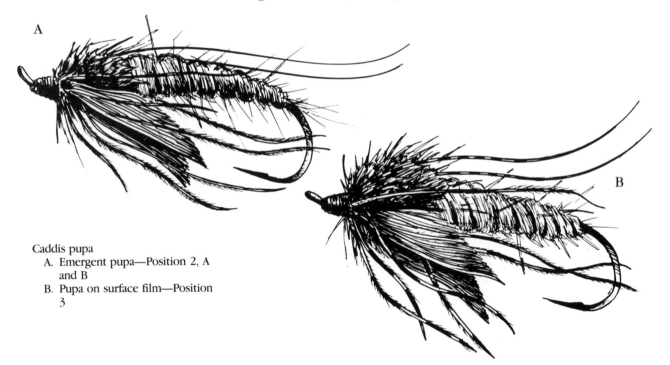

Caddis pupa
  A. Emergent pupa—Position 2, A and B
  B. Pupa on surface film—Position 3

3. **TYING THREAD:** Herb Howard Flymaster to match body color scheme
4. **CEMENT:** same as larva fly
5. **TAIL:** none
6. **ABDOMEN:** Orlon sparkle yarn or similar soft, shiny, synthetic dubbing
    a. rib: none or fine gold or silver wire or tying thread

      b. abdomen should be two-thirds the shank length; extend rear just down on to the hook bend

      c. dub abdomen loosely, but trim off all wild fibers so it appears smooth

7. THORAX: same as larva fly except a little larger in diameter for 2A and B. For 3, make top half larger with either a loop of poly yarn or dubbing to simulate the emerging adult (also assists in holding the pupa in the surface film). Study illustration

8. WINGS: two short sections of duck pointer quills or two small, soft hen-hackle tips. Wings should be one-half the total body length

9. LEGS: one turn of long, soft hen chicken hackle, game hen, grouse, or similar well-marked, soft bird feather. You can also use the same feather with tip removed fashioned into a DeFeo beard-style hackle. In either case, legs should be positioned on the lower sides of pupa from the head-and-thorax area; length should be one to one and a half times the length of body

10. HEAD: continue the thorax-colored dubbing on the head and shape to head's size

11. ANTENNAE (optional): two thin, well-marked feather fibers such as barred wood-duck flank. Position over the head and back of pupa one to one and a half times the length of body

The emergent pupa is fished several ways according to the advancement of this stage and to the area in which the trout seem to prefer to take it. Chances are that the pupa will be eaten most often by the better trout *as it starts for the surface to midway up*. Most larger trout are more reluctant to chase and catch the pupa at the surface simply because it takes more work and exposes them to surface dangers for too small a reward. The water's depth and speed also determine how and where the trout catch the pupa.

Here is how I fish the first two positions. Using a floating line, strike indicator, long leader, long tippet, and Duncan-loop-to-fly knot, I cast the wet, deodorized pupa up and slightly across the stream. The cast distance across is just that which I can easily mend slack line up to the fly-line tip. This enables me to control the straight downstream drift path. If the distance is greater, horizontal control is lost and the pupa *swings* (drags) unnaturally across the current. With either an upstream or downstream cast, I try to stack or put lots of slack in the leader and tippet so the pupa will sink quickly. The cast is placed well above the visual or suspected feeding area so that the pupa will be near or on the bottom as it approaches the trout. I allow the pupa to dead drift deep through the area once or twice, but near the end of the drift, as the fly goes past and downstream of me, I allow just a little vertical drag to develop so that the fly is pulled up toward the surface. Each consecutive cast, working upstream, or across stream, actually fishes the pupa in two positions.

If the trout I see working do not take the deep, dead-drifting pupa (position 2A), there is an excellent chance the trout is looking for the rising, emergent pupa. I position myself so I can slowly lift the pupa up to the surface within the trout's vision, usually beginning the lift about two feet in front of his position. The down-and-across presentation enables this emergent pupa to be fished most effectively. If the lift is made too close to the fish or too fast, it will require too much response for the trout unless he is really hard pressed to find enough naturals. Where trout seem to take the pupa best will usually be *just as the pupa begins to rise.*

In calm or slow water the pupa is allowed to sink on a slack leader. After it is near or on the bottom, I begin to raise the fly by a slow rod-tip lift and a short, slow, strip retrieve. Since the line and leader will be taut the strike may either be seen or felt.

There are dozens of variables in fishing the emergent pupa that will fool or attract trout. Remember that these naturals, although being very fine and fairly fast swimmers, do not naturally swim upstream or across stream once they leave the slack bottom pocket directly adjacent to the bottom structures. So upstream retrieving or horizontal drag converts the pupa into an attractor, not a natural food imitation. The exception to this would be those caddis that crawl out to emerge, when the pupae use a crawling-and-swimming movement along the bottom to reach the shoreline.

In calm waters, ponds, or lakes, the surface-emergent pupa does show more variable-direction swimming, so a certain degree of excess horizontal movement (swimming or crawling) is not unnatural. The caddis species that crawl out to emerge will display much more horizontal or lateral movement than surface emergers in both fast and calm waters. Here again, being able to observe what is taking place is invaluable in determining what, when, where, and how to fish the pupa or any other trout food. Just five or ten minutes of complete observation and concentration on any trout water renders priceless information that no book can give. It is also more fun and satisfying to make discoveries yourself than to have them told to you in a book.

I fish the surface-film emergent pupa (position 3) just below or in the surface film with the same floating line and tackle I use for positions 2A and B. The fly simulates either the first part of the hatching from the pupal skin or the occasional injured or stillborn pupae that occur. In either case, I cast and fish it dead drift and usually directly to a surface-feeding trout. The expanded thorax top is rubbed with Mucilin, Gink, or Dilly Wax so that it will hold the unweighted pupa on or in the surface film. The remainder of the fly should ideally be below the surface film.

As in dry-fly fishing, fishing this stage of the caddis pupa is a visual technique. Both up-and-across and down-and-across presentations in streams work well, as long as there is no major surface drag. This version and method is usually less effective than the swimming subsurface emergent pupa. Watch the surface rise-forms closely before this version is used. If they are quick, splashy, or noisy it is a good bet the trout are chasing fast-swimming pupae up and striking them just as they hit the surface film. The floating surface-film pupa does not excite or trigger these fish and will often pass unseen.

If you see slow, quiet, head-fin-and-tail rises and a residual bubble or two come up a second after the rise is completed, then the surface-film floater is called for. If you watch the riseform and mood of feeding trout, you can determine the better design.

A note on sizes: before I describe the adult-caddisfly designs I use, it might be a good time to refer to sizes, since there is a drastic difference in the size and silhouette of the larva and pupa when compared to the adult caddis. The larva is wingless; the pupa has more dominate leg outlines and small wing stubs. There may be one-half a hook size difference between the larva and the same bug after pupation. The adult's body is one-fourth to one-half a hook size smaller than the pupa, but the wings and antennae of the adult at rest are normally one-half to one time larger still than the body. In flight the difference seems even greater, the wings making the adult appear twice or more the size of the same fly at rest.

Such size variation in the same fly over these phases can be misleading to the average fly tier or fly fisher trying to match a caddis hatch. One size off, especially too large, can put down feeding fish or mean the difference between a few short strikes and many fine catches.

The best advice I can give you is to measure the body of your natural samples of larva, pupa, or adult. Choose a hook size or

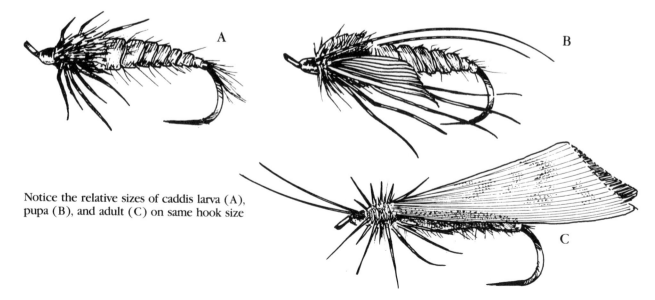

Notice the relative sizes of caddis larva (A), pupa (B), and adult (C) on same hook size

shank length that is correct. Use this same hook for the various stages of the same caddis, varying the proportions of the fly's parts accordingly. Measure the wing length of the adults if available, for example, and add that length to the hook size you have chosen for the body. With this system it is hard to make the most common and defeating mistake—choosing the wrong size.

My most persistent shortcoming in matching the smaller trout foods, such as aquatic and terrestrial insects, scuds, and sowbugs, is choosing a small enough size. It never seems right that trout would prefer or select such tiny foods (size 16 or smaller flies). Yet when trout are feeding during a multiple hatch, they will often ignore the largest bugs for the smallest ones.

The Adult

To match the range of important adult caddis stages (or positions) efficiently, I use four fly designs. These are: adult at rest on surface (position 1), surface-fluttering adult (position 2), spent surface-film adult (position 3), and subsurface, swimming, egg-laying adult (position 4).

Adult caddis resting on surface (microweb wing)

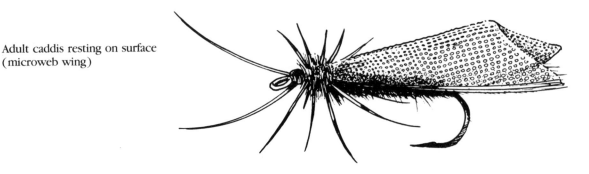

ADULT AT REST (NO. 1 POSITION)

This adult design is basically a low-profile silhouette of an adult caddis with its wings folded. It is used to suggest the newly emerged caddis or one that has returned to the surface to lay eggs, drink water, or die.

1. HOOK: light or extra-fine wire, regular-length or 1XL shank, turned-up or turned-down eye
2. TYING THREAD: Herb Howard Flymaster to match body color
3. CEMENT: clear head cement
4. FINISH: Scotchgard

5. TAIL: none
6. BODY: fine-fibered synthetic dubbing or beaver belly, color to match underbody of caddis and, if present, egg cluster
7. WING: Microweb or feather, colored and trimmed to match tent-wing outline; deer or elk hair may be used where rough water requires more flotation
8. LEGS: deer-mask hair tied as legs as in L & L Microweb Caddis pattern
9. HEAD: same dubbing as body
10. ANTENNAE: two very thin, stiff guardhairs from beaver belly or mink tail tied separated and forward of head
11. Whip-finish and seal with head cement
12. FINISH: lightly spray twice with Scotchgard to enhance overall durability and waterproofing

I fish this design up and across stream in fast water and down and across the slower runs, allowing it to drift naturally or occasionally twitching it during the drift. On calm waters, it is cast ahead of cruising fish and twitched under the surface slightly for best results. Long rods and long, light tippets help perfect this method.

Besides suggesting a newly emerged adult or a returning adult, it also can be fished as a diving or surfacing egg-laying adult if not dressed with flotant. A tiny split-shot at the leader-tippet junction helps greatly when fishing it in this manner. The Scotchgard assists in creating a silvery wrap of air over the fly, which closely simulates the look of a swimming adult.

ADULT FLUTTERING (NO. 2 POSITION)

This design simulates the adult caddis, on or over the surface, that is flapping its wings. I use it to simulate the takeoff of a newly emerged adult or a surface-skittering, egg-laying adult.

1. HOOK: fine or extra-fine wire, regular-length shank, turned-down eye
2. TYING THREAD: Herb Howard Flymaster nylon to match body color
3. CEMENT: clear head cement
4. FINISH: Scotchgard
5. TAIL: none
6. BODY: fine synthetic dubbing or beaver belly, colors to match adult's underbody and egg cluster; body should be tied over rear two-thirds of hook shank
7. RIB: grizzly dry-fly cock hackle dyed to match general leg and wing color, widely wrapped palmer-style over body, fibers sized the width of hook gap

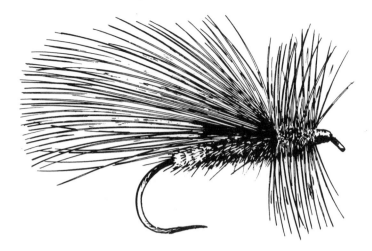

Fluttering-skittering adult caddis
(deer or elk wing)

8. WING: very stiff, natural dun-grey deer hair or coarse polypropylene yarn the color of adult's wing as seen in flight (a shade or so lighter than wing appears at rest). Wing is tied high and full to simulate unfolded, moving caddis wing. Allow the wings to spread out on upper sides as well. Wing hairs should be one and one-half or two times the length of the body

9. HACKLE: one or two very stiff grizzly hackles to match general wing-and-leg color pattern. Fibers' length should be one and one-half times the width of hook gap, and hackle collar should be one-fourth hook shank long for calm water and one-third hook shank long for rough water

10. HEAD: finish off small head with thread and whip-finish

11. CEMENT: add two or three drops of very thin clear head cement or similar penetrating cement to *hackle bases* and thread head

12. FINISH: spray entire fly twice with Scotchgard

I fish this design with a lot of surface action upstream, across, or downstream. Twitching, skittering, skating, and resting it simulates the active fluttering and running adult as she lays surface eggs or takes off. In very rough water I seldom use much action, but in calmer waters I try to imitate the natural's flight and float paths and patterns. This fly is especially effective in the evenings, at dusk, or after dark. A long, light, stiff fly rod and three-, four- or five-weight, double-tapered fly lines greatly assist in fishing this design.

This fly seems to skitter better if the hackle is cut nearly off the bottom of the body and collar and if the wing's length is a little longer than that of the natural.

Front and side views of skittering-diving poly caddis (Borger style)

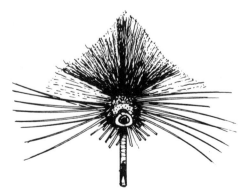

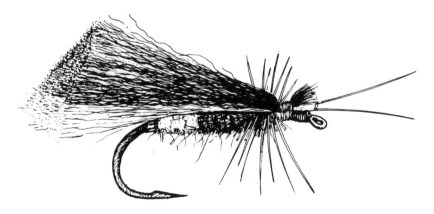

COLOR AND SIZE CHARACTERISTICS

Mayflies

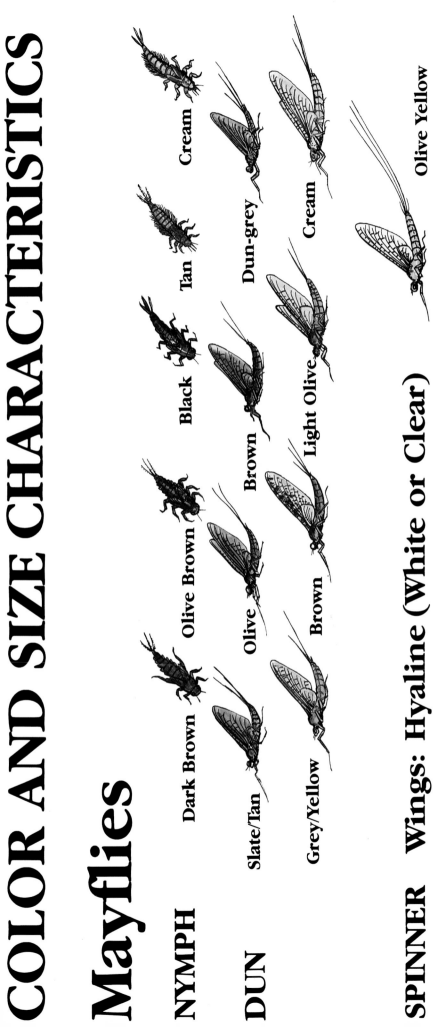

NYMPH Dark Brown Olive Brown Black Tan Cream

DUN Slate/Tan Olive Brown Dun-grey

Grey/Yellow Brown Light Olive Cream

SPINNER **Wings: Hyaline (White or Clear)** Olive Yellow

Reddish Brown Dark Brown Grey

LENGTH RANGE 3 TO 32 MILLIMETERS

Range mm.	3	4	5	6	7	8	10	12	16	20	25	30
Hook Sizes	28	24	22	20	18	16	14	12	10	8	6	4

Stoneflies

NYMPH
(Body/Gills)

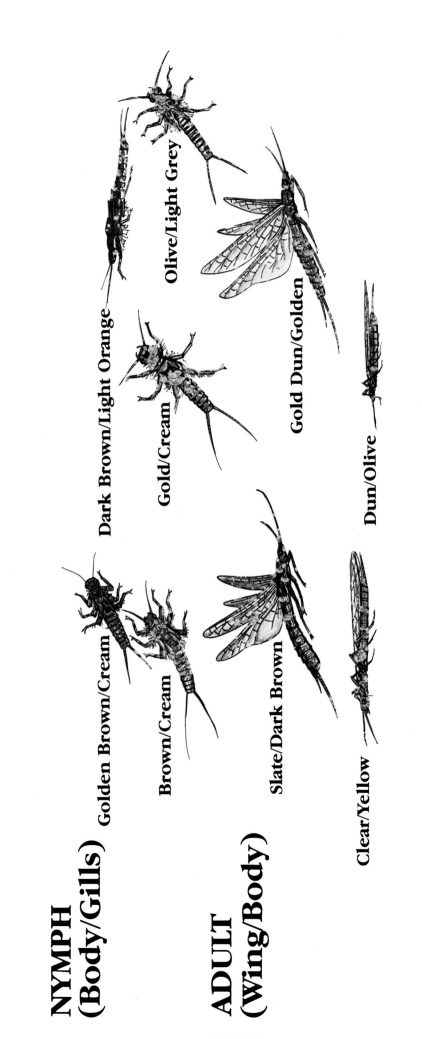

Golden Brown/Cream

Dark Brown/Light Orange

Olive/Light Grey

Brown/Cream

Gold/Cream

Gold Dun/Golden

ADULT
(Wing/Body)

Slate/Dark Brown

Dun/Olive

Clear/Yellow

LENGTH RANGE 8 TO 36 MILLIMETERS

Range mm.	8	10	12	16	20	25	30	36
Hook sizes	16	14	12	10	8	6	4	2

Caddisflies

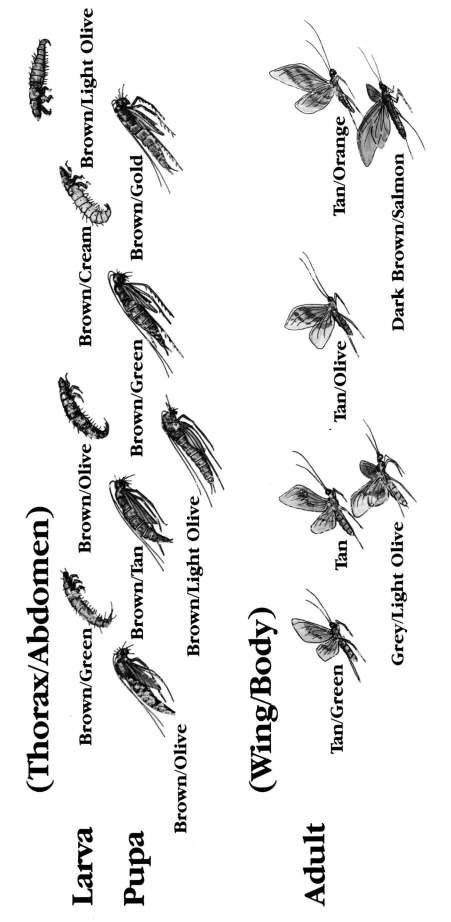

(Thorax/Abdomen)

Larva

Brown/Green Brown/Olive Brown/Cream Brown/Light Olive

Pupa

Brown/Olive Brown/Tan Brown/Green Brown/Gold

Brown/Light Olive

(Wing/Body)

Adult

Tan/Green Tan Tan/Olive Tan/Orange

Grey/Light Olive Dark Brown/Salmon

LENGTH RANGE 5 TO 25 MILLIMETERS

Range mm.	5	6	7	8	10	12	16	20	25
Hook Sizes	22	20	18	16	14	12	10	8	6

Dragonflies

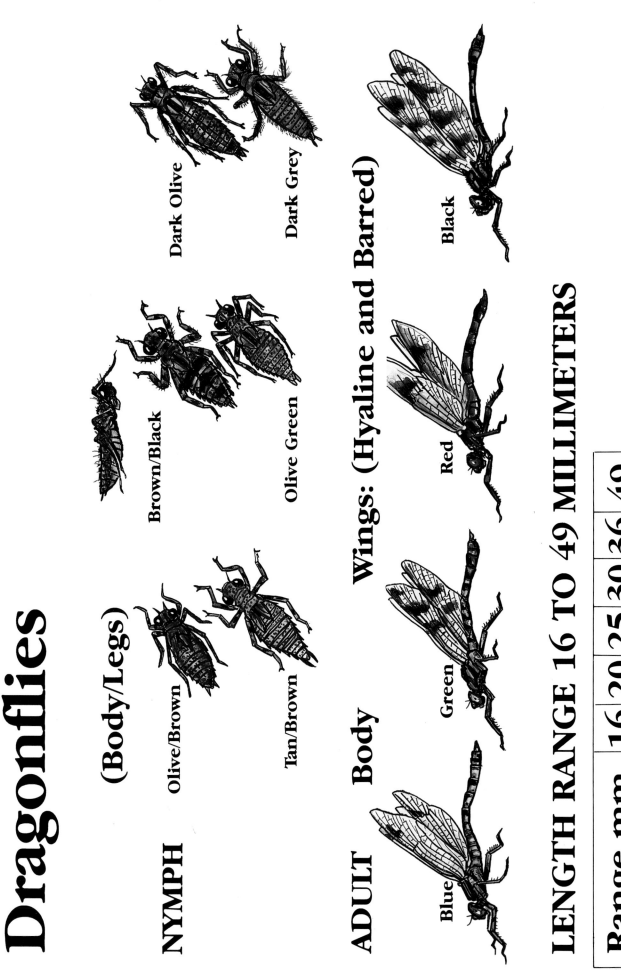

NYMPH (Body/Legs)

Olive/Brown

Tan/Brown

Brown/Black

Olive Green

Dark Olive

Dark Grey

ADULT   Body

Wings: (Hyaline and Barred)

Blue

Green

Red

Black

LENGTH RANGE 16 TO 49 MILLIMETERS

Range mm.	16	20	25	30	36	49
Hook Sizes	10	8	6	4	2	1/0

Damselflies

Nymph   (Body/Gills)

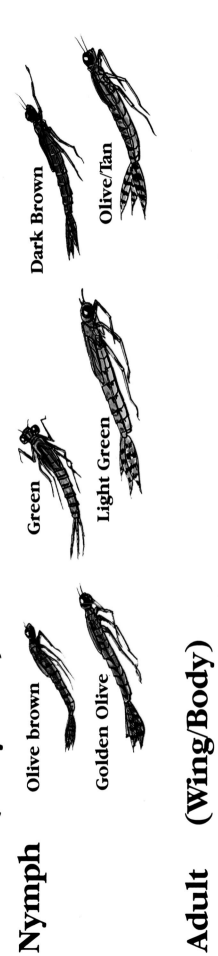

Olive brown

Golden Olive

Green

Light Green

Dark Brown

Olive/Tan

Adult   (Wing/Body)

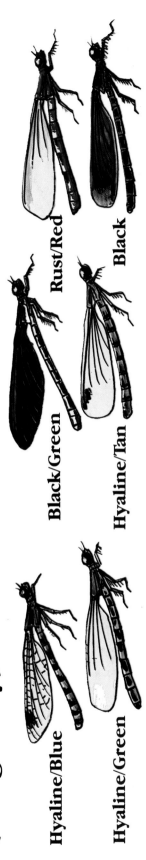

Hyaline/Blue

Hyaline/Green

Black/Green

Hyaline/Tan

Rust/Red

Black

LENGTH RANGE 10 TO 30 MILLIMETERS

Range mm.	10	12	16	20	25	30
Hook Sizes	14	12	10	8	6	4

CRUSTACEANS

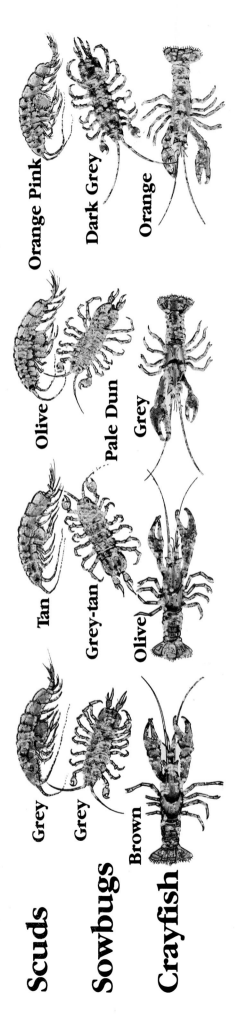

Scuds Grey Tan Olive Orange Pink

Sowbugs Grey Grey-tan Pale Dun Dark Grey

Brown Olive Grey Orange

Crayfish

25mm = 1 inch

SCUD AND SOWBUG							Range in mm.
7	8	10	13	16	20		Range in mm.
18	16	14	12	10	8		Hook sizes

CRAYFISH							Range in mm.
25	37	50	62	75	88		Range in mm.
10	8	6	4	2	1/0		4X Long Sizes

Forage Fish

COLOR PATTERNS

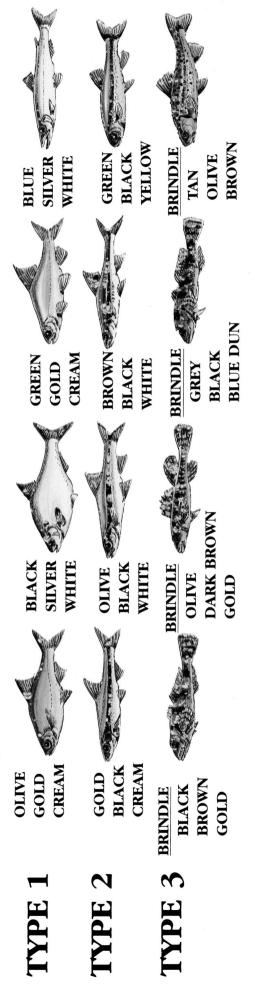

TYPE 1

OLIVE
GOLD
CREAM

BLACK
SILVER
WHITE

GREEN
GOLD
CREAM

BLUE
SILVER
WHITE

TYPE 2

GOLD
BLACK
CREAM

OLIVE
BLACK
WHITE

BROWN
BLACK
WHITE

GREEN
BLACK
YELLOW

TYPE 3

BRINDLE
BLACK
BROWN
GOLD

BRINDLE
OLIVE
DARK BROWN
GOLD

BRINDLE
GREY
BLACK
BLUE DUN

BRINDLE
TAN
OLIVE
BROWN

25mm = 1 inch

Range mm.	25	37	50	62	75	88	100	113
4X Long Sizes	12	10	8	6	4	2	1/0	2/0

Group IV

LEECHES
      MOTTLED PATTERNS
      Brown-Olive-Black-Gold

LAMPREYS
AND EELS

TADPOLES

SALAMANDERS

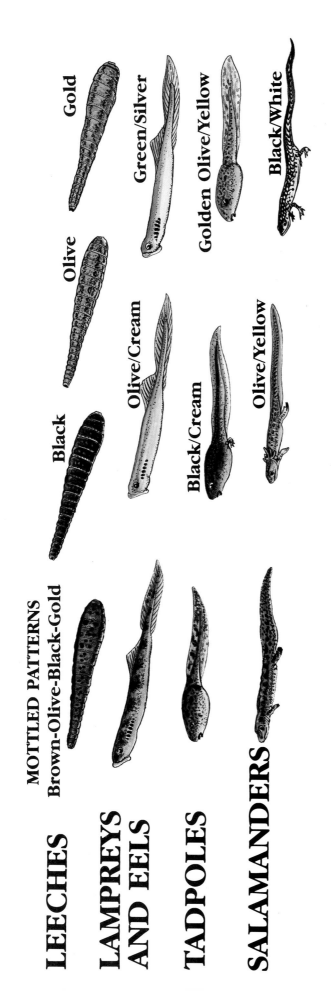

Gold

Olive

Black

Green/Silver

Olive/Cream

Golden Olive/Yellow

Black/Cream

Olive/Yellow

Black/White

25mm = 1 inch

Range mm.	25	36	50	62	75	88	100	113
3X Long sizes	10	8	6	4	2	1	1/0	2/0

THE SPENT CADDIS (NO. 3 POSITION)

I use this caddis design for surface-film fishing when trout are tipping up to sip in all sorts of spent insects from the surface film. There are occasions after high hatch or egg-laying activities when significant numbers of adult caddis expire. Wind, cold, or rain will also do a job on adult insects and force them down onto the water. Eddies, backwaters, and onshore lake winds will concentrate such spent caddis. My friend Larry Solomon, who coauthored with Eric Leiser the fine book *The Caddis and the Angler,* convinced me that spent caddis were very important forms to match. But like the larva, I'm not sure it catches trout that are looking exclusively for dead or crippled caddis.

1. **HOOK:** fine or extra-fine wire, regular-length shank, turned-down eye
2. **TYING THREAD:** Herb Howard Flymaster to match body color
3. **CEMENT:** clear thin head cement
4. **FINISH:** Scotchgard
5. **TAIL:** none
6. **BODY:** small-fibered synthetic dubbing or beaver belly to match the color of the adult's underside; body should be two-thirds the length of hook shank
7. **WINGS:** two pair of hen-hackle tips tied on sides of hook and slanting slightly back and up. The open, spent wings should suggest a dead fly, not a fluttering one. Study a dead, spent, adult sample if you can
8. **LEGS AND HACKLE:** a turn or two of soft hen hackle or other bird feather to match adult's long legs and color scheme. Trim fibers off the top and bottom of the collar. Leave a few fibers on each side to simulate legs
9. **HEAD:** dub head to shape with body dubbing
10. **ANTENNAE (OPTIONAL):** two thin, stiff, mink-tail guardhairs or spade-hackle fibers tied forward and widely separated. If the fly is fished wet slant antennae back over wings
11. Whip-finish and apply cement to head
12. **FINISH:** lightly spray once with Scotchgard

Spent adult caddis
  A. Front
  B. Side
  C. Top

I fish this design dead drift and usually downstream to head-and-tail rising trout. It is a very hard fly to see and so I use a short line, approaching as close as I can.

This fly may be a better choice overall than the mayfly spinner when no particular flies are hatching or falling. Sometimes I have nailed a few bonus trout on it by pulling it under and fishing it wet as an attractor or emerger fly.

THE SUBSURFACE-SWIMMING OVIPOSITING ADULT (NO. 4A AND 4B POSITIONS)

This is a relatively new design to me, and it combines features of the traditional quill-winged flies and soft-hackled wet flies. For decades such wets have been sure trout takers, and they must suggest some of the subsurface adult-caddis egg layers.

It seems to me that trout would well be attracted to both the diving and rising caddis females as illustrated in positions A and B, but the bottom-to-top movement probably triggers more takes.

1. HOOK: regular or light wire, regular-length shank, turned-down eye
2. TYING THREAD: Herb Howard Flymaster to match body color
3. HEAD CEMENT: clear thin head cement
4. UNDERBODY CEMENT: Pliobond
5. WEIGHTING: copper wire wrapped over one-half of hook shank
6. TAIL: none
7. BODY: Orlon sparkle yarn or similar synthetic sparkle nymph dubbing. If it is possible to observe adult female, try to match body and egg-cluster color pattern
8. WINGS: matched duck or mottled hen-pheasant wing-quill segments one and one-half times the length of hook shank, color should be near that of naturals. Position them like semifolded caddis adult wings

Diving-egglaying-drowning
adult caddis

Trout leaping for flying adult caddis

9. **LEGS**: section of grouse, partridge, or pheasant body feather tied DeFeo-style. Fibers should be as long as the wings

10. **HEAD**: use thorax-colored dubbing to shape head in front of wing bases and legs

11. **ANTENNAE**: two thin, soft, feather fibers tied apart back over head, one and one-half times the length of body

12. Whip-finish at hook eye and cement

I would fish this fly in both positions after wetting and deodorizing it with the same method used for the emergent pupa. Normally the egg-laying occurs at the general peak of hatching activity, which can mislead you. That is probably why it has not been a commonly recognized technique for fishing adult caddis.

7
MIDGES AND CRANEFLIES
Diptera

Mighty are the midges—not in size, perhaps, but certainly in numbers and distribution in trout waters. These two-winged, mosquitolike flies are perhaps the single most important aquatic insect that trout eat. Yet most fly fishermen do not realize this, and thus isolate themselves from what I consider the highest plateau of matching the hatch for trout.

124

Midges are typically very small, unglamorous, misunderstood insects. Most fly fishers have had few experiences with midging trout that were not absolutely frustrating . . . so much so that midges are called a "fly-fisher's curse." Few anglers I know ever go to their trout waters to fish specifically for midging trout; most confront such opportunities with aggravation, which stems from having the wrong fly designs and tackle to fish for midging trout successfully.

True midges, which are a small part of the very large order of Diptera, should not be confused with the common use of the term "midge fishing," which refers to fishing all sorts of small terrestrial and aquatic insects. Diptera, of which there are several thousand known species, contains mosquitos, craneflies, gnats, deerflies, and midges.

Diptera means "two wings" (one pair of wings per insect), which is the key to distinguishing adult midges from other orders of aquatic insects important to trout.

Midges and similar families of Diptera live in the widest range of water conditions, far exceeding the tolerable environments for trout. It is safe to say that any water that supports trout will be capable of supporting vast populations of midges. Unlike most of the more well known aquatic insects, the midges usually have two or more generations annually. Actually, lots of prime midge water, such as spring creeks, shallow, fertile lakes, and lowland rivers will have continuous hatches of one or more species every day of the year. Midges are the foundation of many trout lakes. This fact alone is enough to explain their importance to the trout and the angler. Midge hatches that I've observed seem to be predominant during the colder months usually considered poor for matching the hatch for trout. I have had my greatest experiences midge fishing at my home in Arkansas, and in Montana, from late October to early March. Midges hatching in these wintery periods have been frequently called "snowflies."

The midges are very much like the caddis in the general life-cycle stages. That is, they have a complete four-stage metamorphosis, which includes the egg, larva, pupa, and adult. The adult is an air-breather and the egg, larva, and pupa are aquatic.

The egg stage has little or no significance to trout. Once the eggs hatch, the larvae distribute themselves along the bottom structures of the lake or stream and feed on live and decaying plants. They grow quite rapidly and begin to interest trout when they reach three millimeters or more in length. The larvae, which are usually slender and wormlike in shape, do not have body parts as distinctive as the immature insects discussed earlier. However, they are capable of swimming with whiplash body movements in particular directions, especially in calm or very slow waters.

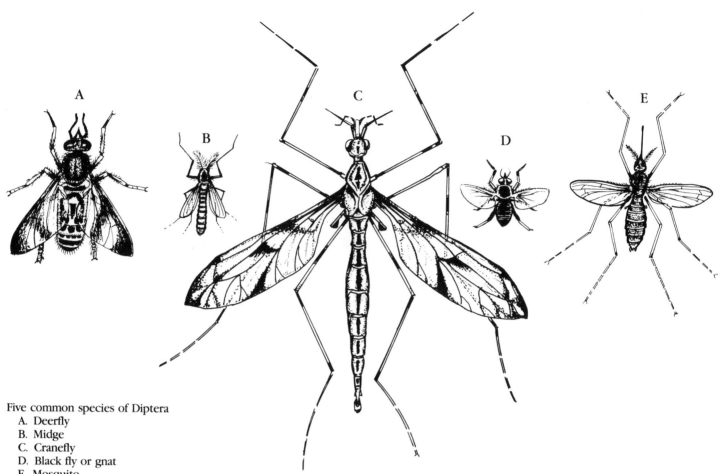

Five common species of Diptera
  A. Deerfly
  B. Midge
  C. Cranefly
  D. Black fly or gnat
  E. Mosquito

Lake- and pond-dwelling species, particularly of the Chironomidae family, are most active in the twilight and dark hours. They leave the bottom and swim up to the surface en masse. Each sunup they swim back to deeper water to resume their secluded deep feeding. The rise to the surface I suspect is to reach water richer in oxygen and perhaps some microscopic foods not available in the deeper water. There is little doubt trout will actively cruise just below the surface at twilight and night hours on these lakes to feed on larvae.

In flowing waters, larval colonies inhabit the bottom. They live in aquatic plant beds, algae, crevices in rocks, and in the soft aggregates of muds. Unless the larvae are very abundant and concentrated or other foods are scarce, trout seldom forage actively for them in these areas. Fishing a midge larva imitation in streams is usually impractical; it is very difficult actually to match the natural's placement and action.

The following physical characteristics distinguish the midge larva:

1. the body is wormlike and segmented with no distinctive thorax or abdomen as with the caddis larva

2. no visible legs or wingpads
3. no distinctive gills on body

The midge larva begins pupation when it is fully grown. The stillwater species remain free-swimming while most of the flowing-water species attach pupal cases to bottom structures. During pupation, like the caddis, midges quickly undergo dramatic physical changes as legs, wings, and enlarged abdomen develop.

The midge pupae of many of the lake and stream species swim or rise from the bottom and hang vertically just below or in the water's surface film. The pupa then splits out of its pupal skin or case and emerges as the winged adult. This pupal emergence is the most dramatic and significant opportunity for trout to feed on the midge. Pupae are quite vulnerable and usually so concentrated that trout do not pass them up.

Characteristics of midge (Chironectidae) larva

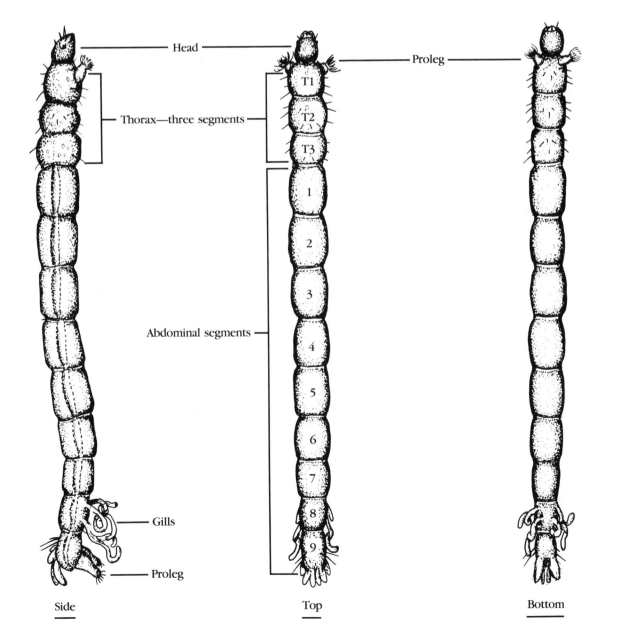

Head

Thorax—three segments

Proleg

T1

T2

T3

1

2

3

Abdominal segments

4

5

6

7

8

9

Gills

Proleg

Side   Top   Bottom

To a lesser extent, but still important, is the subsurface emergence in some stream species. These pupae hatch from the pupal case that is affixed to the bottom structure. The adult then swims to the surface. Such emergence does not trigger the same classic and rewarding fishing the surface-film emergers do, because the subsurface pupa-to-adult transformation disperses the flies much more.

The following physical characteristics distinguish the midge pupa:

1. enlarged head and thorax appear to be fused as one
2. plumelike gill filaments on head and tip of abdomen
3. enlargements under top of thorax contain folded legs and wings
4. abdomen is much smaller in diameter than thorax and appears well segmented

Characteristics of midge (Chironectidae) pupa

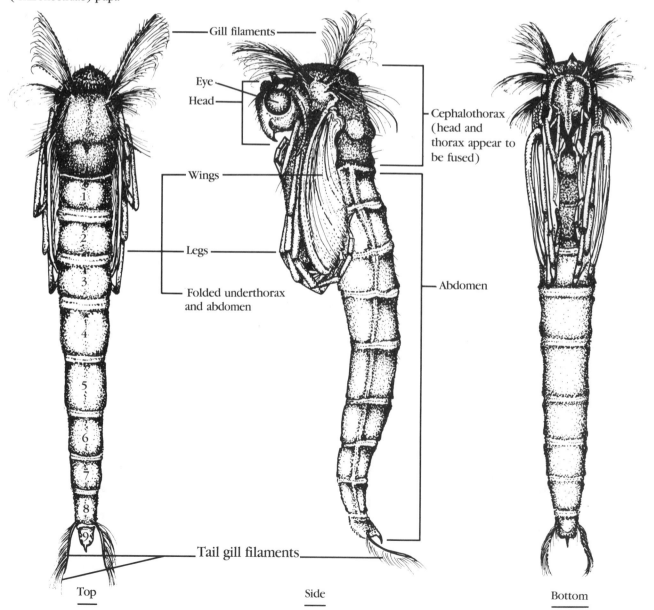

Gill filaments

Eye

Head

Wings

Legs

Folded underthorax and abdomen

Cephalothorax (head and thorax appear to be fused)

Abdomen

Tail gill filaments

Top

Side

Bottom

Once the midge pupa splits its skin down the back, the adult pushes itself out of the pupal skin. Emergence usually takes but a few seconds, but during very cold weather it is slower, sometimes taking a minute or so. The adult midges quickly unfold their wings, which dry and harden while the flies sit on the water's surface. Many flop their wings, testing and strengthening them before flight.

At times, midge adults—especially on calm surfaces of lakes or along the borders of streams—will be congregated as the result of a slight breeze. They seem to stick or clump together before they can escape the surface by flight. Trout are more apt to feed on these clumped adults than on scattered individuals.

The adults normally form mating swarms in vertical columns over or nearby the home water at this time or at some time within twenty-four hours following emergence. The females come back to the water and lay their eggs on the surface or just below.

Characteristics of adult male midge (Chironectidae), side and top views

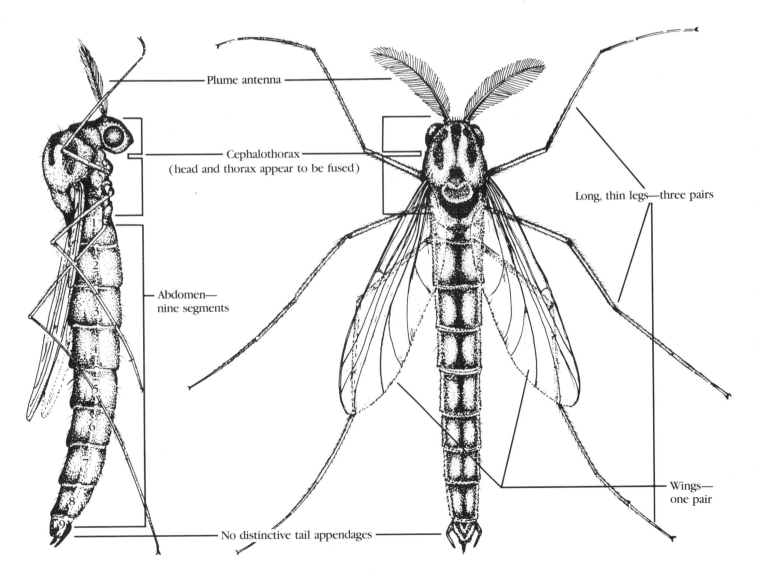

Plume antenna

Cephalothorax
(head and thorax appear to be fused)

Abdomen—
nine segments

Long, thin legs—three pairs

Wings—
one pair

No distinctive tail appendages

Both sexes die within a few hours after mating, but do not necessarily fall to the water as do mayflies. There is normally little or no significant trout feeding done on the egg-laying or dying adults.

The identifying physical characteristics of adult midges are:

1. one pair of wings. When at rest, the wings are set flat and separated at slight angles to the body
2. six very slender, long legs, two to two and one-half times longer than body
3. thorax and head very much enlarged and humped compared to abdomen
4. two large plumelike antennae, especially large on most males
5. no tail
6. smaller abdomen is well segmented

Identifying, Matching, and Fishing the Midge

The larva. Look for concentrations of wormlike midge larvae in aquatic-weed beds, accumulated silts and sands, on the sides of algae-covered bottom objects, and only occasionally in the surface film of lakes and streams. They are generally easy to identify since they are colorful, distinctive, small, slender, wormlike forms with few distinguishable appendages.

It is almost impossible to accurately simulate active midge larvae under most conditions. Trout normally forage on both passive and active larvae mostly when found in large concentrations. Imitating their position, action, and competing with naturals is a relatively unproductive way to midge fish. Perhaps most of the success I and others have had fishing larval imitations can be attributed to creating more of an attractor effect. I'm sure many midge-larva imitations are taken by wild trout thinking they are either pupae or other aquatic insects such as tiny scuds or small, swimming, mayfly nymphs. While species of midge larvae ten millimeters long or longer are far more practical to imitate than the smaller ones, fishing midge-larva imitations is extremely difficult for most of us to do effectively.

I do advise you to collect and observe live midge larvae under magnification and in a clear vessel of water. They are unique and their behavior and action must be seen to appreciate the problem of imitation. Yet perhaps with your personal observation you can solve this tough problem.

Midge larva living and swimming in aquatic vegetation. Larvae swim with an extreme whiplash action.

The pupa. Midge pupae are the most important form of this insect for the fly fishermen to recognize and imitate. I capture most of those that trout will eat by seining the water and surface film with a fine-mesh net. Sometimes I will check aquatic vegetation and the sides of bottom structures for holding pupae. Trout stomach samples are very significant for pupal identification, matching, and fishing. Sometimes there will even be live pupae still lodged in the gill rackers and throat of a freshly caught trout. I note carefully their size, shape, and color.

The midge pupae, particularly emerging ones that swim or rise to the surface film to transform into adults, are the most vulnerable and attractive midge forms to trout. They are easy to imitate with artificial flies. As the pupae rise en masse and collect in the surface film of a lake or stream, they attract trout of all sizes, which can scoop them up with minimum effort.

The rise and emergent subsurface float of the pupae is not lateral but quite straight upward. The pupae emerging in a stream will be carried by the current downstream and are somewhat helpless. I fish the emergent-pupa imitation rising to the surface or still in the surface film of lakes. I fish the pupa in flowing waters straight downstream, dead drift, with no lateral or across-current movement. If across-current fly movement happens, the trout usually ignore or reject the fly.

As the pupae begin to emerge, some mid-depth trout feeding is often visible, but the best clue is smooth, almost prolonged rising at the surface. I watch for this typically slow, back-dorsal-fin-and-tail move to tell me that midges are being taken. The surface might also contain adults just out of the pupal membrane. I look closely and at a low angle to the surface for the new adults. Adult trout feed on pupae to adults probably at a rate of fifty to one.

The adult. Adult midges can be captured and identified with relative ease by using some sort of small aquarium fish net. Their size and color are practical keys to what the pupae look like, and, of course, they are positive proof of the nearly invisible presence of emerging midge pupae.

The midge-adult imitations are not normally easy or effective to fish. Most midge adults (from practical sizes 18 to 28) are far

Trout seining on surface film for emerging
midge pupa

less practical for trout to catch and eat than pupae. Usually, smaller, "showy" trout and chubs will give the impression that significant feeding on the small adults is taking place. Sometimes, too, there will be a multiple hatch, and larger trout may be eating another adult insect dispersed among the midges. You must watch closely to keep from being misled under these tricky circumstances. Methods that I have had some limited success with are the twitched live adult, the clumped midges, and spent midges. I'll discuss these in the fly-pattern section.

A Typical Midge Life Cycle

1. Adult female midge deposits eggs on or below water's surface.
2. Hatching eggs produce tiny midge larvae that swim to various bottom areas.
3. Midge larvae in lakes or streams feed on plant material, living on or in the bottom and on aquatic plants. Some larvae also swim free, moving about the bottom and rising to calm water surfaces at night.
4. Mature midge larvae pupate, undergoing a drastic physical change. Some pupate by attaching to the bottom, others remain free swimming.
5. Within a few days of the beginning of pupation, the midge pupa reaches maturity and swims or floats upward toward the surface.
6. Pupae stick in surface film and hang there vertically before beginning the final emergence into adults.
7. The pupal skin splits down the back, opening up above the water's surface, and the adult slips free of the pupal skin held in the surface film.
8. New adult midges rest momentarily on the water's surface until the wings are unfolded, inflated, hardened by the air, and ready for flight. Pupal skin remains in surface film.
9. Adult flies off water and immediately or within a day joins other adults in a mating swarm over or nearby the site of emergence.
10. Female midges return to the water to deposit eggs after mating, then die.

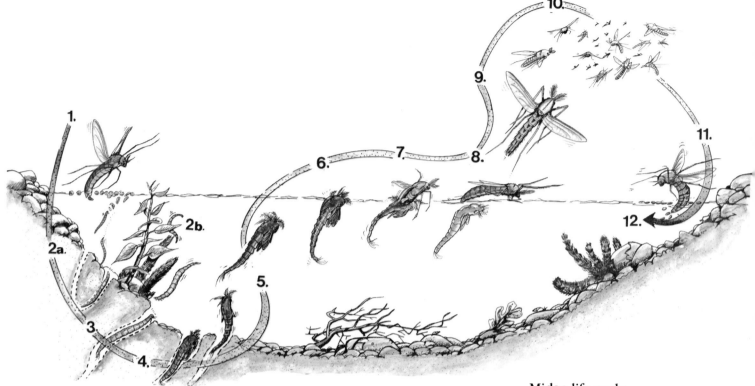

Midge life cycle

My Favorite
Midge Fly Designs

Matching and fishing midge imitations are very precise methods greatly dependent on the size and action aspects of hatch matching. Shape and color seem far less important with midges than with any of the other important aquatic insects. The midges' average size range runs from size 14 to 28 hooks, and the most common practical sizes are 18 through 26. Duplicating size and action on hooks smaller than size 26 becomes very unreliable and impractical for most of us. Remember to keep these imitations sparse and delicate. If you use a magnifying glass while tying, it will help tremendously.

Midge life cycle and fly designs
1. Midge larva—Position 1
2. Midge pupa—drifting and rising—Position 2
3. Midge pupa floating on surface film—Position 3
4. Stillborn adult midge hatching—Position 4
5. Adult clumper midge—Position 5

The Larva

The various larvae of Diptera are mostly legless, slender, and wormlike. They are quite often brightly colored red, light green, purple, cream, golden olive, tan, or black. The larvae are found and fed upon for the most part in or on bottom structures or congreated near the water's surface. My larva-fly design can be fished in either area conveniently and effectively.

MIDGE LARVA (NO. 1 POSITION)

1. HOOK: extra-fine wire 3XS or 3XL. The 3XS is for larger hook needs; 3XL for more accurate imitation of the larva's shape. I use the short-hook design where larger trout are expected, trying, for example, a size 18 fly on a size 14 hook
2. WEIGHTING: no. 1/2 or 1 Buss Fuse Lead Wire or soft, fine, copper wire wrapped six to twelve turns at midshank; weighting is used on both deep and surface larva flies
3. TYING THREAD: finest nylon, Midge, or Herb Howard Danville Special, color of midge body or white
4. CEMENT: thinned Pliobond for underbody; clear head cement
5. TAIL (OPTIONAL): should be only a tiny tuft of muskrat underbody fur, tip of ostrich herl, or similar material, approximately one-sixth of body length
6. ABDOMEN AND THORAX: beaver belly, Fly Rite Poly II, or Andra Spectrum to match natural's color. Both generally equal in diameter
   a. rib: fine gold or copper wire together with a length of nylon or silk thread close to body's color. Rib is wrapped over both abdomen and thorax. Study with a 4X glass the natural larva segmentation for correct rib-pattern proportion
   b. dub entire length of body with dubbing materials; keep the body slender and almost uniform in diameter throughout. Trim off body any excessively long fibers after body is ribbed
7. HEAD: thread-finish head, whip-finish, and cement

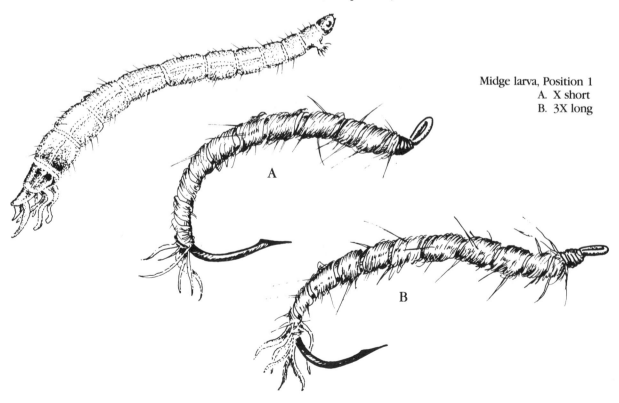

Midge larva, Position 1
A. X short
B. 3X long

This very simple larva fly is fished on a very long (thirty-six-inch to forty-inch), light tippet either deep along the bottom with a weighted leader or suspended near or in the surface film. Grease the leader to within six to twelve inches of the fly if you fish it near the surface. Pull it slightly every so often to animate it in still-waters. I fish it deep, totally dead-drift, casting downstream, in flowing waters. It is almost impossible to imitate an active midge larva's swimming action, so it is best to use only very short line pulls if any for still waters.

The Pupa

The pupa is the most significant imitation when fishing for most actively midging trout. It is comparable to the emerging forms of the mayfly nymphs and the caddis pupae, yet it is usually even more attractive and vulnerable to trout than either. The surface-emerging pupa is far more easily captured and probably available much more often than the others.

My pupa design is constructed on a light-wire, extra-short or extra-long hook for the same reasons as the larva.

MIDGE PUPA (NO. 2 AND 3 POSITIONS)

1. HOOK: same as larva
2. WEIGHTING: for position 2, I use no. 1/2 Buss Lead Fuse Wire, six to twelve turns at the rear of the hook shank so pupa will be more apt to set tail down and head up as it rises or swims. For position 3: no weighting
3. TYING THREAD: Midge or Herb Howard Flymaster, color to match or blend with overall body color
4. CEMENT: same as larva
5. TAIL: very small tuft of muskrat-belly underfur or ostrich herl, one-fourth as long as body
6. ABDOMEN: beaver-belly underfur, Andra Spectrum, or Fly Rite Poly II to match color of body
   a. rib: fine gold, silver, or copper wire
   b. make abdomen one-half the body length and very thin
7. THORAX: same as abdomen, except somewhat more enlarged. Dub it much looser than abdomen. Note: the body colors of a pupa will often be different in intensity or color—usually the abdomen will be lighter colored than the thorax
8. GILLS: over top and front of abdomen, small tufts of muskrat, beaver-belly underfur or ostrich herl. Gills should be one-half the length of thorax. Note: legs and wings are not included as they are still encased in thorax
9. HEAD: simply finish off with thread and whip-finish. Coat lightly with head cement

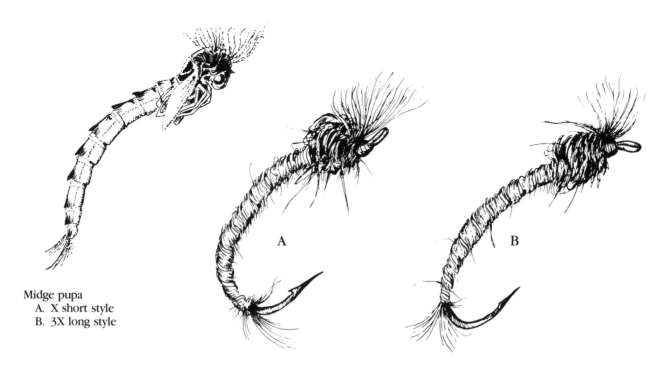

Midge pupa
 A. X short style
 B. 3X long style

I fish the swimming-midge pupa (position 2) prior to emergence by allowing it to sink on a long, fine tippet (thirty to forty inches long). Sometimes a small lead strip, sleeve, or split-shot greatly enhances the sink rate, especially in very deep or fast-moving waters.

When the midge pupa has reached the right depth I begin to retrieve or raise it slowly in calm waters, or just allow it to free drift in current. It is extremely important in this type of midging that the take is quickly detected. I watch either the floating position of my leader or a small, fluorescent, inch-long indicator floating on my leader for the slightest indication of the commonly unseen and unfelt take of a deeply fished midge pupa. Trout softly inhale the pupa with no urgency or violence.

Position 3 of the pupa is fished just beneath or hanging in the surface film and imitates the emerging pupa. It is not weighted nor is it necessarily dressed to float either. It is most effective entirely under the film, dressing it defeats this preferred position. I do not fish such a fly blindly, but always to a specific, rising trout. It is a waste of time to cast this pattern randomly over water that does not have rising trout—it would be like shooting in the general direction of a flock of ducks and hoping for the best.

Normally my long leader tippet will suspend the pupa, but sometimes in moving water or when it is windy it is necessary to dress the tippet with Mucilin or another silicone paste. This holds the fly up very well without the pupa itself floating.

I fish this pupa on stillwater and moving-water surfaces where I observe trout feeding on midges. You recognize such feeding by the presence of midge adults resting on or flying off the surface and trout rises that are slow, smooth, and rhythmic. Their backs, dorsal, or tail fins often protrude in a horizontal rise path. Seldom will there be much if any head splash or residual bubbles.

On calm lake waters, trout will constantly cruise slowly and rise to these emerging pupae. The cast and presentation must be in the path but well ahead of the feeding trout. Sometimes a slight twitch will be effective just as the pupa comes within taking range of the trout. Other times the trout only want a still-fished imitation in the same position.

In streams, trout will hold, maintaining a shallow, horizontal position to intercept the squirming chains of drifting pupae. They tip and sip. I cast this pupa downstream to the rise, about two or three feet above the fish's holding position. I'm ever so careful not to let my wading wake disrupt the drift pattern of the pupa. The closer, lower, and quieter I can be, the greater my effectiveness. The pupa must drift straight downstream. *The pupa must not swing across at all.* Just as the pupa approaches the trout, I slow it a little so that it will rise up. This usually triggers a rise response. Also I try to time the rises of an individual trout so that I reduce the gamble of competing with the other midge pupae and the whims of the trout. At times just a dead-drifted pupa, particularly right under the surface film, will be best. Be sure to try both presentations.

Once the drifing midge pupa is past the trout's station I slowly move my rod left or right so that the fly line does not float over the trout, then I softly lift the fly for another cast.

For most midge fishing, hooking a trout is a delicate, simple matter of slowly and smoothly lifting the rod tip until the trout's weight is felt—almost like pulling the leader and hook taut in a spider web. Most midge-hooked trout must be fought very passively to keep the trout from overreacting and breaking or pulling off.

HATCHING OR STILLBORN PUPAE (NO. 4 POSITION)

This position is often most effective during very sparse hatching activity or where lake wind or stream current causes an accumulation of crippled or dead emergers. Although the design is relatively complex, I still tie it sparse.

1. HOOK: extra-fine wire, regular-length shank, ring or turned-up eye
2. TYING THREAD: Midge or Herb Howard Danville Special, color to match or blend with natural's color
3. WEIGHT: none
4. CEMENT: same as other larva and pupa positions
5. TAIL: tuft of muskrat-belly underfur or tip of ostrich herl, one-half to three-fourths the length of hook shank. Actually this simulates pupal skin that has been vacated but still adheres to the adult's body. Should be light tan or light grey in color

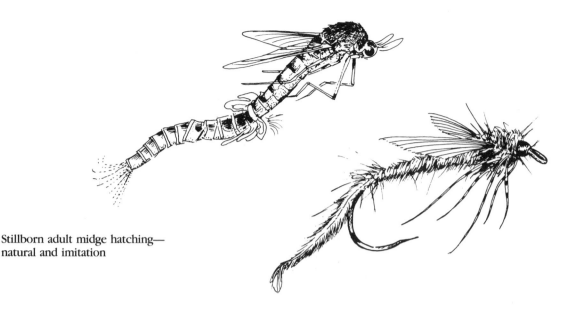

Stillborn adult midge hatching—
natural and imitation

6. ABDOMEN: beaver-belly underfur or Andra Spectrum, color to
   match adult natural; dub rear one-half of hook shank
7. THORAX: same as abdomen except larger
8. WINGS (OPTIONAL): one or two ostrich herl or tiny hen-hackle
   tips, one-half the length of hook shank, set to sides and
   back of thorax
9. LEGS (OPTIONAL): a few fibers of soft hen or partridge hackle,
   just to simulate a few legs freed from the pupal case
10. HEAD: thread tied off at hook eye and whip-finished; add
    head cement

I put Mucilin or a similar waterproofing paste or grease on the
thorax, wings, and legs of the stillborn emerger. This allows the
fly to rest low on top of the water with its abdomen and case and
hook bend below the surface film. I fish this fly also only to specific risers. I cast it to intercept cruising lake risers or dead drift
straight downstream to a riser in a stream. Sometimes this design
fishes well as a wet fly in eddies, at the side of riffles, and behind
or beside protruding boulders or logs.

The Adult

The fly described below simulates two or more surface-floating
midge adults clumped together. It is most effective on smooth-
surfaced lakes, ponds, spring creeks, and sloughs. During the late
stages of a midge emergence the midge adults will be grouped
together when a fresh breeze blows over the calm surfaces. Trout
will on occasion take these adults if their numbers and groups are
excessive.

MIDGE ADULT CLUMPERS (NO. 5 POSITION)

1. **HOOK:** extra-fine wire, regular-length or 2XL shank (Mustad 94833 or 94831)
2. **TYING THREAD:** Midge or Herb Howard Flymaster to match or blend with natural's color pattern
3. **WEIGHT:** none
4. **CEMENT:** same as other midge positions
5. **TAIL:** three or four cock-hackle fibers three-fourths the length of shank
6. **BODY:** short-fibered ostrich or peacock herl. Wrap around entire length of shank
7. **HACKLE:** two dry-fly grizzly natural or dyed to match color scheme. Hackle palmered over herl body
8. **HEAD:** finish with thread and whip-finish

This fly should be sprayed or brushed with fly flotant. I fish it to rising trout in the same manner as the stillborn. On occasion I twitch it very slightly to better attract a cruising trout's attention.

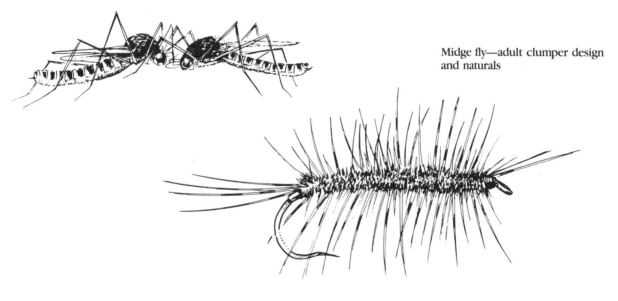

Midge fly—adult clumper design and naturals

Craneflies

Craneflies are exceptionally large Diptera that should be considered individually from the more typical midges such as mosquitos and blackflies. The larval and adult craneflies are abundant, available, and very attractive to many trout. The pupal form is more or less out of reach because it exists only on the perimeters of its home water.

The cranefly larva is a long (one to two inches) thick, meaty, morsel that burrows in and around bottom structures of lakes and streams. When it is dislodged, it either tumbles and rolls along the bottom in a protective curl or sharply reacts *by elongating with fast, strong, efficient swimming motions similar to an eel or leech.* Cranefly larvae also swim to better locations or to the land to pupate. In all three circumstances, trout will feed on the larva.

Cranefly adults, which resemble giant mosquitos, actively mate and lay eggs along the edges of their home waters. This activity attracts trout, which will dash up and out of the water to snap up a dancing, fluttering cranefly adult.

My Favorite Cranefly Fly Patterns

The Larva

I use two designs to simulate the cranefly larva. One for the bottom-living (or loose) larva and the other for the swimming form of the same larva.

DAVE'S CRANEFLY LARVA (NO. 1 POSITION)

This larva fly simulates the natural that is on or tumbling along a stream bottom. *I never use it for lakes.* The natural larva is a rather thick, soft, meaty worm that appears to be almost transparent, although it may be colored cream, dirty orange, dirty grey, tan, or light olive.

1. HOOK: standard-wire, 3XL (Mustad 9672)
2. TYING THREAD: Herb Howard Flymaster to match natural's darker body parts
3. WEIGHT: lead wire
4. CEMENT: same as midge patterns
5. TAIL: none
6. BODY:
    a. soft, fine-textured Orlon and nylon sparkle dubbing to match body's general color. Blends of colors are much better than one solid color to accomplish match
    b. overbody is one long, very fine, pale or bleached grizzly saddle hackle with fibers removed from one side of stem. Select a hackle with short fibers (appropriate for a fly about two hook sizes smaller than hook used). This is over-

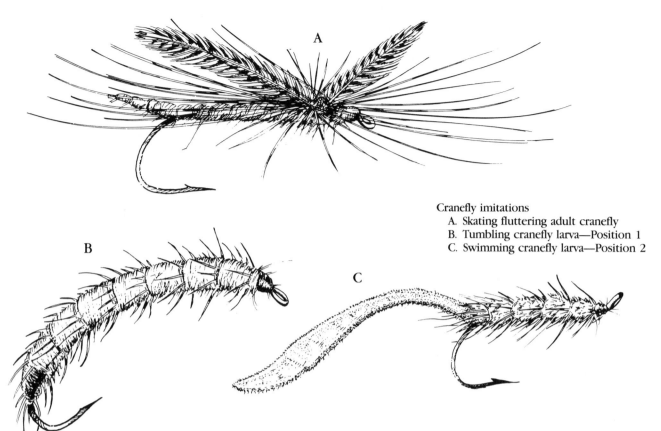

Cranefly imitations
A. Skating fluttering adult cranefly
B. Tumbling cranefly larva—Position 1
C. Swimming cranefly larva—Position 2

wrapped after the body is dubbed so that the hackle palmering is full length of the body
7. HEAD: finish off at hook's eye and whip-finish; cement with clear head cement

I fish this design right on the bottom, dead drift, with a long leader in shallow, moving water. A sinking-tip line and short leader best fishes this larva imitation in deeper, swift water. It should be rolled and tumbled along the bottom, especially in riffles and pocket waters.

DAVE'S CRANEFLY LARVA (NO. 2 POSITION)

The swimming cranefly larva elongates and flattens its tail and wiggles rhythmically, moving relatively fast. It is often hard to imagine the fat, sluggish, jellylike larva coming suddenly alive, changing its shape, and swimming so efficiently, but it does!

1. HOOK: regular-wire, 1XL shank, turned-up or ring eye (Mustad 9049)
2. TYING THREAD: Herb Howard Flymaster in matching or blending colors
3. WEIGHT: six to fifteen turns of lead wire about the diameter of hook wire used
4. TAIL: chamois skin bleached or dyed or colored with felt pen to match natural's color. Cut to shape as shown and attach to hook bend. This actually simulates the larva's swimming body

5. **BODY**: Orlon-nylon sparkle dubbing (nymph blend) to match natural's body color (same as chamois tail). This is sparsely dubbed over hook shank up to hook eye
6. **OVERBODY**: same as Position 1
7. **HEAD**: thread-finish at hook eye and whip-finish, cement wraps with clear head cement

This design, when wet, closely simulates the shape, action, and texture of a swimming cranefly larva. Swimming larva is two to two and one-half times longer than nonswimming form. I fish it in both calm and flowing waters with rhythmic *inch-long* strips at various levels and in various directions. This design is a fine fly to interest very large trout with. It looks like the swimming cranefly larvae, leeches, worms, eelets, salamanders, and so on, so it's fine, suggestive versatility can be a big bonus for big trout.

The Adult

The adult cranefly, which resembles a giant mosquito, often triggers some dramatic trout feeding. When these adults mate and lay eggs over the water, their fluttering and dancing sometimes titillates trout into spectacular leaping responses. My favorite design is dressed to simulate this fly action, and when compared to the big standard skaters and variants that also fish well for a cranefly adult, this one floats, moves, and hooks fish far more effectively. The secret is using a parachute hackle rather than a standard hackle collar at midshank.

DAVE'S ADULT CRANEFLY

1. **HOOK**: regular-length, extra-fine wire, turned-down eye (Mustad 74840, 94833, or 94834), sizes 12 through 14
2. **TYING THREAD**: Herb Howard Flymaster to match natural fly's body color (tan, cream, or orange)
3. **TAIL**: none
4. **BODY**: Fly Rite or Nymphblend dubbing
5. **WINGS**: two grizzly cock hackle tips dyed to match natural's wings (tan, coppery, dun, or brown)
6. **HACKLE**: one or two stiff, wide, spade hackles or very large neck hackle to match leg and wing colors. Grizzly plus brown, ginger, or dun is an excellent two-feather mix. Hackle is wound parachute style over body (study illustration carefully)
7. **HEAD**: thread-finish the head very small, then whip-finish and cement
8. **FINISH**: spray with Scotchgard

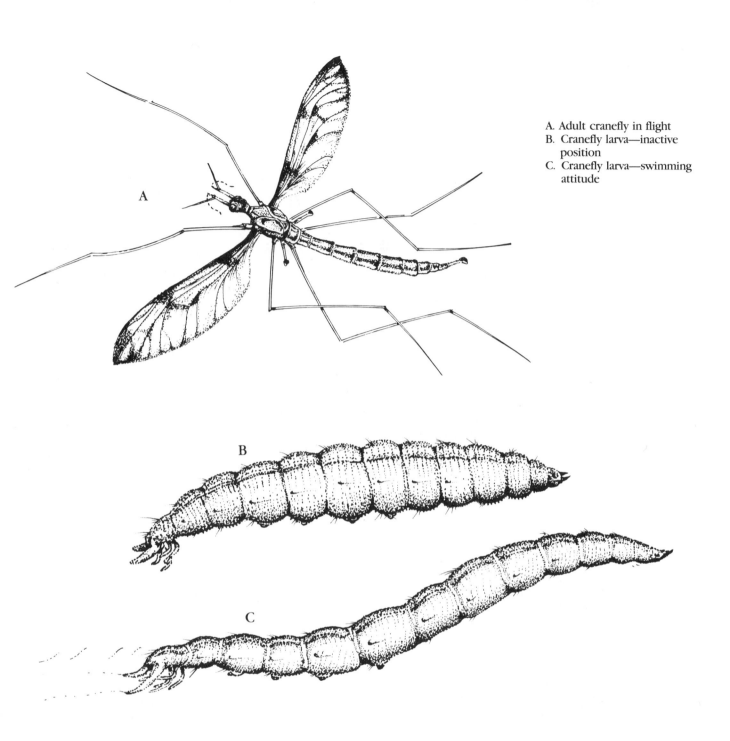

A. Adult cranefly in flight
B. Cranefly larva—inactive position
C. Cranefly larva—swimming attitude

I fish this adult "paracranefly" with a long rod and twelve-foot leader. It is cast downstream and high, allowed to flutter down, rest just a second or two on the surface, then erratically twitched or skated over the surface. It is extremely effective when cast repeatedly to an area. This fly is effective both on rough and smooth water surfaces. Be sure to strike slowly and deliberately when a trout leaps on the fly—too fast and you will miss many more than you will hook. This is one dry fly that works very well all day even when no naturals are visible . . . or to locate large, moody fish.

8
DRAGONFLIES AND DAMSELFLIES
Odonata

Members of the order Odonata, the dragonflies and damselflies are extremely important food sources for most trout living in slow-moving, weed-rich streams, ponds, sloughs, and lakes. They should be as well known to lake fly fishers as the mayfly, caddis, stonefly, and midge are to stream fishermen. Both insects generally average larger in size and live longer in their immature (aquatic) and mature (terrestrial) forms than do members of the other four insect orders discussed in previous chapters. This significant difference, plus the fact that most are active predators, increases their exposure as well as attraction to trout. I class them as ideal foods both to imitate at the tier's bench and to fish imitations of. I have pleasant memories of catches of large trout made by swimming damselfly and dragonfly nymphs off the bottom in front of foraging, spotted, submarinelike trout.

Dragonflies

These large, active predators are truly dragonlike in behavior and appearance. They derive their suborder name, Anisoptera, from a description of their adult wing shape: *aniso* means "unequal," and it refers to the dragonfly's pair of narrow forewings and pair of much wider hindwings.

The dragonflies have a three-phase life cycle—egg, nymph, and adult—which typically spans two to four years. After the eggs incubate for a period of up to two weeks, they hatch into the aquatic nymph. These nymphs catch, kill, and eat any lesser form of invertebrate or small fish. The nymphs rapidly grow to sizes attractive to trout. Most species reach an impressive twenty-five to forty-five millimeters by the time they reach maturity as nymphs.

Dragonfly nymphs are capable of crawling, darting, and free swimming. They typically live and hunt around aquatic plants, rough rubble, heavily sedimented bottoms, or submerged tree limbs or roots. Some types use elaborate camouflage methods to ambush their prey; others pursue their prey. These fierce predators seldom are found in large concentrations, as they are very competitive even within the same generation. However, their size, degree of exposure, and long nymph cycle make them a prime target for alert, cruising trout.

The important, physical structures common to all dragonfly nymphs are:

1. six long, spiderlike but tightly based legs
2. no tail
3. no outer surface gills
4. a complex labium (mouth) that is hinged and designed to spear or seize prey. It is folded under the head and thorax.
5. two very large, compound eyes that almost touch each other and dwarf the nymph's head

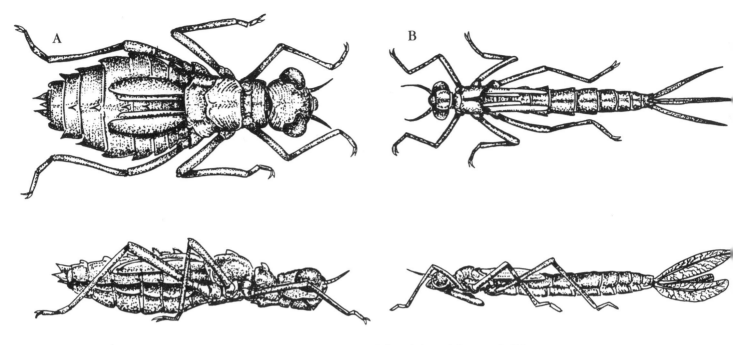

Side and top views of dragonfly nymph (A) and damsel fly nymph (B)

Side and top views of dragonfly nymph anatomy

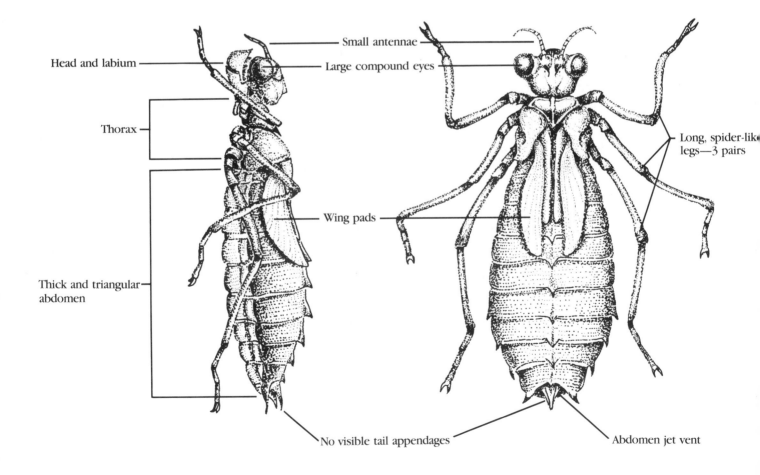

Head and labium

Small antennae

Large compound eyes

Thorax

Long, spider-like legs—3 pairs

Wing pads

Thick and triangular abdomen

No visible tail appendages

Abdomen jet vent

6. two very small antennae
7. body sections very thick and compressed, almost triangular in cross section

Nymphs are easily captured by seining lakes or stream edges or inspecting aquatic and submerged structures. Since they have such long life cycles, large nymphs are available for capture, identification, and inspection any time of the year. However, late spring seems to be the best time.

The adults emerge from the mature nymphs in the spring or early summer of the last year in the life cycle. The nymph crawls out of the water onto concealing aquatic and terrestrial vegetation. It's skin dries from exposure to the air and splits down the back. The adult makes a slow, laborious exit from the skin that often takes several hours. Once free of the nymphal skin, it unfolds and inflates its wings, which harden from exposure to the air. Its body greatly elongates in the process. Usually within twelve to twenty-four hours, the transformation is complete and the air-breathing adult dragonfly is ready for terrestrial life. The newly emerged adult is somewhat wobbly of leg and wing for the first few hours and days. At such times they will fall off of lakeside foliage or weakly fly out of control onto the water's surface. At such times they make a very nice morsel for any trout in the area.

After the dun-colored adults are a few days old they take on the lustrious colors typical of their species. These range from brilliant rusty reds through burnt oranges, emerald greens and blues, yellows, purples, and blacks. The females usually have larger abdomens and lack the brilliance of the males. The adult stage lasts two to five months, during which period the adult kills and eats insect prey and reproduces.

The adults are most vulnerable to trout during their first "test flights" following emergence and when laying their eggs on and below the water's surface. The remainder of the time they are usually far out of reach of trout—high above the water surface and out over land, living more like hawks than aquatic insects.

The important physical structures common to all dragonfly adults are:

1. two pair of strongly veined, glassy wings of equal length that are always separated horizontally at rest and in flight
2. forewings narrower than hindwings
3. two very large compound eyes that touch or very nearly touch at the top of the head, thus the eyes are the dominant features of the head
4. six small, weak legs tightly grouped on thorax
5. long, slender, vividly segmented abdomen with no tail

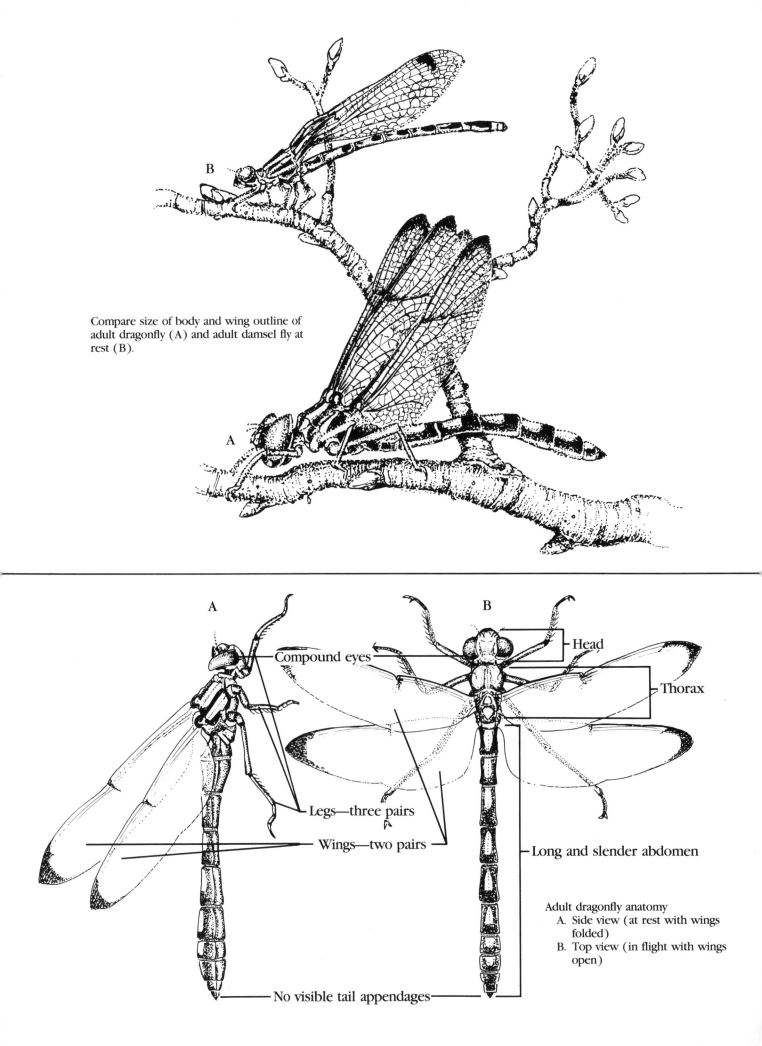

Compare size of body and wing outline of adult dragonfly (A) and adult damsel fly at rest (B).

A

B

A

B

Head

Compound eyes

Thorax

Legs—three pairs

Wings—two pairs

Long and slender abdomen

Adult dragonfly anatomy
A. Side view (at rest with wings folded)
B. Top view (in flight with wings open)

No visible tail appendages

A Typical Dragonfly Life Cycle

1. Male adult attends and/or guards female during egg-laying.
2. Egg-laying female deposits eggs on or below the water's surface and along edges of lakes and streams, usually among aquatic or terrestrial structures.
3. Eggs incubate and hatch in one to three weeks.
4. Immature dragonflies are predacious nymphs that widely distribute themselves on bottom structures and plants, such as (4A) bottom rubble and decaying plants, or (4B) live, submerged, standing aquatic and terrestrial plants.
5. Dragonfly nymphs feed and grow rapidly. Each species has specific hunting, hiding, and moving modes, from crawling to burrowing to swimming.
6. All dragonfly nymphs are active and fierce predators. With their extendible mouth, they spear, hold, and kill all types of aquatic insects, other invertebrates, and even fish fry.
7. Spring or early summer of the last year of the life cycle the dragonfly nymph crawls out and up on various structures in or adjacent to the water. The skin dries and splits open down the back. The adult dragonfly begins a long, laborious emergence out of the constricting, dried, skin membrane. It then becomes an air breather.
8. After three to twelve hours, the adult is free of the nymphal skin. It then proceeds to fill out its wings and exoskeleton, which harden by exposure to the air.
9. The new adult begins to fly and take on its typical color and feeding routine in about twelve to thirty-six hours after the emergence began.
10. Male dragonfly secures the female and fertilization begins. Such mating may occur at several intervals with other mates during the adult's summer activity.
11. Female returns to water with or without male and lays her eggs.
12. The eggs incubate and hatch, completing the dragonfly's life cycle.

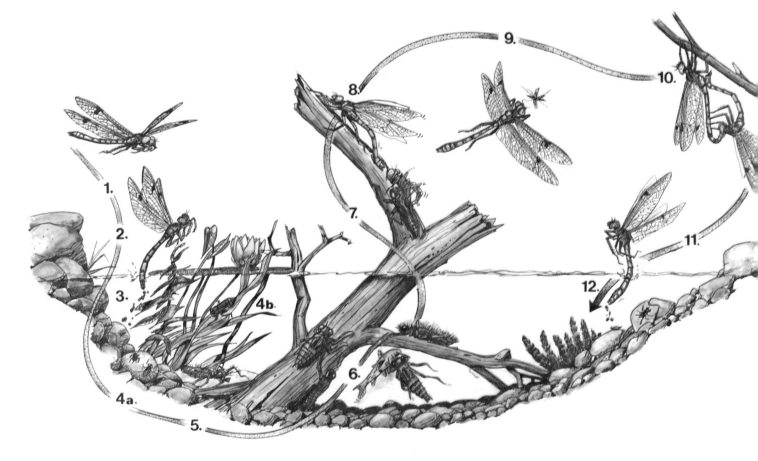

Dragonfly life cycle

My Favorite
Dragonfly Fly Designs

The good news here is that the dragonfly can be imitated and fished simply and effectively with just two basic fly designs. Usually there are not many different species available to create selectivity among trout. Several sizes and color patterns for each stage will do beautifully in eighty to ninety percent of the dragonfly trout waters I know.

SWIMMING MATURE DRAGONFLY NYMPH

Dragonfly nymphs are heavy, well-compressed insects that have, in cross section, irregular triangular bodies. When they swim they fold their spidery legs, the joints pressed tight against the body. By using a special anal breathing and propulsion valve on the end of the abdomen (associated with their internal gill system) they draw in water and squirt it out rapidly to propel themselves in quick one- and two-inch darts through the water. I'm often amazed to see a one- to two-inch-long dragonfly nymph boldly jet-swimming in open, clear water as if it were the only creature in that body of water. Trout eat some dragonfly nymphs by picking them off the stems of aquatic plants and bottom structures. However, this is not the best time, place, or method in which to use the dragonfly-nymph imitation. Most dragonfly nymphs reflect their surroundings in their dull, mottled color patterns. Browns, greys, greens, olives, and dirty blacks are the most common. There seems to be two basic shapes: 1. a short, wide, heavy-bodied nymph that seems to prefer hiding and slow crawling, and 2. a more elongated, streamlined nymph that seems to crawl and swim about much more.

Dragonfly life cycle and its imitations
  A. Crawling nymph—Position 1
  B. Swimming nymph—Position 2
  C. Fluttering adult—Position 3

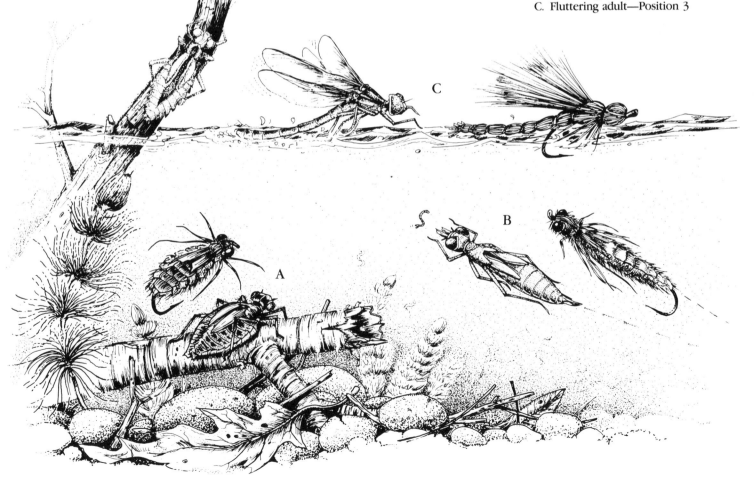

1. **HOOK:** no. 1 type: regular-length shank, heavy wire, turned-down eye; no. 2 type: 3XL shank, heavy wire, turned-up eye

2. **TYING THREAD:** Herb Howard Flymaster or waxed Monocord to match body color

3. **CEMENT:** five-minute epoxy and Pliobond for underbody

4. **BODY SHAPE, FOUNDATION, AND WEIGHT:** section of lead wire equal in diameter to hook wire. This is looped to sides of hook shank, thread-wrapped, and epoxied to form wide body foundation

5. **ABDOMEN AND THORAX:** dubbing blend of coarse synthetics and natural muskrat or rabbit fur; blend colors to simulate those contained overall in natural's body color pattern. I often mix olive, brown, grey, and black to create a basic natural color most common on lake and sluggish stream bottoms.

6. **RIB:** dark brass or dark, varnished, copper wire

7. **TOP OF ABDOMEN, THORAX, WINGCASE, AND HEAD:** Swiss Straw with natural's base color and marked with waterproof felt-tipped pen

8. **LEGS:** various cock- or hen-pheasant back feathers, dyed if necessary, to match nymph's color cast

9. **EYES:** large pair of melted nylon monofilament beads or pair of decorative plastic beads

10. **HEAD:** dubbing and Swiss Straw

Dave's fly designs for the dragonfly life cycle
  A. Crawling nymph
  B. Swimming nymph
  C. Fluttering adult

This nymph should sink rapidly so that it can be worked up and off the stream or lake bottom in short, quick, one- to three-inch line strips to simulate natural's swimming motion. I cast it out from shoreline aquatic cover or parallel to the same. Depending on the depth, I use either a floating, sinking-tip, or full-sinking line. The weighted nymph sinks and fishes best on the full-floating line with a knotless, tapered, nine- to twelve-foot leader. Usually the size 8 to 1/0 nymphs work well on 2X, 3X, or 4X tippets. You can expect excellent results either fishing the nymph blind or casting, sinking, and retrieving it up in front of a visible trout that is holding or cruising.

Midlake or midstream dragonfly-nymph fishing is far less effective than working the edges of weedbeds and points. Along lily-pad edges and beaver-cut fallen logs and limbs are perfect spots to swim the dragon nymphs. Sloughs and surface-reaching moss beds in slow-moving spring creeks and streams are best areas to find trout looking and willing for big dragon nymphs. A nylon-loop snag guard is a useful addition when using these nymphs around such structures.

When the tight-line swimming nymph is taken by a good trout the strike is likely to be abrupt and violent. I hold the stripping line gingerly and deliberately strike slowly after the trout takes. This avoids almost certain breakoffs if the fish are large. Hook points should be kept very sharp and barbs low.

FLYING AND FLUTTERING DRAGONFLY ADULTS

Adult dragonflies are most vulnerable to trout during the first twenty-four hours after the emergence, when they are slow to gain their physical balance and strength of leg and wing. They fall off their perches and/or flutter down weak-winged onto the water's surface. On the surface they flop, twitch, and flutter trying to get off the water. Such actions really light up a big trout's lateral-line sensors.

Mating and egg-laying adults as well as some surface-insect hunting adults will put themselves again within reach of the alert trout. This pattern, which is a cross between a bass hairbug and a dry fly, seems to work well for these circumstances.

1. HOOK: salmon low-water or salmon dry-fly hook
2. TYING THREAD: Monocord or single-strand nylon floss to match natural's body color
3. CEMENT: Pliobond and rod varnish
4. TAIL: none
5. ABDOMEN:
   a. elk-rump hair tied to form extended body to match natural's color and length. Extend one to one and a half shank lengths beyond bend

    b. underbody: strand of monofilament for reinforcement
    c. rib. Monocord or single-strand floss
6. **THORAX AND HEAD**: deer-body hair tied as illustrated to form
   these two parts
7. **WINGS**: bucktail or squirrel-tail hair tied extended out sides of
   thorax. Hair should be at right angles to thorax and in a horizontal plane. Such wings cause the fly to flutter slowly
   down on water when cast, as flying or fluttering natural
   would do
8. **LEGS**: tips of deer hair used for thorax and head
9. **COATING**: underbody parts painted with thinned Pliobond.
   Thorax, abdomen, and head painted with rod varnish for
   durability and to imitate natural's luster. When dry, spray entire fly with Scotchgard

This fly is not usually cast randomly, but spotted in areas where
you see trout catching adults. Try to eliminate excessive false
casting to prevent twisting of leader. I also look for landing sights
popular with adult dragonflies, such as a single twig, weed, stem,
or protruding rock. I then cast the fly high over such a spot and
let it flutter down. Once on the water, I attempt to skip and flutter and twitch the fly to imitate the distress of the water-trapped
adult. I have even had trout in such key landing zones leap out
and meet the falling fly or leap out and down on the fluttering
fake on the surface.

Another neat and fun trick is to cast the fly over a limb, let it
dangle just over the water a few seconds, then flip it off the
branch into the water and brace yourself! Trout and bass go nuts
over this technique, which simulates the newly emerged wobbly-
wing adult on a misdirected maiden flight.

Damselflies

Damselflies (suborder Zygoptera) are much better known to
most trout and trout fishers than dragonflies, and true to their
common name are much more delicate in appearance than the
large and fierce-looking dragonflies. They derive the scientific
name from their wing-base shapes: *zygo* means "yoked," and the
damsel's wings are more necked or yoked than those of the other
aquatic insects discussed in this book.

Dragons and damsels usually occur naturally and abundantly in
trout waters that are food rich and not very turbulent, such as
slow-flowing, spring-fed streams, beaver ponds, lakes, and lowland rivers. Adults are most visible and active on warm, clear, summer days, while other adult aquatic insects usually prefer more
moderate temperatures, cloudy days, or twilight hours of the
same season. Damselflies average one-half to two-thirds smaller in

size than dragonflies but are usually many times more abundant, especially in waters that have heavy and dense growths of bottom-to-surface aquatic vegetation.

Damselfly nymphs in these areas, like dragonfly nymphs, are active, aggressive predators, preying on smaller invertebrates. They love to feed on midge larvae and waterfleas. While all damsel nymphs are capable of almost minnowlike swimming performances, some spend a major portion of their nymphal stages creeping spiderlike through the aquatic jungles, and others dart fishlike in and out of their aquatic covers in search-and-capture feeding activities.

Like their relatives the dragonflies, the damselflies have three stages of development: egg, nymph, and adult. They usually live as nymphs from one to two years and spend their last spring and summer as air-breathing, feeding adults. At this time they mate and lay eggs on water structures above, on, and beneath the surface. Both the nymph and adult are typically far more delicate and slender than the dragonflies. Adult damselflies seem to be more greatly oriented to and dependent on life modes very near the water than are the far-ranging dragonflies. Thus, the damsels are consistently more visible to the trout and the fly fisher.

A Typical Damselfly Life Cycle

1. A. Adult males and females live and mate over or very near stillwaters or slow-water streams.
   B. When adult pairing and mating occurs, males usually assist females in egg-laying efforts on aquatic plants above and below the surface.
2. Egg clusters sticking to stems hatch in a few days or weeks and tiny damsel nymphs scatter down and through aquatic vegetation. Some swim, others creep or crawl around.
3. Damsel nymphs from birth are active predators on most other small invertebrates, particularly tiny aquatic insects.
4. Mature damsel nymphs begin a general concentrated movement to the perimeters of their water homes as the water warms in the spring and early summer.
5. The mature damsel nymphs crawl up and out of the water on aquatic plant stems or adjacent terrestrial structures. Their nymphal skin dries, splits and the air-breathing adult emerges. This emergence often takes from one to six hours to complete.
6. The adult takes flight within about twenty-four hours. Unlike

Damselfly life cycle

many of the other aquatic insects important to trout, they are
weak fliers initially. But with age, they develop excellent flight
ability.

7. Throughout the next thirty to ninty days, weather permitting,
an adult damsel lives an active adult life, catching and feeding
on small flying insects and mating.

8. Once paired and mated, the adults return to the aquatic plant
beds and deposit their eggs. Some females even crawl down
the stems depositing their egg clusters in deeper water.

9. The eggs incubate and hatch, completing the damselfly's life
cycle.

The important physical structures common to all damselfly nymphs are:

1. three large, distinctive, paddlelike tails that are actually tracheary gills
2. no gills, plumes, or hairlike projections on the abdomen or thorax
3. abdomen long and slender and thorax very short and larger with very tightly folded, high, dorsal wingcases
4. no distinctive head antennae; complex, large mouth appendage tucked under head
5. six long, spidery legs
6. large pair of compound eyes on a short head as wide or wider than thorax.

Damsel nymphs range widely in shape and color, but most have a very distinctive, skinny, long, spidery look. They usually reflect the color and pattern of the area they live in. Olives, greens,

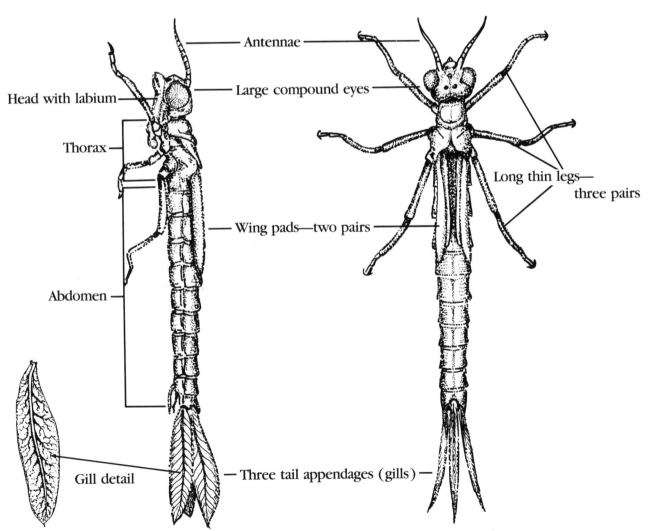

Characteristics of damsel fly nymph anatomy

Antennae

Large compound eyes

Head with labium

Thorax

Long thin legs— three pairs

Wing pads—two pairs

Abdomen

Gill detail

Three tail appendages (gills)

browns, and dirty blacks are typical colors. When they swim, they characteristically tuck in their legs and wiggle, much like a fish. The large paddlelike gills on the end of the abdomen certainly must assist in these agile swimming motions. For years I watched damsels swim about thinking them to be small minnows or trout fry in high trout lakes in Wyoming and Montana.

Live damsel nymphs can be captured along water edges, especially in dense leaves, stems, and roots of aquatic vegetation. Sides and undersides of submerged logs, tree limbs, and coarse sediment beds are good areas to catch nymphs also. Note their size and shape first then place them in the water and watch how they move away.

Just after emergence the damsel adult is a watery pale, wobbly-legged, wobbly-winged insect. In a day or so the brilliant colors of the male and wing banding appear. Females usually are less colorful and have slightly heavier abdomens. Damsel adults are most vulnerable to feeding trout just after emergence, during windy or chilly days, and during the egg-laying periods. Some trout become excellent at catching both damsel and dragon adults

Characteristics of adult damsely fly anatomy

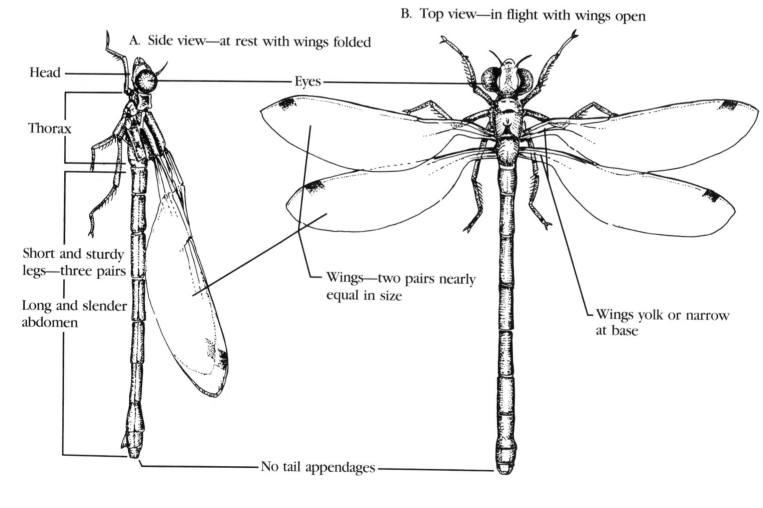

B. Top view—in flight with wings open

A. Side view—at rest with wings folded

Head

Eyes

Thorax

Short and sturdy legs—three pairs

Long and slender abdomen

Wings—two pairs nearly equal in size

Wings yolk or narrow at base

No tail appendages

that are hovering over the water's surface. Most adults that are eaten, though, are taken on the surface.

The important physical structures common to all damselfly adults are:

1. two equal pairs of long wings; each wing has a distinctive, narrow stalk or yoke at the base of the thorax
2. abdomen very long and slender, distinctly segmented, two to three times the length of the thorax or even longer than the wings
3. no tails or easily visible antennae
4. at rest, wings are folded over and to rear of thorax, appearing to be one wing
5. eyes large, but separated on the top of the head by a distance equal to or greater than the width of one eye; eyes and head together are wider than either thorax or abdomen
6. six short, rather weak, crowded legs, seldom longer than thorax and head area

My Favorite Damselfly Fly Designs

The damselflies are large, active, daytime insects during both the nymphal and adult stages. They are probably more attractive and more frequently fed upon in trout waters that contain both damsels and dragons than are the dragons. I would always start with a damsel imitation first if I had to guess which would be the most productive of the two insect imitations to use.

DAVE'S DAMSEL NYMPH

I tie this nymph in two designs, the straight body and the wiggle body. Both seem to be very effective, but the wiggle-nymph would probably be best to fool very large and selective trout. I have found the smaller size 4XL hook to be far superior to a larger 2XL or 3XL hook for tying nymphs to be used in very clear water for selective trout. The smallest hook size possible allows me to use the finer leader tippets needed for such situations.

1. HOOK: standard body: 4XL, regular wire, turned-down eye. Wiggle-body: regular-length shank (Mustad 94842 or 94840) and (for abdomen) use any small, inexpensive, ring-eye hook

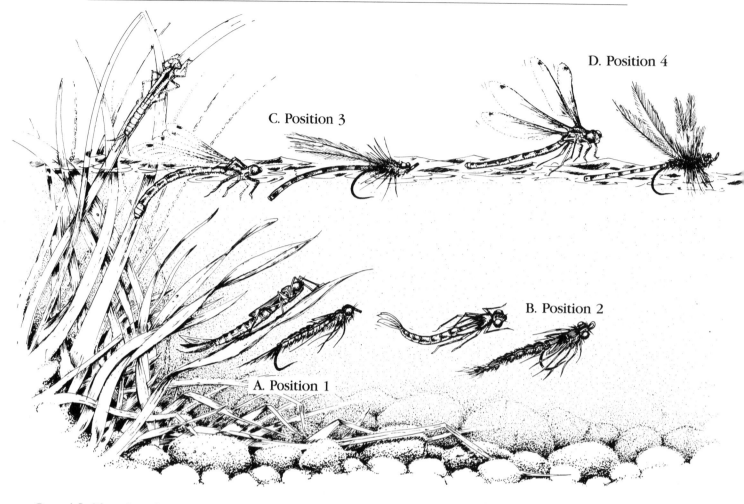

D. Position 4

C. Position 3

B. Position 2

A. Position 1

Damsel fly life cycle and its imitations
- A. Crawling damsel nymph and standard body nymph—Position 1
- B. Swimming damsel nymph and wiggle nymph—Position 2
- C. Spent or egglaying adult and Dave's spent wing adult—Position 3
- D. Fluttering adult damsel and fluttering adult—Position 4

2. **BODY WEIGHT:** six to ten turns of lead wire on abdomen
3. **HINGE:** bead wire (for wiggle-body only)
4. **CEMENT:** Pliobond
5. **TAILS:** three tips of very soft ostrich herl or a small bunch of marabou herl tip ends
6. **ABDOMEN:**
    - a. rib: fine gold wire
    - b. back: Swiss Straw or turkey wing quill section
    - c. body: sparkle synthetic nymph dubbing
7. **THORAX:**
    - a. wingcase: Swiss Straw or turkey wing quill section
    - b. body: sparkle synthetic nymph dubbing
    - c. legs: soft hen or grouse hackle
8. **HEAD:**
    - a. eyes: two connected melted beads of nylon monofilament
    - b. top of head: Swiss Straw
    - c. synthetic sparkle nymph dubbing

For the wiggle-body I put the hinge between the joint of the abdomen and thorax. Wingcase extends just back over the abdo-

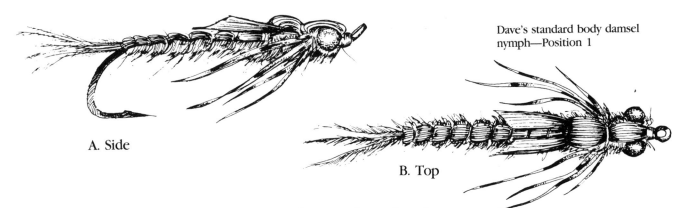

A. Side

B. Top

Dave's standard body damsel
nymph—Position 1

men. A common mistake is to tie this nymph too fat—the more
slender it is tied, the more realistic it appears when being fished.
Whenever possible, capture and study live damsel nymphs up
close and in the water swimming. Like scuds, they look totally different in hand and when swimming free.

The damsel nymph has been one of my most effective designs
wherever these aquatic insects are likely to be eaten by trout. I've
seldom experienced poor fishing in trout lakes, ponds, sloughs,
and spring creeks when I have fished this design properly. I use
a floating line, a nine- to twelve-foot, knotless, tapered leader and
a twenty-four- to forty-eight-inch tippet. The nymph is cast out
and allowed to sink deep or rest on the bottom. I then swim it
in irregular-length line strips and rod twitches toward the water's
edge or along shorelines. It is especially deadly if sprung up in
front of a cruising trout you have sighted. I seldom fish these
nymphs in fast-flowing midstream areas or dead drift. I nearly always actively swim this nymph along the perimeters of stillwaters
or slow-water areas of streams.

Many rich springcreeks and ponds contain hordes of tiny
(hook size 16 to 24) scuds, water fleas, midge larvae, and sowbugs. Fishing these midgets deep and naturally is often a futile,
frustrating practice. But almost without exception, there are
hordes of damsel nymphs there, too, swimming about, like the

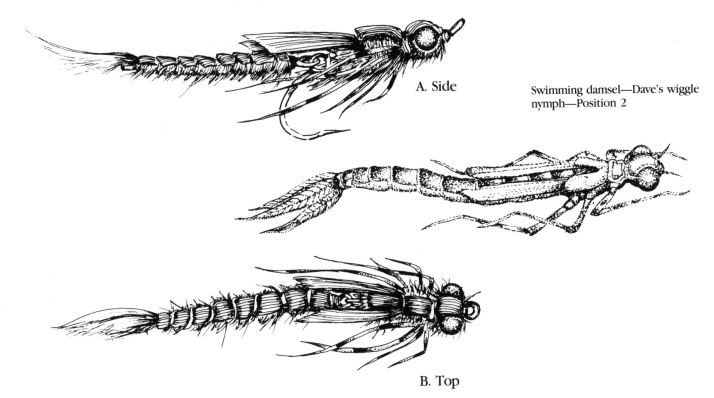

A. Side

Swimming damsel—Dave's wiggle
nymph—Position 2

B. Top

trout, enjoying the bounty of goodies. By using the much larger and easier-to-fish damsel nymph, I have had far greater success with large fish.

DAVE'S SPENT-WING ADULT DAMSELFLY

1. **HOOK:** Mustad 94842 or salmon dry-fly hook
2. **TYING THREAD:** Herb Howard Flymaster to match body color
3. **CEMENT:** Pliobond and rod varnish
4. **ABDOMEN:** large, stripped, grizzly cock-hackle stem dyed or colored with felt pen to match the natural's body color. Hackle stem forms entire length of abdomen tied on one-fourth of the rear length of hook shank and extended past bend two full hook-shank lengths. Put the large end of stem to the rear
5. **THORAX:** synthetic dubbing to match natural's color
6. **WINGS:** four narrow dun or grizzly cock hackles tied spent out from sides of thorax. Wings should be three-fourths the length of total fly
7. **LEGS:** grizzly hackle collar trimmed on top and bottom, hackle dyed to match natural's leg color
8. **HEAD:** same dubbing as thorax
9. **EYES:** two beads of melted nylon monofilament

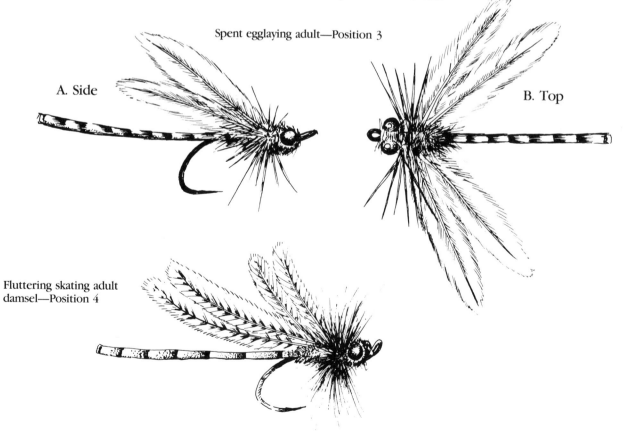

Spent egglaying adult—Position 3

A. Side

B. Top

Fluttering skating adult damsel—Position 4

Brook trout taking damsel nymph

This spent-wing fly imitates the fluttering-down and water-trapped adult. Adult damsels or dragons do not naturally land or rest on the water's surface like caddis, stoneflies, or mayflies. They partially sink and their wings are always in open, spent positions. This fly works best when cast around the edges of any structures protruding out of the water that trout might hide under or swim by. I often twitch or dap this fly in lakes. Like the damsel nymph, be sure it is tied very slender and sparse. In streams, I have some success with this design fished wet. I put it under just as it comes near or up to any trout cover, such as a log, boulder, or tree limb.

9
CRUSTACEANS

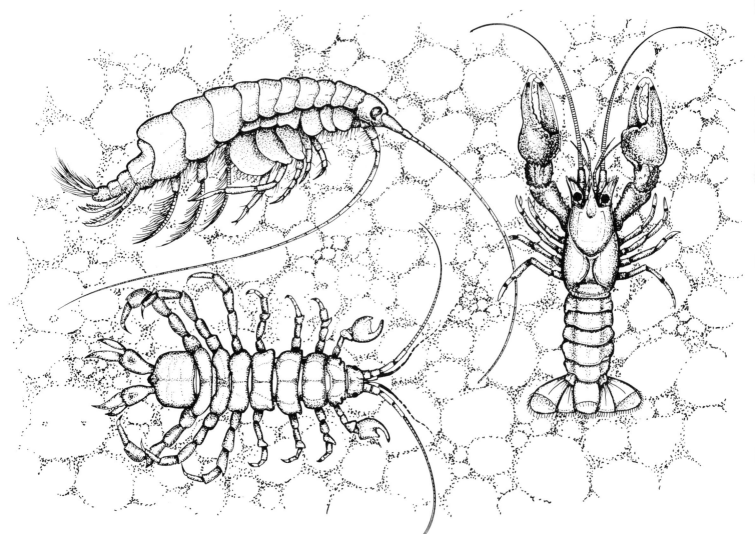

I consider the crustaceans one of the three major groups of aquatic trout food. Most high-quality trout waters that I know of would not successfully support the fish without populations of scuds, sowbugs, or crayfish. Their numbers and vulnerability are unequalled by the other two major groups, aquatic insects and fish. The simplicity of their forms and life cycles make successful imitation usually quite easy for the fly tier and fly fisherman. Even the superb flavor and rich orange-red color of wild trout are largely due to these crustaceans.

It was imitating these trout foods that I had my most consistent success as a beginning fly fisherman some twenty-five or thirty years back. Their forms, actions, and locales are more suited to the limited fly selection and casting and line manipulation ability of the newcomer than any other class of trout food. Yet the most highly skilled fly tier and fly fisher will never find these forms anything but challenging and enjoyable to imitate.

Scuds

Scuds are small (5 to 25mm), shrimplike, freshwater crustaceans that occur naturally in most trout waters and have been successfully introduced into many man-made trout tailwaters, lakes, and reservoirs. Where they thrive, there is a significant enrichment in the size, growth rate, and eating quality of resident or carry-over trout. They are often called freshwater shrimp because of the similarity in looks and behavior to the saltwater shrimp, and because they contribute a pink to deep-orange color to the flesh of trout that eat them. This color is due to a fatty organic compound called carotene, which all crustaceans have and salmonids uniquely acquire through eating them and accumulating it in their tissue. Scuds, shrimp, and crayfish often turn pale to dark orange after they die as a direct reflection of the presence of this compound.

Scuds, upon close inspection, have a rather horizontally flattened, strongly segmented body with a slight vertical arc, or curved back. They have several types of appendages on their heads, thoraxes, and abdomens, totaling fourteen pairs. Their scientific name, Amphipoda, means "two types of legs." These are located on the lower parts of the body segments and give scuds a distinctly leggy look. Out of water they are almost helpless, having to lay on either side and assume a fetal position; more active

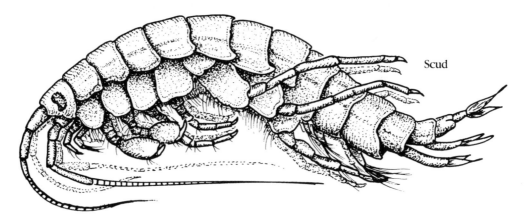

Scud

scuds out of water will kick and flip in a tight circle. When they are in the water they use their legs to swim forward and their tails to dart backward when frightened. In either case, they swim with their bodies almost straight. Scuds also have an almost amusing trait of randomly swimming on their sides or upside-down as well as upright—as if they were not aware of gravity or bottom and top.

Scuds are very active crawling and swimming scavengers, especially during twilight, nighttime, and cloudy days. I have often observed large individuals as well as groups of scuds swimming in open water directly exposed to predators. They prefer to rest and feed in aquatic plant beds, the calmer edges of streams, and along coarse-gravel bottoms. To capture live scuds, just use a simple fine-mesh nymph or aquarium net to seine these areas with. Often they can be captured by pulling up a handful of aquatic plants or stream-bottom gravel. They reproduce during the milder seasons and are capable of generating and sustaining enormous populations.

There can be wide variations in size and color among the same species in the same generation and locale. This is because the males are smaller than the females and because the individual's diet and growth rate will vary a great deal. At various intervals, they undergo metamorphic skin-shedding periods, and their color drastically changes from a pale tannish-pink to olive-grey to dark-grey, and so on as the new skin hardens and ages. I'm convinced trout strongly prefer the "fresh" or soft-shelled scud that has just shed its skin and has yet to have its new skin harden up, which is also true with sowbugs and crayfish. It is, I feel, a matter of more odor, less color camouflage, and a more pleasing texture to mouth and swallow.

I can't think of a better aquatic food for the fly tier and angler to imitate, because the shape, size, color, and swimming characteristics of scuds allow a fantastic latitude. They swim and crawl in all directions at many different speeds.

Trout are always receptive to these wonderful foods, and there is seldom one day a year that scuds don't form some portion of the trout's diet. Eight years of examining the stomach contents of thousands of trout across North America has convinced me of this. I suspect many artificial nymphs and wet flies are taken by trout because they are often fished more like scuds than the food forms they are supposed to imitate.

The important physical characteristics of scuds are:

1. head and first thoracic segment fused
2. seven thoracic and six abdominal segments
3. seven pairs of legs, first two pairs are clublike claws
4. six paired appendages on six abdominal segments
5. two long, distinctive antennae on head that curve forward and down

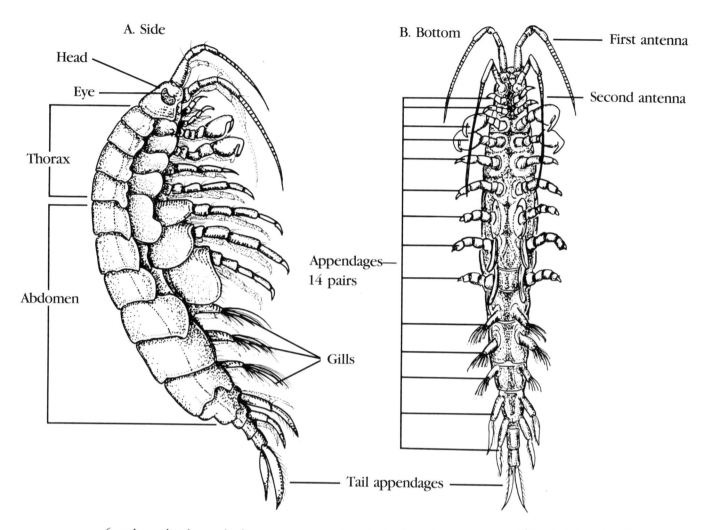

A. Side

Head

Eye

Thorax

Abdomen

B. Bottom

First antenna

Second antenna

Appendages—
14 pairs

Gills

Tail appendages

Characteristics of scud anatomy

6. when dead, scuds form a strong, closed, fetal body position, which is C-shaped and resembles an armadillo

DAVE'S SWIMMING SCUD (SHRIMP)

This one scud design will suggest or imitate all of the important freshwater shrimp and scud species that trout feed upon in both flowing waters and stillwaters. Only the sizes and colors need to be altered. This design is tied both forward or backward swimming (see illustration).

1. **HOOK:** Mustad 94842 or regular-length shank, extra-light wire, turned-up eye
2. **BODY WEIGHT:** lead or copper wire
3. **CEMENTS:** Pliobond for underbody and clear head cement
4. **ANTENNAE:** wood duck or mallard barred flank-feather fibers
5. **LEGS:** soft partridge hackle or hen hackle
6. **RIB:** fine gold or silver wire
7. **BACK:** strip of Swiss Straw or clear poly bag material
8. **BODY:** blend of sparkle Orlon yarn or nymph blend dubbing, muskrat belly or beaver belly, (Spectrum color natural). I prefer a light dun-grey with undertones of tan and olive for an all-around standard

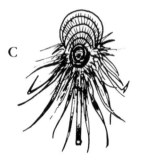

Dave's swimming scud (shrimp)
A. Forwarding swimming design
B. Backward swimming design
C. Front view of Dave's scud

It is extremely important to obtain a straight-bodied shape to best simulate a swimming scud or shrimp. The backward-swimming design usually fishes best, but many shrimp and scuds are taken by trout as they leg swim forward. I prefer to fish these designs with a lightweight, floating fly line (three, four-, or five-weight), nine- to twelve-foot, knotless leader with strike indicator and thirty to forty inches of tippet. The open Duncan loop knot to the fly is an absolute must.

In both streams and lakes I fish the swimming scud near bottom structures and plant beds. In lakes I cast out, allow the weighted fly to sink near or to the bottom, then begin a slow, erratic, short-pulsed line strip with my rod pointed at the fly and rod tip about six inches off the water. I watch the floating indicator and the angle of line between the rod tip and water—either or both will give me a better indication of a take than feeling the take.

In flowing waters I cast up and slightly across or straight downstream. (Often as you wade, your boot soles will dislodge quantities of scuds, sowbugs, snails, and nymphs. The trout below will hold and work this bonus chum line.) In either case I use a very slack leader presentation so that scud can quickly sink. The fly is dead-drifted as much as possible until it reaches a point far downstream, then I allow it to swing around and rise up. I often impart very short, erratic, line-strip twitches. I watch the floating indicator at all times to detect the strike or take. Usually it just pauses, dips under, or slightly twitches when the scud is taken by a trout. When I detect such, I strike with a quick line strip and a very slight rod-tip reaction.

Scuds in various natural positions

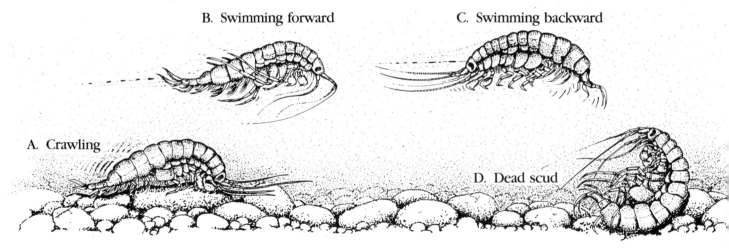

B. Swimming forward

C. Swimming backward

A. Crawling

D. Dead scud

Sowbugs

Sowbugs (Isopoda), sometimes known as cressbugs or pillbugs, are closely related to the scuds in general size, habitat requirement, and life cycle. They probably run a close second to the scuds for importance in distribution and numbers in trout waters. They are rather wide, flat creatures with seven pairs of equally spaced legs that extend at right angles from their sides. They have two large, long antennae and two flaplike tails.

Aquatic sowbugs closely resemble their terrestrial counterparts, the roly-poly sowbug, in shape and crawling action. They only crawl on bottom structures and are practically helpless if off the bottom until they sink back to the bottom again. Like scuds, they prefer oxygen-rich, hard, limestone waters abundant in aquatic vegetation.

They are basically nocturnal scavengers but are much more active than scuds in daylight during very cold water periods. Although they are found in good numbers in some trout lakes, they are *far more significant to imitate in flowing waters*. This is because in lakes it is almost impossible to imitate their crawling action, whereas in streams they often break free of the bottom and drift along.

Their life cycle is very simple and the angler only needs to imitate the general size, color, and action of the adults, which can be found in and on the shallower bottom structures. Trout catch them off the surfaces of these structures, dislodge them from clumps of aquatic vegetation, and intercept others that have washed free of these structures in currents or windy lakes. To capture samples I just pull up a small handful of aquatic vegetation or seine very near the bottom while overturning some of the gravel or disturbing aquatic plants.

Sowbugs in their natural bottom habitat

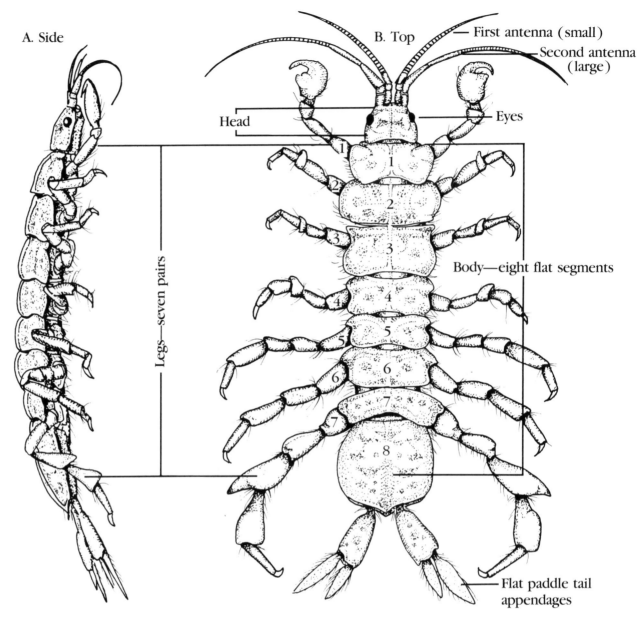

A. Side

B. Top

First antenna (small)

Second antenna (large)

Head

Eyes

Legs—seven pairs

Body—eight flat segments

Flat paddle tail appendages

Characteristics of sowbug anatomy

The important physical characteristics of sowbugs are:

1. body has eight distinctive, flat segments
2. head contains one large and one small pair of antennae
3. rearmost segment has two flat, paddlelike tails
4. underside of body has a distinctive white area

DAVE'S SOWBUG

1. HOOK: Mustad 94842, extra-fine wire, regular-length shank, turned-up eye
2. TYING THREAD: Herb Howard Flymaster, color of body
3. BODY WEIGHT: lead wire same diameter as hook wire or slightly larger. A base for the wide, flat sowbug body is construct-

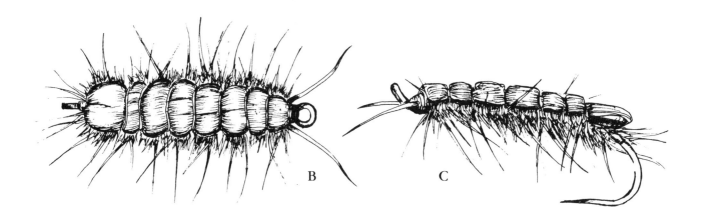

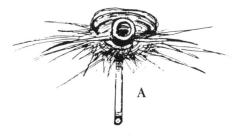

ed by looping the lead wire along the sides of the hook, overwrapping it with thread, and coating it with five-minute epoxy.

4. CEMENTS: five-minute epoxy, Pliobond, and clear head cement
5. RIB: fine gold or silver wire
6. TAIL: two short, grey fibers off the leading edge of a duck primary wing feather
7. BODY: blend of fifty-percent grey fox-squirrel back hair and thirty-percent silver-grey muskrat-belly fur and twenty-percent foxtan or sienna (yellowish-brown) sparkle Orlon yarn
8. BACK: Grey or tan Swiss Straw or polypropylene
9. LEGS: A few guardhairs of the grey fox-squirrel blend picked out on sides of body

Dave's sow bug
A. Front
B. Top
C. Side

The sowbug fly is normally not useful in lakes but quite useful in streams. Since sowbugs either crawl or drift and tumble out of control with the current, the fly should be fished on or tumbling just above the bottom. I use the same line, leader, indicator, tippet, and knot as described for the scud and the same slack-leader presentation. However, I fish this fly dead drift and with no swing or action. The bug is best fished right on the bottom structure and with just the normal current movement. The trout usually take this fly very softly and you must watch the strike indicator with a keen eye.

A typical feeding position called tailing: The fish is foraging among vegetation and gravel for scuds and sowbugs.

Crayfish

The crayfish (Decapoda) is a sizable, important, and rich food for trout in a great many lakes and streams. They are often the foundation for significant trout growth, yet few fly fishermen regularly depend upon imitating them to catch trophy fish. Their large size, bottom-dwelling behavior, and nocturnal activity make them somewhat difficult to imitate properly with traditional fly-tying methods.

Crayfish have five pairs of legs (*deca* means "ten," and *poda* means "legs") on their thoracic segments. The first pair is usually much larger with large, strong-jawed pinchers used for holding and eating. Although they are scavangers, they also can be fierce predators, preying on small fish and many other aquatic creatures, including other crayfish.

They inhabit all types of trout water, preferring bottom structures that allow them to dig holes or dens beneath the structures. Shallow, coarse-rubble bottoms and aquatic plant beds seem to be ideal for supporting large numbers of these solitary, nocturnal creatures.

Crayfish have a simple multiannual life cycle in which they are most active in growth, movement, and reproduction during the months of warmer water. They are almost dormant when the water temperature falls below forty-two degrees and are seldom found outside of their dens during these periods. As the water warms, they become active and easy prey for foraging trout. This is particularly true during two periods: when the water temperature is just below ideal (normally between fifty-five and sixty-five degrees) they are active but sluggish crawlers or swimmers; and when the water temperature is ideal for fastest growth and they are regularly shedding their hard shells for growth room. At that

Crayfish

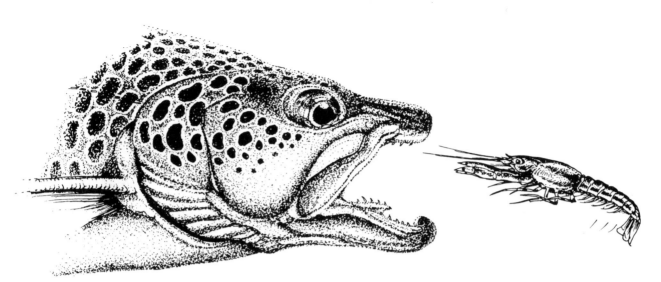

Crayfish swim backward rapidly when threatened by a large enemy, in this case a trout.

time they are helpless, soft-shelled creatures—and absolute delicacies for trout. Certainly this is the most ideal stage and time for fishing their imitations.

Crayfish move in two ways: they normally crawl about forward, but when threatened they crawl backward with their claws raised in a defensive posture. When startled or attacked they fold their legs in and use their tails to swim in a fast, darting, backward motion to the nearest bottom-structure protection. In their soft-shelled condition, these movements are made in very slow motion, which makes the crayfish sitting ducks for fast, opportunistic trout. When they are hard shelled, trout often catch them but go through a series of biting, head shaking, and releasing actions to soften up the hard shells and disable the flesh-cutting pinchers. When they are hard shelled, trout usually prefer the smaller crayfish and the females, which have smaller pinchers. But when they are soft shelled, trout will eat any size with zest.

Look for live crayfish under shallow streamside or lakeside bottom structures such as large, flat rocks, moss beds, old cans, and tree bark or logs. They are much easier to find and capture at night when most will be out of their dens foraging for food or shedding their skins. A simple aquarium fish net is excellent for capturing these backward-swimming creatures. Take care not to allow the large specimens to pinch you; it can hurt and result in a minor cut.

The important physical characteristics of crayfish are:

1. five strong pairs of thoracic legs, first three pairs have clawed ends
2. first pair of legs is much larger and has strong pincher claws similar to a crab
3. two beady, stalklike eyes on the front top of head
4. a strong, segmented tail with a flaplike paddle at the end
5. one very long, stalked, whiplike antennae with one much shorter pair between them; each of the shorter antennae is split into two parts so that it appears as if there are two pairs of short antennae

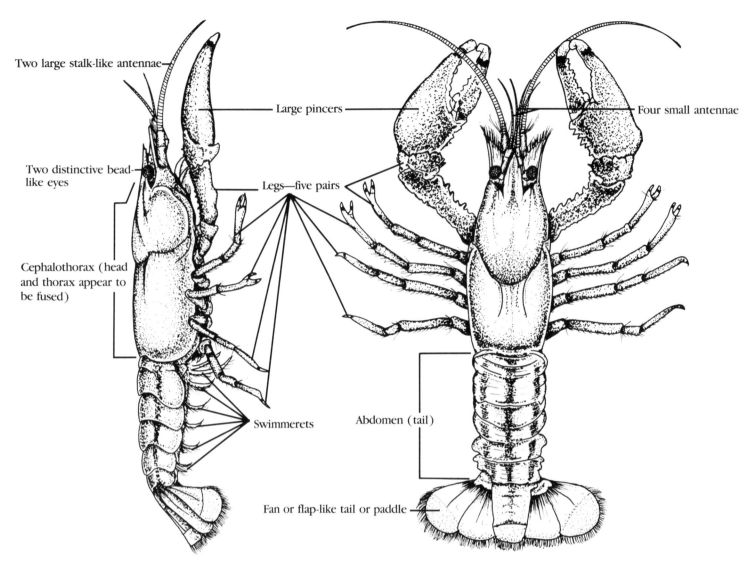

Two large stalk-like antennae

Large pincers

Four small antennae

Two distinctive bead-like eyes

Legs—five pairs

Cephalothorax (head and thorax appear to be fused)

Swimmerets

Abdomen (tail)

Fan or flap-like tail or paddle

Characteristics of crayfish anatomy, side and top views

DAVE'S SOFT-SHELLED CRAYFISH JIG FLY

This crayfish imitation is designed to look, act, and feel like a live soft-shelled crayfish. It is an unorthodox fly design, as it is more of a jig than a fly in its construction and fishing method. Yet I am convinced that anything less is not as effective an imitation of the crayfish's natural position and action.

1. **HOOK**: jig hook or turned-down eye, 4XL standard hook bent down at a forty-five-degree angle just behind eye to create jig-hook effect
2. **WEIGHT**: lead split-shot pinched directly around hook wire at a forty-five-degree angle to neck of hook and epoxied
3. **CEMENT**: five-minute epoxy and Pliobond
4. **TYING THREAD**: single-strand nylon floss, color to match body of fly

5. **PINCHERS**: two pair of grizzly or cree soft cock-neck or saddle hackles dyed to match natural's color scheme
6. **EYES**: pair of melted nylon monofilament beads
7. **ANTENNAE**: small- or medium-size rubber hackle
8. **FRONT OF HEAD**: small clump of dyed northern deer hair
9. **BACK AND TAIL**: Swiss Straw, color to match natural
10. **RIB**: medium brass or gold wire
11. **BODY (TAIL OR THORAX)**: synthetic dubbing blend to match color of side and underbody of natural
12. **LEGS**: soft grizzly hackle dyed to match natural's color scheme

This design is tied so when fished it appears to be crawling or swimming backward as the natural does when pursued by a trout. The split-shot near the hook eye causes the fly to sink rapidly and swim or crawl like a real crayfish. All the materials used are water absorbent and soft to look and feel much like the soft-shelled naturals. Study this design very closely before attempting to tie it.

I fish this soft-shelled crayfish two ways. In streams, I use a floating, bass-bug taper line, long leader, and relatively heavy tippet. I cast the crayfish at any angle and crawl it slowly, occasionally jigging it slowly, as if it were a natural trying to escape by swimming. I've found the slower and more deliberately I fish it the better it works. The more helpless soft-shelled crayfish are sluggish and often vulnerable day or night in streams, so the trout are always more than willing to accept a well-designed and properly fished imitation. I consistently catch large trout with this fly, although it is not pleasant to cast.

In lakes I use a High-Density sinking-tip fly line and a heavy, three-foot leader. The crayfish fly is cast to or parallel to the shoreline and allowed to sink to the bottom. I slow strip the line and use short, quick, rod-tip twitches to jig the fly in—but always keeping it right on the bottom.

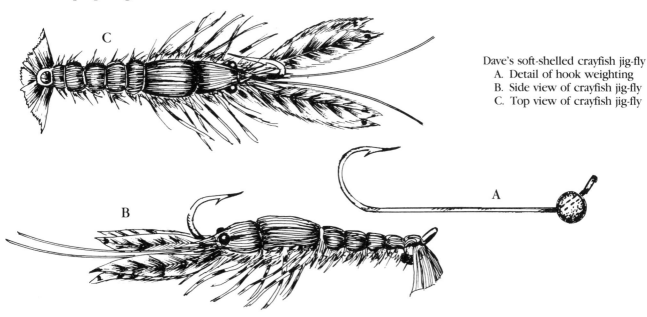

Dave's soft-shelled crayfish jig-fly
A. Detail of hook weighting
B. Side view of crayfish jig-fly
C. Top view of crayfish jig-fly

10
FORAGE FISH

As they mature, trout usually feed increasingly on forage fish. This is due to the necessity to ingest larger amounts of rich foods efficiently to sustain growth, size, and energy requirements. The smaller and more seasonal aquatic foods such as insects are not usually abundant enough or large enough to meet these demands. So "minnows," or smaller fish, are usually the most abundant and dependable food source in natural trout lakes and streams.

The paradox is that most fly fishermen want to catch at least a share of the big trout in their waters, yet few use anything but imitations of small food forms. Less glamorous and heavier-tackled streamer-fly fishing is not very popular.

The important trait of a great gamefish, *being a supreme predator,* is exactly what makes large trout so aggressive, fast, and belligerent when hooked. It is time to reevaluate our opinions on streamer fishing for trout. Matching the minnow is as fascinating, challenging, and sporting as matching the hatch—if the approach to understanding forage fish, imitating, and fishing the imitations is given the same attention to detail.

Over the years many of my most exciting experiences with trout have been the result of using streamers to fish large and small waters. The method is extremely active, not passive like many of the smaller-fly methods. In the past few years I have routinely fished streamers to evaluate new waters and to locate concentrations of trout or large solitary fish. Even when fish are tipping and sipping in the sophisticated spring creeks, a well-fished streamer brings the real muggers out there. Some fly fishers are discovering that these larger trout are taking advantage of the vulnerable hatch-feeding activities of dace, chubs, small trout, and other fish to pounce on them with almost no effort.

All trout are natural predators, and I have seen weeks-old rainbow, brook, brown, and cutthroat fry eat their newly hatched cousins greedily. From the first, trout live with, often side by side, other small trout, minnows, suckers, and other fish. Year-round they share the same water and are always accessible and vulnerable. Larger trout only survive in fishable waters by staying deep to hide from anglers and other large predators. When they feed, they prefer to grab a big, quick, easy mouthful of another live fish. Those trout that break or slip up on this routine are usually caught and killed by anglers.

Perhaps the crudeness attached to streamer fishing was once justified as the flies were crude in design, weight, and imitation. Most were surely simple attractors, and a few were good simulators. Rods, lines, and leaders used to fish them were heavy, insensitive, and not much fun for casting, fishing, or fighting a trout. Today that is mostly changed with a whole new approach to flies, rods, lines, leaders, casting, and fishing techniques.

Resident or migrating fish and minnows of all types and sizes in trout waters have life cycles of three to nine years. Trout prefer to feed on the one- to six-inch-long forage fish, but on occasion will eat other trout, suckers, and chubs up to twelve-inches long. Like trout, these fish make spawning runs and are influenced strongly by seasons, temperatures, and water conditions. Being cold-blooded creatures, they are less active in very cold and very warm waters. It is most important to understand when these fish

Trout feeding on trout fry

are present and where they exist in a particular area; exact identification is less important.

In order to best relate to you a working understanding of trout forage fish, I've worked out a general classification of shapes, color patterns, actions, and preferred habitats. A lot like aquatic nymphs, these fish can be simply classified by their shapes, action, and mode of living. Such a system clearly directs the fly tier

A. Bucktail
B. Muddler
C. Feather (hackle) wing

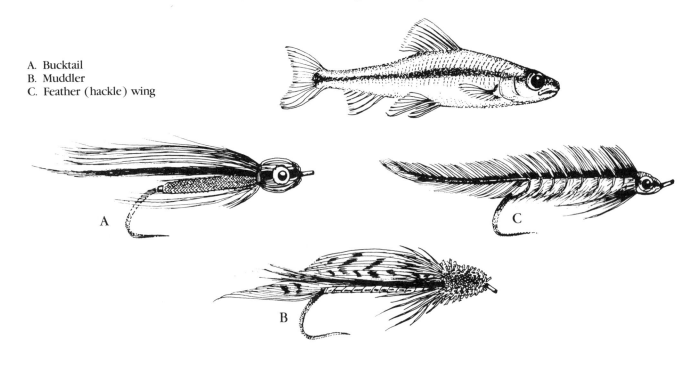

and angler once he has recognized the resident forage fish trout are feeding upon.

Thanks to a whole new world of innovative tying methods and materials, effective imitations with very realistic shapes, looks, and actions are a piece of cake for today's fly tier. The matuka-style wing for hackle body feathers and the use of marabou feathers have been major breakthroughs for tying these imitation fish. Mylar threads, tinsels, tubing and prismatic Mylar tapes give us the touch of light-reflecting scales unique only to live fish. These techniques and materials have helped bring about this new period in streamer-fishing for trout.

The four basic forage fish types are:

1. the deep-sided, thin-backed, large-metallic-scaled fish. These fish are lake- and river-dwelling open-water, fast-swimming, school-oriented, and derive their mirrorlike re-

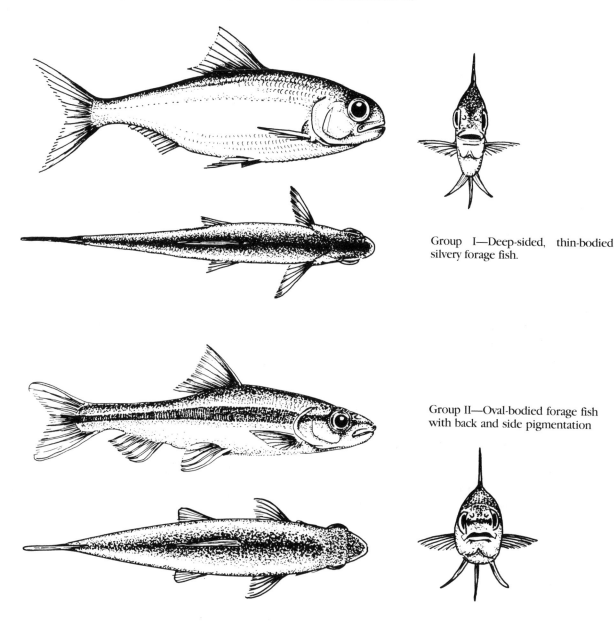

Group I—Deep-sided, thin-bodied silvery forage fish.

Group II—Oval-bodied forage fish with back and side pigmentation

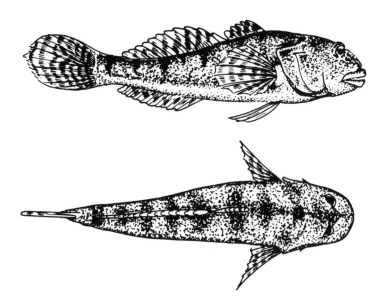

Group III—Bottom-dwelling forage fish, heavily pigmented and with compressed bodies

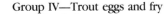

Group IV—Trout eggs and fry
  A. Newly layed egg
  B. Hours-old egg doubled in size from water absorption
  C. Eyed egg, near hatching
  D. Newly hatched yolk sac fry
  E. Swim-up fry

flective colors from the pale colors of open water. Examples are shad, smelt, herring, alewives, and shiners

2. the long, oval-bodied, free-swimming fish that are solitary or small-group fish, which derive their color pattern from close proximity to the sides and bottoms of streams and lakes. Examples are chub, dace, whitefish, sticklebacks, carp, and trout

3. the compressed-bodied, wide-bellied, bottom-dwelling fish. These fish live near, on, and under the bottom structures of lakes and streams and display intricate back and side color patterns to camouflage themselves on the stream or lake bottom. Some examples are sculpin, catfish, darters, and suckers

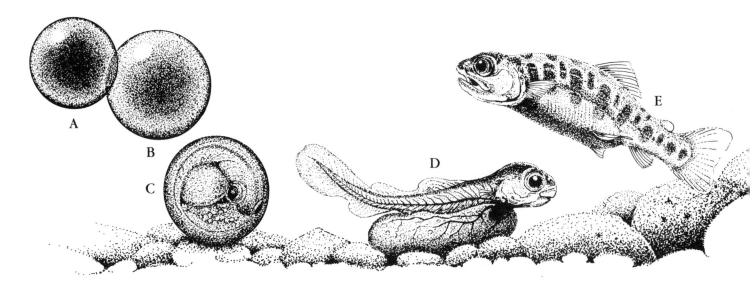

4. the eggs, newly-hatched egg-sac fry and swim-up fry of all salmonids. These bottom and near-to-bottom eggs and fry are a very important forage source for trout in many waters. Examples are eggs of salmon, char, and trout, and the newly-hatched and swim-up fry of these. Also included here are the eggs and fry of suckers

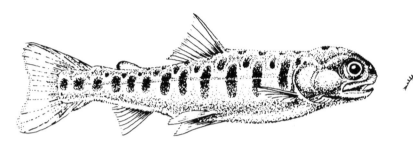

Advanced stage free-swimming trout fry

Group I. These fish are generally close-schooling fast swimmers that frequent large, open waters. They are generally flat, thin fish with very silvery scales on their sides and undersides and have backs colored similar to the water's color. Few species have any characteristic bands, stripes, spots, or other body markings. Trout feed on them by attacking the schools and chasing them or driving them to the surface. Threadfin shad, alewives, and smelt are the three best-known fishes of this group.

This group is usually most successfully imitated on trout lakes by casting to surface attacks or deep trolling. They are prone to congregate at stream inlets to lakes where they feed and run up to spawn. In rivers, particularly below dam tailwaters, they are fished with a crippled action down and across the stream at various depths. A massive amount of these fish are shocked, stunned, or killed going over or through intakes and turbines at dams and are greedily eaten as they drift helplessly in tailwater currents and eddies.

I've developed two Group I designs to imitate these fish. The primary requirements are to accurately simulate the wide silhouette, flashy side, and action of these fishes. Such streamers must also be tied to fish from top to bottom with panic-swimming or crippled-dying actions. All these fish have very distinctive, large eyes and *so must the imitation!*

WHITLOCK MATUKA MARABOU AND MYLAR MINNOW

1. **HOOK:** silver (nickel) or gold plated, 3XL or 4XL shank, ring or turned-down eye, sizes 10 to 3/0

2. **TYING THREAD:** white single-strand nylon floss or Monocord
3. **BODY WEIGHT** (OPTIONAL): lead wire
4. **CEMENTS:** clear head cement and Sportsman's Goop Cement (for doll eyes)
5. **EYES:** plastic doll eyes or yellow and black enamel
6. **BODY:** white, cream, or yellow chenille
7. **RIB:** Gold or silver beading wire
8. **WING:** One white, light cream, yellow, or gold turkey marabou feathers and three to six narrow gold or silver Mylar strips
9. **OVERWING:** four to six ostrich herls dyed color of minnows back (blue, green, or gold, for example)
10. **GILLS:** bright-red hackle-base fluff
11. **CHEEKS:** two small, grey-silver mallard-drake breast feathers, natural color or tinted the color of minnow's side

Group I imitations
A. Whit Matuka Mylar and Marabou Minnow
B. Whit Prismatic Mylar and Marabou Minnow

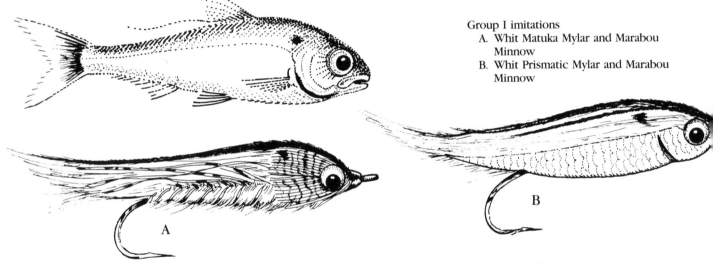

Without body weight and with doll eyes this design has a neutral buoyancy. Without doll eyes it is a slow sinker. With lead body weighting it sinks fast. Tied regular matuka style using the Mylar and marabou it simulates a swimming minnow. Tied the same, but with matuka wing on the side of the hook it uniquely simulates a crippled or dying minnow. The Mylar strips are added as you rib the marabou feathers matuka style.

PRISMATIC MYLAR MINNOW

This is a "second-generation" design from the Whitlock Marabou Matuka and Mylar Minnow that closely imitates the reflective highlights of the wide, large, flashy side scales of these minnows. The prismatic Mylar type is an absolute must for this design. It is also much easier to tie but has a bit less durability and live swim-

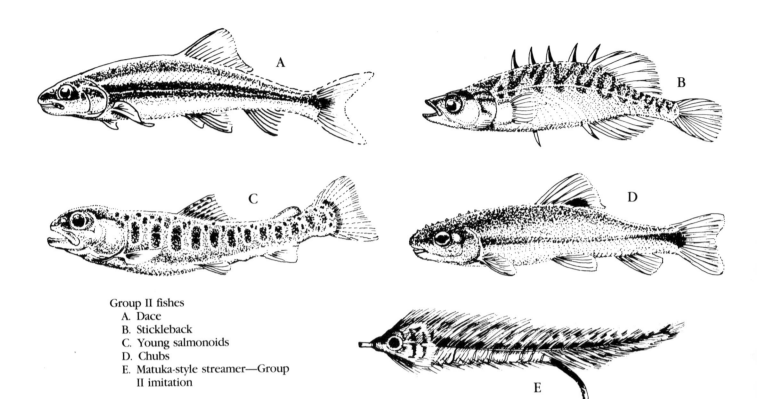

Group II fishes
  A. Dace
  B. Stickleback
  C. Young salmonoids
  D. Chubs
  E. Matuka-style streamer—Group
     II imitation

ming action than the Whitlock Marabou Matuka and Mylar Minnow.

1. HOOK: silver (nickel) or gold plated, 3XL or 4XL shank, ring or turned-down eye, sizes 10 to 3/0
2. THREAD: white single-strand nylon floss or Monocord
3. BODY WEIGHT (OPTIONAL): lead wire
4. CEMENTS: Clear head cement and Sportsman's Goop Cement (for plastic doll eyes)
5. EYES: plastic doll eyes or black, white, and yellow enamel
6. BODY: prismatic Mylar tape, silver pearl, pale gold, or dark gold
7. GILL: red prismatic Mylar tape
8. WING: one turkey marabou feather color of minnow's side (white, light bluish-green, and pale gold are most common)
9. OVERWING: three to six ostrich or peacock herls, color of minnow's back
10. CHEEKS: two mallard silver-and-black barred breast feathers, natural feather color or dyed to match wing color

On eyes for both designs, the plastic doll eyes add visual appeal. Glue them to the cheek feather with Goop for best results. If you decide instead to paint eyes on cheek, first apply a base coat to the area with thin, clear cement. Allow to dry, then paint on eye with enamel.

Group II. These fish are much more oval bodied than Group I fish. Although free swimming, they are less inclined to form large schools and live in open water. Their coloration and activity is more oriented and specialized to stream- and lake-bottom shore-line environments. There is generally much more diversion in their species and life cycles than there is among the members of Group I. Many are even troutlike in their life styles, and thus often share the same territory in trout lakes and streams.

All have multiple-year life cycles, so there is always a great variety of sizes for trout to feed on—from one-half to six-inches long or longer. Most are spring spawners and take on more intricate, even bizarre, color patterns during these spawning runs. Generally, the color pattern throughout the year includes the backs reflecting the water and bottom color; the sides have dark lateral stripes, weak parr marks, or mottling; the stomachs range from medium to very light cream or white on most vertical surfaces. The eyes are medium size and while they are usually not nearly as prominent as those of Group I fish, they are still important to imitate.

Most of these fish feed on aquatic and terrestrial insects, but some prey on other small fish or are vegetarians. When chased by trout they use both swimming speed and erratic maneuvering to escape, darting to the shallows, hiding under bottom structures, or taking to the surface. A healthy Group II fish is extremely hard for a trout to overtake and kill in shallow water or water with obstructions in it. Like trout, their activity is closely related to water conditions and seasons, especially the dace, chubs, whitefish, perch, shiners, fall fish, and sticklebacks.

To best imitate their shape, coloration, and action, I greatly prefer the feather-wing matuka style over bucktail, free marabou, or hackle wings. The matuka style allows me to blend the more complicated color pattern of the body with the best results. Painted eyes on the feather cheek or thread head further enhance the complete natural look of my Group II design.

MATUKA MINNOW—GROUP II

1. **HOOK:** ring or turned-down eye, 3XL to 6XL shank streamer hook in bronze or black
2. **TYING THREAD:** single-strand nylon floss or Monocord, color to match or blend with minnow's color
3. **CEMENTS:** clear head cement, Pliobond and Goop
4. **BODY WEIGHT** (OPTIONAL): fine or medium lead or copper wire
5. **MATUKA RIB:** gold or silver beading wire
6. **BODY:** blend of sparkle Orlon, Kodel polyester, and seal or African goat to match minnow's underside and stomach
7. **BODY RIB** (OPTIONAL): if minnow has bright scales, use gold or silver oval Mylar tinsel over body but not included in matuka-wing ribbing

8. MATUKA WING: four to six soft, wide, flexible cock- or hen-chicken hackle or grouse or pheasant flank feathers. Variegated cree, furnace, grizzly, plain, and badger hackle can be mixed in their natural colors or dyed to achieve almost any body-side-back pattern of the natural minnows in Group II. Plain or grizzly marabou can be effectively substituted for Matuka-wing feathers if you need more swimming, slow-fishing performance in calm waters.

9. GILL: red hackle-base fluff

10. CHEEK (OPTIONAL AS NEEDED): pair of appropriately marked and colored feathers to simulate fish's head and gill-plate area. I use mallard-breast and pheasant feathers mostly

11. EYES: plastic doll eyes glued on or eyes painted on cheek or thread head of streamer

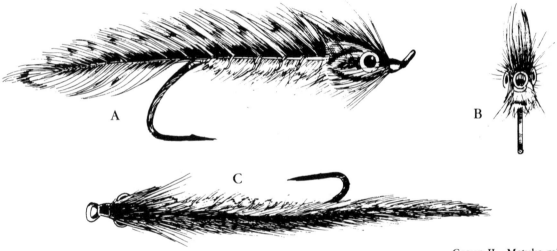

Group II—Matuka minnow
A. Side
B. Front
C. Top

I fish this imitation from top to bottom with floating, sinking-tip, or fast, full-sinking lines, depending on the water and the fishing situation. Casting from shoreline at right angles to shoreline and retrieving with erratic, fast action is often a very effective method in streams and small lakes. In large streams, you can cast up and across, letting the fly sink, and then retrieve it down and across the stream with either an even swimming motion or with rod-tip twitches. There are also times when a dead-drift presentation is very effective, particularly if the water is swift and broken with eddies and obstacles. Here again, as in all these examples, I'm trying to trigger trout response by simulating a forage fish in some kind of plight.

Group III. Members of this group generally are solitary bottom dwellers under normal stream and lake conditions. Their shapes are generally less streamlined than members of either Group I or Group II. They have strongly-pigmented back and side color patterns, which alter to camouflage their exposed upper forms. Usually there is a distinct back barring or brindle mottling on minnows in this group. They have undersides (including underside of head) colored pale grey, green, cream, or white.

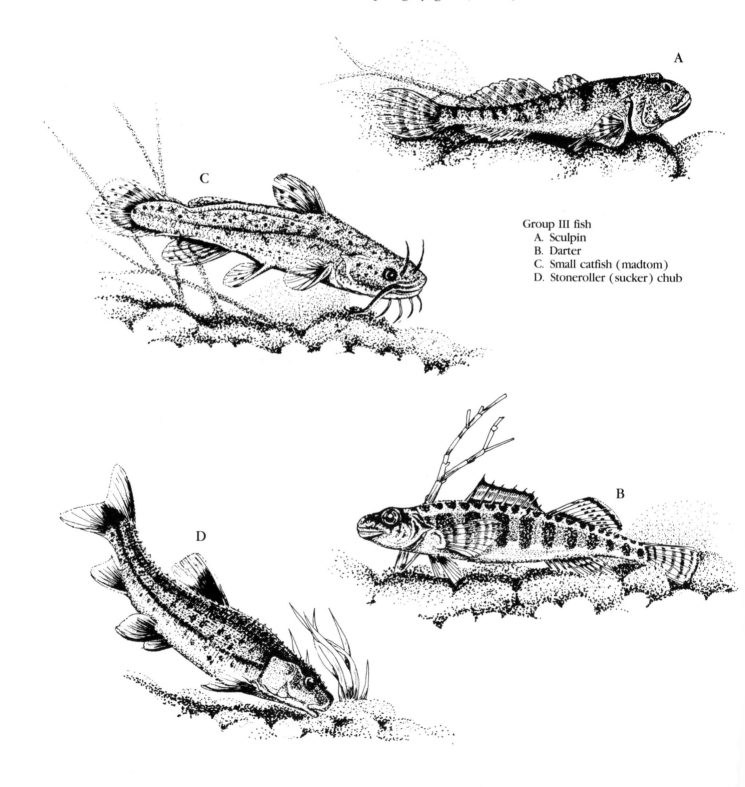

Group III fish
  A. Sculpin
  B. Darter
  C. Small catfish (madtom)
  D. Stoneroller (sucker) chub

These fish usually feed on aquatic insects, other fish, crustaceans, aquatic worms, and snails. A few, such as the hogsucker, are vegetarian.

Group III fish also have mutliple-year life cycles and generally, like trout, inhabit the lake and stream areas most plentiful with food, cover, oxygen, and ideal temperature. They range in size from one inch to six or eight inches or longer. Lengths of three to five inches seem to be most favored by large trout, particularly brown and lake trout (char).

This group seems to provide the most consistent forage fish for large trout in all types of streams. I feel this is because they are, like large stonefly nymphs, the easiest and most available food for a big trout to find, chase, catch, and eat. Large trout seldom need to leave the bottom or expose themselves to catch minnows of this group. Sculpins, for instance, are slower, weaker swimmers than are Group I or Group II fish, and they generally do not flee upward or to the shallows when chased.

When properly imitated and, more importantly, properly fished in these areas, trout eat them. Imitations of Group III forage fish are very effective on above-average to trophy-size trout. The method is to keep the streamer on the bottom with a vulnerable panic, distress, or crippled action. Short leaders and fast-sinking-tips or full-sinking lines with heavily weighted flies are usually the winning combination when fishing the Group III designs.

MATUKA BOTTOM MINNOWS

This basic design of clipped deer-hair head and matuka-feather wing-and-body should be shaped to pattern and weighted to look and act like the various bottom-dwelling forage fish that reside in the trout lakes or streams you fish.

1. HOOK: heavy wire, 3XL to 6XL shank, ring or turned-up eye, bronze or black finish (Mustad 9672, 9674, 36620, or Partridge salmon low-water hook), size 10 to 3/0
2. WEIGHT: lead wire
3. CEMENT: Pliobond and rod varnish
4. MATUKA-WING RIB: gold or copper wire
5. BODY: Orlon sparkle wool and African goat hair blended to match underside of body
6. MATUKA WING: four to six soft, webby, flexible cock hackles or grizzly-barred marabou (cree, grizzly, and variegated-cree cock neck), natural or dyed, and mixed to match the minnow's back and side color pattern
7. GILL: red Orlon sparkle wool or bright-red hackle-stem fluff
8. PECTORAL FINS (OPTIONAL): pair of duck, chicken, or pheasant fan-shaped feathers to match natural's size and color

9. HEAD: mule or white-tailed deer hair, natural and/or dyed to match minnow's color pattern. After deer-hair head is trimmed to shape of minnow's head, it should be coated with thinned rod varnish; this assures a durable but flexible head

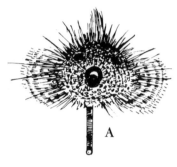

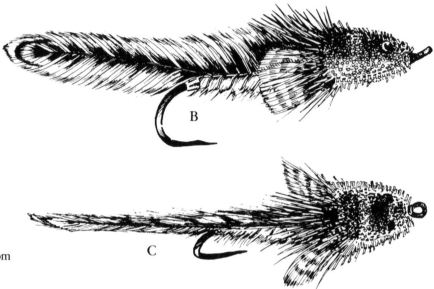

Group IV imitation—Matuka bottom minnow
A. Front
B. Side
C. Top

I fish these heavily weighted streamers with two- to 6-foot leaders with an open Duncan loop knot and a high-density sinking-tip line (ten- or twenty-foot sinking tip) in most streams and along shallow lake shorelines. For deep, large streams or lakes, I use a full-sinking line or a High-Density shooting taper fly line. *The fly must be given time to sink*! I usually cast up and across the stream and let the line and fly sink on a slack downstream drift. The streamer is fishing then, as it swings deep around and below me, hopefully very close to or tapping on the bottom. As the fly and line stretches out below me or reaches the bottom in a lake I point my rod tip down and begin a series of slow, erratic strips to imitate the minnow's deep- or bottom-swimming motion. Take care not to retrieve too fast or the fly will "swim" too shallow.

Group IV. Salmonid eggs and fry make up this group. Wherever trout, char, salmon or other large fish in any numbers lay eggs in trout water, they create a major food source for foraging trout. The eggs are eaten while being laid or when washed out of the nests. As those surviving incubate and hatch, the emerging yolk-sac fry and the more developed swim-up fry are caught and eaten with great relish by resident trout. In many Pacific Coast streams from California to Alaska, streams that run into the Great Lakes, and in a few Atlantic Coast streams, a major annual food source for trout are these eggs and new fry.

Trout seem to be totally vulnerable to well-tied and properly fished Group IV imitations during spawning and hatching periods. Even the largest wild trout are very gullible when they have eggs and fry to eat. At one time I felt this was a rather poor fly-fishing method, but, while not as traditional, it requires equal timing, skill and technique, and equally well-tied flies as any other method I know of.

The main considerations are fishing the right size and color of eggs during spawning season and knowing where and how the eggs are naturally taken. The same considerations, but to a less demanding extent, go for the yolk-sac and swim-up fry.

SINGLE-EGG FLY

This is an extremely simple but most effective design. Salmon eggs usually run five to seven and one-half millimeters in diameter; trout and char eggs three to five and one-half millimeters. The color range embraces a pale yellow-orange to a bright, rich red. The most common error with these flies is to make them too large, which drastically reduces their effectiveness. Trout can be as particular about single eggs as they can be about hatching mayflies or midges!

1. **HOOK**: gold or nickel plated, 5XS single-egg shank, turned-up eye, sizes 8 to 14
2. **TYING THREAD**: single-strand nylon floss or Monocord, color of egg
3. **WEIGHT**: none
4. **EGG BODY**: extra-fine dineer nylon tow floss or chenille the color of the egg

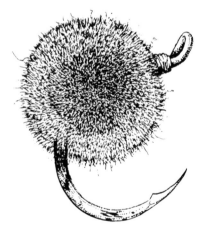

Group IV—Single-egg fly

The hook on this pattern is too short and the egg body too bulky for much extra weight, but it must be fished rolling downstream on the bottom. Lead split-shot or lead strips must be used just above the leader's tippet. The lead should tap the bottom to make the egg act like the real thing.

The Single-Egg Fly is best fished through and below the area downstream of the spawning activity and down into the nearest holding water. Trout will hang just below the spawning area. I cast this fly either upstream or downstream and allow it to sink and roll at current speed on the bottom, *which is usually two or three times slower than the surface current*. The tapping lead helps slow the drift and roll of the egg. The take will be easy and soft, like a take of a small, natural-drifted nymph. But don't be fooled—even big trout savor just one small egg at a bite!

YOLK-SAC AND SWIM-UP FRY

This simple design imitates the period from egg hatching until the large yolk sac is absorbed by the fry. Most such fry will run from one-half inch to one and one-half inches in length.

1. HOOK: low-water Atlantic salmon, size 8, 10, or 12
2. TYING THREAD: Herb Howard Flymaster 6/0, white or yellow
3. BODY WEIGHT: fine lead wire
4. CEMENT: clear head cement and rod varnish
5. EYES: black and yellow enamel
6. BODY: silver and gold Mylar thread
7. EGG SAC: bright yellow-orange hackle-base fluff
8. THROAT: red Mylar thread
9. WING (BODY): small, dyed, plain or grizzly marabou blood feather
   a. yolk-sac fry has pale amber body
   b. advanced yolk-sac fry has tan, gold, or olive body with faint parr marks
   c. swim-up fry is tan, gold, or olive with distinct parr marks
   Dyed grizzly marabou is perfect
10. HEAD: thread, built up and painted dark on top with two large eyes painted on sides

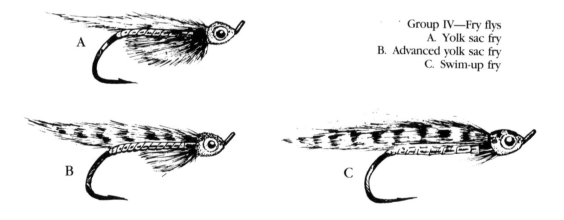

· Group IV—Fry flys
A. Yolk sac fry
B. Advanced yolk sac fry
C. Swim-up fry

I fish the Yolk-Sac Fry in the same area and with the same method as the Single-Egg Fry. Usually they are present sixty to ninety days after the eggs are laid. I fish the Swim-Up Fry imitation on a long, fine leader and floating line below the nesting areas and in eddies. Dead drift, slightly twitching, and raising the fly to the surface are the most effective actions. When the fry are emerging they are weak, erratic swimmers. To fill their air bladders they dart to the top frequently the first hours after their emergence from the incubating gravels.

A large amount of all four groups of forage fish daily share close or identical habitat with trout in both small and large streams and lakes. Yet they are seldom harassed or attacked by trout; only at certain intervals are trout triggered to kill and eat these fish. Trout hunger and the presence of forage fish will cause feeding action, but the fly fisherman isn't always present to take advantage of these easy-to-fish times. However, the catalyst that most often triggers these scenes can be artifically created just by the way you

Brown trout chasing sculpin as it flees for a rock crevice on the stream bottom

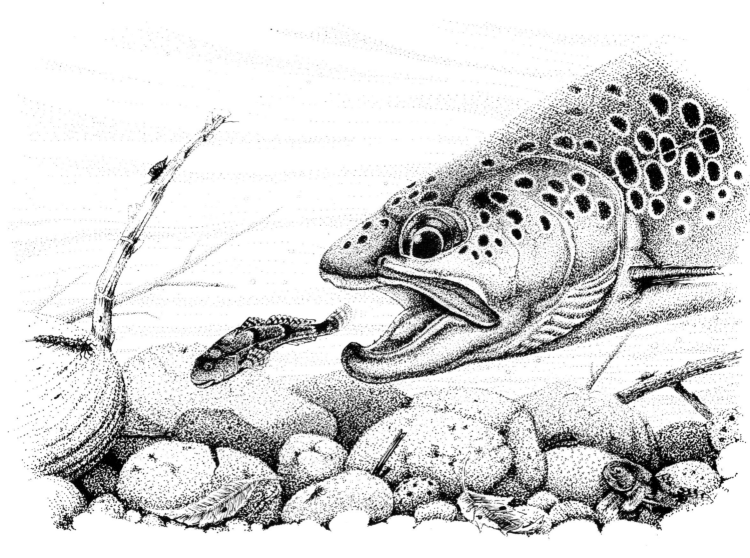

present and fish these minnow imitations. It is done by introducing a circumstance that alerts the trout. Minnows that move deliberately up, down, or across stream *while facing upstream,* do little to attract trout. By simulating a fish in a state of distress, panic, or helplessness, the predatory instincts of trout are turned on. A noisy surface splash and abnormally fast or slow erratic movement up, across, or down in the surface are prime attack catalysts. Flash and abnormal swimming postures are also important. Another trigger is the fast, erratic swimming of the streamer from very shallow water out over very deep water. Cast the streamer hard up against the shoreline and immediately swim it in fast or erratic strips across the current or at right angles to the shoreline.

With aquatic-insect imitations, the angler tries to imitate the most natural movements; with forage-fish imitations, abnormal movements are usually the most effective.

11
LEECHES, EELS, AND SIMILAR TROUT FOODS

Following aquatic insects, crustaceans, and forage fish, there is a fourth group of aquatic trout food. This group mainly consists of long, slender, swimming animal forms such as leeches, eels, lampreys, snakes, salamanders, and tadpoles. Such slinky, slimy, creepy creatures probably seem to most anglers to be baits that bass, pike, and catfish would favor. Yet practically every rich trout lake or stream has one or more of these foods in enough abundance to stimulate significant and consistent foraging for them by large trout.

Perhaps the most commonly imitated of these lesser-known foods is the leech. Though all sorts of leech patterns exist and catch trout effectively, to me they look very little and fish very little like a real leech. Like the traditional, heavily hackled dry flies that in almost no way have the action, shape, or silhouette of the real mayfly dun or spinner, most leech designs just don't appear realistic to me.

I think that this fourth group of trout foods and the various imitations of them usually trigger opportunistic feeding by large trout. I think so because often poorly designed and tied imitations are devastating in trout waters where these foods seldom exist. Few fly tiers and anglers I know actually tie or fish specific imitations of these food forms.

For several months earlier this year I developed a system to study and learn about these creatures' looks, habits, and actions in their natural environment. I set up a thirty-gallon Pandora's Box aquarium. Most of my friends, and particularly my wife, Joan, would get cold chills watching these creepy, slithering, crawling, swimming creatures. But the set-up allowed me to learn a lot that would have taken years at least to observe in nature. The best thing that I learned is that most of their shapes and actions are similar. Almost none of the popular leech patterns was much more than crudely suggestive of the real thing.

All the members of this group swim with an undulating rhythm that uses a back-and-forth or up-and-down head-to-tail wiggle. When swimming, they streamline their bodies by tucking in their legs or fins. In the case of leeches, they even elongate as much as twice their resting length. Most swimming is done very near or on the bottom in both lakes and streams. Water snakes will swim on the surface or rise to the surface to breath. Only the blind leeches swim any distance off the bottom and then only in such calm or very slow-flowing waters as ponds, lakes, and sloughs. All rest or stay on the bottom when not swimming: none suspend when not swimming. Salamanders will crawl along the bottom and up on structures. They swim when disturbed or frightened. Tadpoles, which are the immature forms of frogs and toads, act a lot like salamanders, especially after their legs have developed while they still have full tails. All these creatures are mostly nocturnal, especially during the warmer seasons, except the tadpoles and leeches. These two seem to be equally active in anything but excessively shallow and brightly sunlit water.

While black seems to be the most popular leech-pattern color, few of the trout foods in this group are pure black. Most are patterns of dirty browns, tans, olives, and dark greys brindled with

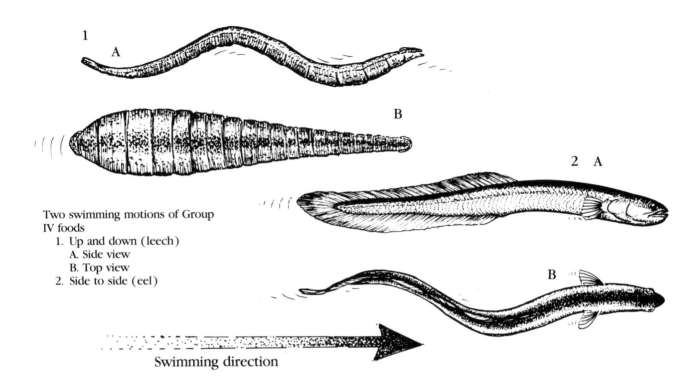

Two swimming motions of Group
IV foods
　1. Up and down (leech)
　　A. Side view
　　B. Top view
　2. Side to side (eel)

Swimming direction

stripes or bars of dark brown, black, or dark olive. Most have spots in burnt orange, gold, yellow, red, or black. Most have dark backs and sides and lighter undersides. Few actually contrast with their environment; most are chameleon-like and camouflage to their present environment color. For instance, a lamprey in deep, clear, open water will be almost a minnowlike silver. The same lamprey will be a muddy brindled, olive-brown when it is in a small, dark-bottomed stream. Thus, imitations should be dressed with color schemes that match the water's color or the bottom's color, particularly if live samples are not available for reference.

Leeches

Leeches are probably the best-known member of this group among fly fishermen who specialize in lake fly-fishing and large trout. Leeches are invertebrates that inhabit most trout waters in good numbers and some variety. Contrary to popular opinion, few species are actually bloodsuckers on warm-blooded animals; most are parasites on cold-blooded fish, reptiles, snails, or they live off dead animals and plants.

While lacking eyes, they have well-developed senses of smell and touch. They have a tough, smooth skin over a multisegmented body and a highly developed muscular system, which also pro-

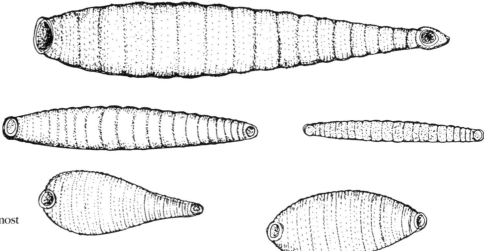

Underside view of the most common leech shapes

vides skeletal support to their bodies. Most have the ability to drastically alter their body shapes from short and thick to long and slender while swimming. When swimming, they elongate their bodies, forming a long, pointed head and front and a wide, thin, flattened rear end, which seems to serve as a tail. They swim with up-and-down undulations of the entire body. In still water they swim at a speed of about one foot per two or three seconds. The swimming pattern *is not erratic,* but very rhythmic and smooth.

It is usually the swimming form that trout eat. Both head and tail ends of their bodies have strong suction devices for holding to their host or the bottom structures when at rest. The free-swimming leeches interest trout most and they range from one to six inches in length, with two- to three-inch lengths most attractive to trout. Free-swimming leeches I've seen in trout waters and found in trout stomachs were patterned with medium-to-dark, dirty shades of brown, olive, tan, and slate grey.

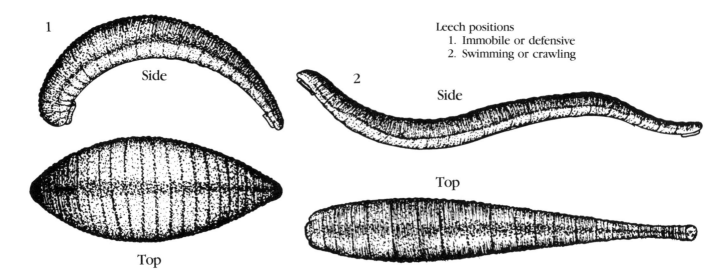

1

Side

Top

Leech positions
1. Immobile or defensive
2. Swimming or crawling

2

Side

Top

Top

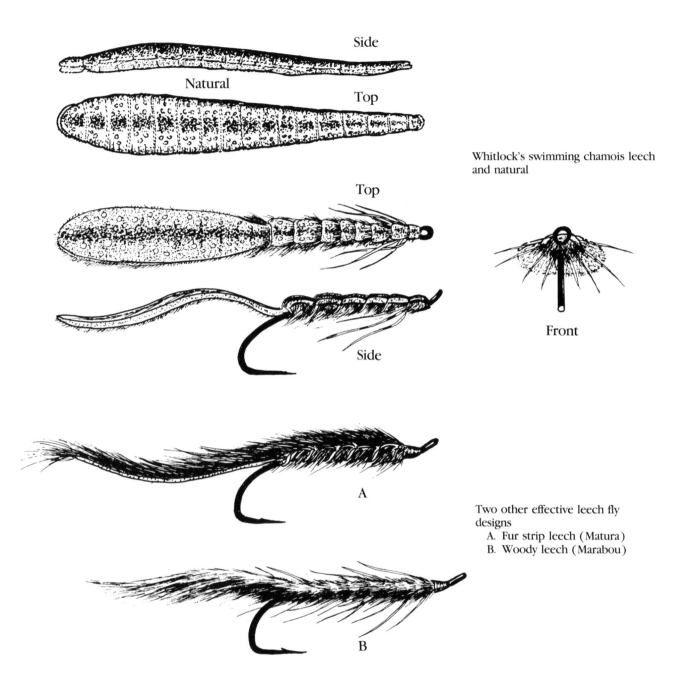

Side

Natural

Top

Whitlock's swimming chamois leech
and natural

Top

Front

Side

A

Two other effective leech fly
designs
  A. Fur strip leech (Matura)
  B. Woody leech (Marabou)

B

Lampreys

Lampreys are snakelike or eellike, blood-sucking, parasitic, primitive fish that have cartilage skeletons and no scales. They are best identified by the round, sucking, disk mouth and the long, double dorsal fin, which merges directly with their tails. Also they have a series of horizontal gill holes just behind their heads. No

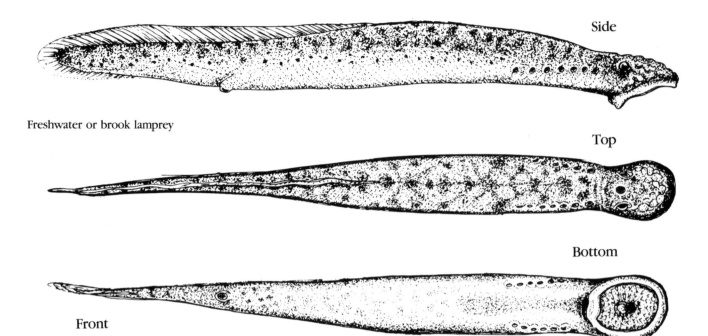

Side

Top

Bottom

Freshwater or brook lamprey

Front

pectoral or pelvic fins are present. Their early life is spent as wormlike larvae buried in mud and sand bottoms of freshwater streams. When they emerge they become free-swimming lampreys and are from two to six inches in length, depending upon species and environment. They mainly attack and are parasites on fish. Trout eat them until they are about eight inches in length.

Lampreys are more fishlike than leechlike in their coloration and swimming actions. The body and the tail fin wiggle from side to side for swimming movements. Most of the time lampreys swim close to or hide next to or under bottom structures in lakes and streams. They range from silvery to dirty dark olive or brown with a lighter side and underside much like the color scheme of a fish.

Eels

Eels are primitive fish that are very snakelike in appearance with no scales and a long dorsal fin that merges directly into a tail that merges into an anal fin. They also have a pair of pectoral fins directly behind the gill openings. Eels have strong teeth and jaws and are both active predators and scavengers of most other fish and similar aquatic creatures.

Eels spawn in salt water and live their adult lives in fresh water, while most lampreys spawn in fresh water and many species live their adult lives in salt water. Practically speaking, the lampreys would be a much more abundant and ideally sized trout food than the American eel, which is less abundant and almost too large to eat by the time it reaches most inland trout lakes and streams. The smallest true eels I have seen were about eight inches in length and two-thirds of an inch in diameter. A trout of four pounds could easily eat this size.

Eels swim like fish, using side-to-side body movements and their tails to move forward. They are swift, strong swimmers that prefer living near or on the bottom of lakes and streams. They are especially nocturnal in their movements and feeding.

A typical freshwater eel

Front

Side

Top

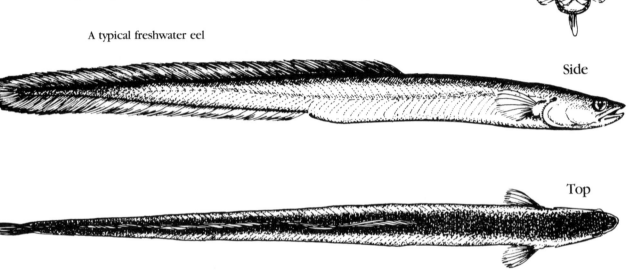

Salamanders

Salamanders are lizardlike amphibians. They are bottom dwellers in lakes and streams and are often very abundant in trout waters, especially spring creeks and weed-rich small ponds. Being soft, harmless, crawling and swimming, cold-blooded creatures, they are very easy for trout to catch and eat. There is a great variety of colors and sizes, but most salamanders are one to six inches long and chameleonlike in general coloration.

When undisturbed, they walk or crawl over the bottom and even out on dry land. When a trout encounters one, the salamander either tries to hide under or in bottom structures, or it swims briskly away to either shallow water or another cover. The main considerations for tying and fishing imitations is to keep them long and slender and to fish them on the bottoms of streams and lakes.

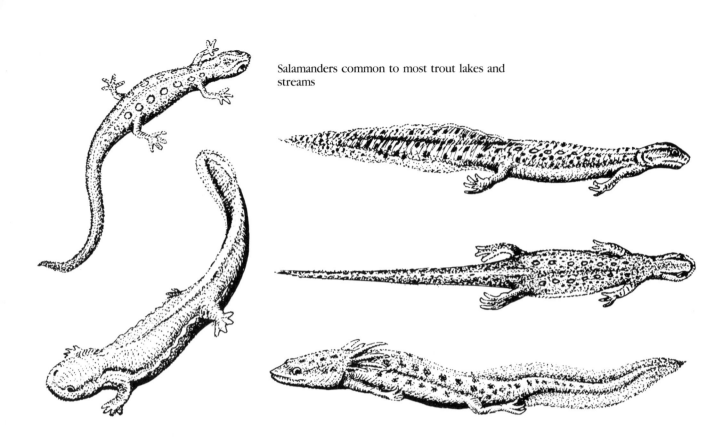

Salamanders common to most trout lakes and streams

Tadpoles

Tadpoles are immature stages of various frogs and toads. They resemble eels and salamanders in shape, coloration, and general swimming action. Their heads and bodies are larger and much more rounded than their long tails.

Tadpole skin is soft, scaleless, and generally dark olive, brown, and black—similar to the bottom environment of the streams and lakes they live in. The tadpole stage lasts one year or less, and tadpoles are usually most abundant and active on the perimeters of trout waters in the spring and summer months. They typically congregate after hatching and remain in loose groups or bunches in the warmest, shallow, calm waters. They swim directly on or just above the bottom, never suspending themselves as fish do.

As tadpoles mature they reach lengths from one to six inches and develop two pairs of legs very similar to those of a salamander. As they mature further, their eellike tail is absorbed and they leave the water as immature frogs or toads.

Trout feed near or off the bottom on all sizes and stages of tadpoles, just as they would other foods in this group or swimming aquatic-insect nymphs. The presence of frogs or toads along the perimeter of trout waters is an excellent indication that tadpole imitations might be most effective.

Tadpole fly: The head is made of deer hair and the tail is of soft webby hackle or marabou.

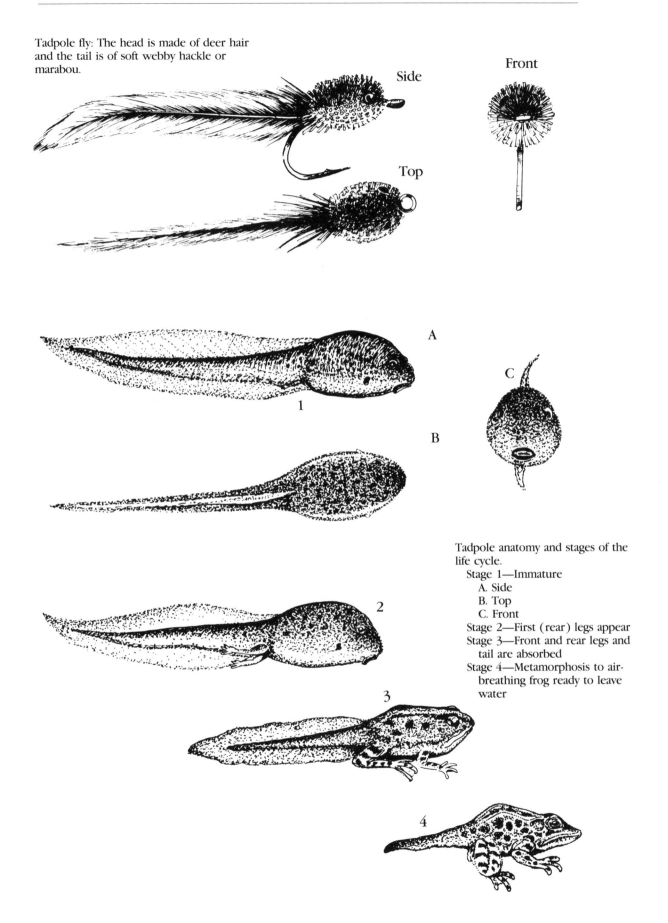

Side

Front

Top

A

B

C

1

2

3

4

Tadpole anatomy and stages of the life cycle.
Stage 1—Immature
  A. Side
  B. Top
  C. Front
Stage 2—First (rear) legs appear
Stage 3—Front and rear legs and tail are absorbed
Stage 4—Metamorphosis to air-breathing frog ready to leave water

Water Snakes

Water snakes are slender-bodied, air-breathing, legless reptiles that utilize the shallow water of various trout lakes and streams, particularly those of lower elevation and south of the Canadian border. There are a number of small aquatic and semiaquatic snakes that feed on fish and insects common to trout streams. When they are small and active, they are most attractive to large trout while surface swimming at night. Trout also will take water snakes when the snakes are diving deep to catch aquatic insects and small fish.

Snakes are very long and slender with soft scales and large mouths. They swim with a complete side-to-side, head-body-and-tail wiggle similar to the eels and lampreys. Usually they are four to twelve inches long and have distinct light and dark banded patterns the length of their bodies. The dyed grizzly or variegated cree saddle hackle is an ideal material to imitate water snakes.

Water snakes
  A. Surface-swimming
  B. Diving

My Favorite Group Four Fly Designs

WHITLOCK CHAMOIS SWIMMING LEECH

This design was developed from my aquarium observation to imitate the swimming leeches' shape and lifelike texture. It closely simulates the fluid up-and-down body movements the leech makes as it swims. It is also an excellent design to use for swimming cranefly larvae, swimming worms, lamprey, and eels with appropriate but simple variations in size, color, and shape.

1. HOOK: ring eye or turned-up eye, limerick bend, regular-length shank, heavy wire (Mustad 3658-B)
2. TYING THREAD: single-strand nylon floss or Monocord, color of leech body
3. BODY WEIGHT: lead wire and/or small pair of bead-chain eyes; weight must be on front third of hook shank for proper sinking and action
4. TAIL AND BODY: chamois leather strip cut to the shape of an elongated swimming leech; dye basic body color and spot or bar with waterproof felt-tip marking pen
5. HEAD: a small amount of fur dubbing same color as body, wrapped over body and tied down at mid-third of hook shank and over lead and bead eyes
6. COLLAR (OPTIONAL): long, soft, grouse or hen hackle color of body; one or two turns just behind bead eyes adds a bit of head action and helps mask hook outline

It is most important that the leech head be weighted so when it is slowly stripped it moves in up-and-down, head-and-tail undulations. I use the open Duncan loop knot to further enhance this important natural action.

To fish this leech design I prefer a sinking-tip fly line and a four- to six-foot leader in most lakes and streams where the water is three to ten feet deep. For more shallow-water leeching, I like to use an intermediate density (neutral-buoyancy) fly line and a six- to nine-foot leader to swim the leech over bottom structures and moss beds. I cast it out, let it sink near the bottom, then begin a *steady* series of one- or two-inch line strips to animate the Chamois Leech's swimming action. Of course, in streams the leech need not be stripped in but just twitched by the rod tip as it drifts down and across the current. In deep pools, I will sometimes let it go downstream and deep on a dead drift, then place the rod tip under the water and slowly, with regular inch-long strips, work it back upstream right on or near the bottom.

WHITLOCK LAMPEEL MATUKA STREAMER

This design doubles as an effective and realistic imitation of small lampreys and eels. Both have long, slender bodies with wide, flat, thin tails, and they have very similar swimming actions. This streamer is designed to have a reasonably natural eel or lamprey body-and-tail swimming movement.

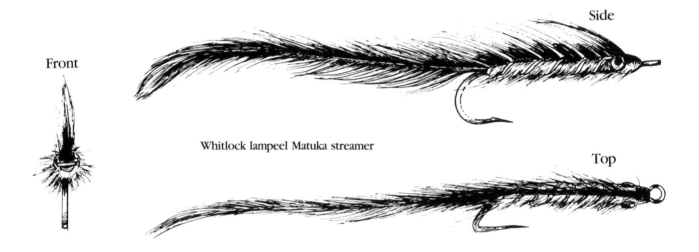

Front

Side

Whitlock lampeel Matuka streamer

Top

1. HOOK: ring or turned-up eye, 3XL or 4XL shank, limerick bend, size 8 to 3/0
2. TYING THREAD: single-strand nylon floss or Monocord, color of natural's body
3. BODY WEIGHT: lead wire and clear head cement
4. STOMACH: light-colored sparkle synthetic dubbing to match natural's stomach color
5. MATUKA RIB: silver or gold wire
6. BODY: two wide, soft, webby flexible, saddle hackles, two or three times longer than hook shank, color pattern should be that of side and back of lamprey or eel
7. HEAD: body and stomach tied right up to the hook eye so that little or no thread head is visible (study illustration for correct proportions)

Side

Top

Front

Whitlock's eelworm streamer

I fish this streamer deep and fairly slow in both lakes and streams with a sinking-tip or full-sinking line and four to six feet of leader. The open Duncan loop knot greatly assists in sinking and wiggle action.

WHITLOCK EELWORM STREAMER

This streamer design works well as an all-purpose Group Four imitation. By altering its size, color pattern, and fishing method it imitates well most of the eellike trout foods I know of as well as being a splendid attractor for large trout.

1. **HOOK**: ring or turned-up eye, 1XL or 2XL shank, limerick bend
2. **SNAG GUARD**: Mason nylon monofilament strand, same diameter as hook wire
3. **BODY WEIGHT**: pair of bead-chain eyes and lead wire
4. **CEMENT**: Pliobond and five-minute epoxy
5. **TAIL**: two or four slender, flexible-stemmed saddle hackles, three times as long as hook shank, tied flared out or in (optional) for action. Hackle color and pattern should be that of natural's body and tail. I prefer grizzly or variegated cree, natural feather color or dyed to match natural's body
6. **BODY**: coarse synthetic dubbing mix to match natural's body and head color

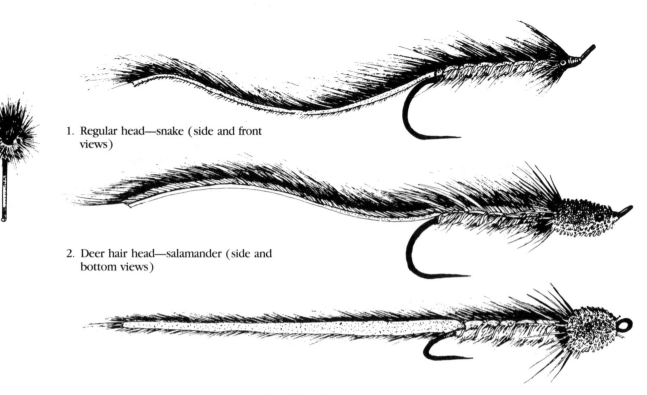

1. Regular head—snake (side and front views)

2. Deer hair head—salamander (side and bottom views)

7. **RIB**: wide, soft hackle, same color and markings as tails, sparsely palmered over body
8. **HEAD**: same as body, except just a little larger around bead-chain eyes

This fly should be weighted just in the head so that it will sink or dip head first with tails high. It works well even in the smallest creeks and ponds in three- to six-inch lengths. At night and/or in large waters, such as the Missouri River, I use a six- to nine-inch Eelworm Streamer, which takes trout from two pounds to ten pounds and more. I fish this fly with an open Duncan loop knot and four to six feet of leader and a High-Density sinking-tip (ten-foot sinking portion) line on or just over the bottom. I use either a jigging up-down-up action or a strip-pause-strip action off the bottom. This fly also works well bounced and rolled downstream on a slack line.

FUR-STRIP MATUKA STREAMER

The Fur-Strip Streamer does an excellent job of suggesting the size, shape, texture, and action of Group Four trout foods. Tanned hair on skin leathers such as rabbit, muskrat, mink, squirrel, and others makes excellent material for this streamer.

1. **HOOK**: turned-up or turned-down eye regular-length shank, limerick bend, sizes 8 to 3/O
2. **TYING THREAD**: single-strand nylon floss or Monocord to match natural's body color
3. **WEIGHT**: lead or copper wire
4. **CEMENT**: Pliobond
5. **TAILS AND BODY**: a strip of rabbit, muskrat, squirrel, or similar tanned leather with hair on to match color, length, and shape

of natural's body and tail. Cut strip with a sharp razor blade after marking on skin side of hide, taking care not to cut hair off leather

6. MATUKA RIB: brass, gold, or copper wire
7. EYES (OPTIONAL): small pair of bead-chain eyes
8. HEAD (OPTIONAL): flared and clipped deer hair.
9. FINISH: Cement head with rod varnish or thinned sportsman's goop for a durable, soft head.

This is an extremely simple fly to make, and it fishes so well it is almost too good to be true. Its hallmark is slow breathing and swimming action. It does well for a leech, salamander, eel, lamprey, snake, or tadpole if tied, sized, and fished accordingly. This design seems to fish best for me with a slow retrieve in calm waters.

Trout approaching a swimming leech

12
THE FLY BOX

T he contents of an angler's fly box can tell you a lot about what sort of a fly fisher he might be. It can tell you how, where, and when he fishes. I just love to sneak a peek into the vest pockets of as many fly fishermen as I can; it's like walking into someone's home unexpected—I feel very vulnerable when someone investigates *mine!* I have been really shocked at times to see what some "experts" wrote they carried and did not! Part of the impetus to write this book came after I let Nick Lyons prowl through two or three of my fly boxes, and I realized that their contents and organization told Nick more about my perspectives than three days astream. Nick shortly after suggested I compose this book to describe how I identify, match, and fish the major aquatic trout foods.

My fly boxes are usually stocked so that I can effectively fish most of the waters across the country. I use a flexible, multiple-box system that allows me to imitate the major foods through the various seasons and in the various water types. At least sixty percent of my fishing time is spent on new waters or waters I fish infrequently from coast to coast. Even on my home waters, the Norfork River and White River tailwaters in Arkansas, there is a seasonal shift in aquatic foods as well as the trout's feeding preferences and feeding cycles. One small box of a dozen or so patterns will not necessarily serve a person who just fishes one water all season. There are four major aquatic trout food groups, and several options within those groups, that trout will prefer due to their whims as well as water and weather conditions.

No fly box stocked with a "universal magic dozen killer flies" exists, unless it is twelve sticks of dynamite! However, I have found some extremely effective selections that will serve me satisfactorily in almost any North American water.

I wear a well-designed fabric or leather shorty-style vest, which has limited pocket space. I could comfortably carry more fly boxes, but the standard vest is too long for my height and usual style of wading too deep (and falling regularly), and the lower pockets seem always to be dripping wet. It's a miserable thing when you open up a fly box and you have to wait several minutes for it to drain enough to pick out a soupy fly! The shorty solved most of this problem, but it reduced my carrying potential about thirty to forty percent. So I had to reorganize my fly boxes into a more workable system. As it turns out, it was the best thing that could have happened.

My vest pockets will carry two (four if jammed) medium-large boxes ($3\frac{1}{2} \times 6 \times 1$ inch) and two small boxes ($3\frac{1}{2} \times 2\frac{1}{2} \times \frac{1}{2}$ inch). I love the beautifully crafted metal Wheatley boxes with both spring-lid compartments and clips. They seem to improve with age and are quite functional and versatile for most fly designs except large streamers and skaters. The new molded-plastic fly boxes with various designs of durable white foam-plastic inserts are probably the most practical and functional fly boxes, however. They are very light, durable, and easy to use. They also float and don't cost an arm and a leg each. I like the white foam-plastic inserts for organization, visibility, and accessability of very small flies such as midges and tiny spinners. (Extra inserts also serve as ideal storage files as well as allowing a quick switch to a different fly system.) The metal clips on most metal boxes are too coarse and too few to do a good job of storing the smallest flies.

Usually, unless I know a particular design or pattern will be most effective, I load my boxes with one to three of each size of a particular pattern. Larger flies, such as a size 4 nymph or a size 2 matuka are both more durable and take up more space than other flies—so I carry only one or two of each. But with a size 20 spinner or a size 16 nymph, I will carry three or more. I use the metal clips to store only one or two of each size of nymph, wet, or streamer. If I carry extras, I put them in a "general-storage" compartment in that box or a simple small plastic box in my vest. Three well-made, durable flies of a particular size and design seem to be enough for me for any day's fishing.

One of the most common questions I receive from audiences or readers concerns what fly designs I actually carry as I trout fish across the country. This list is really very general, and, not all the flies listed in this chapter are described in the text of practical suggestive and realistic imitations, but the ones that are do represent the same philosophy of imitation of the four groups of aquatic trout foods that I abide by. They are more suggestive in nature, which gives me a versitile capability or allows me to take advantage of some unorthodox trout reactions.

BOX NO. 1:
General Utility Box

I carry this box in my vest wherever I trout fish. It is stocked with a selection of general aquatic and terrestrial imitations in a range of medium-small (size 16) to medium-large (size 4) patterns. Most fly designs in this box simulate the largest possible range of foods, water situations, and seasons.

NYMPHS

size 16 to 4, 3XL carried on clips with extras stored in one compartment)
  TYPE A (weighted, simple, impressionistic, soft-fur bodied)
  1. Dave's Red Fox Squirrel Nymph, sizes 6–16
  2. Gold-Ribbed Hare's Ear, sizes 10–14
  3. Polly's Casual Dress, sizes 6, 8
  4. Soft-Hackled Flies:
      Partridge and Muskrat, size 14
      Partridge and Peacock, size 14
      Partridge and Primrose Muskrat, size 16
  TYPE B (weighted, impressionistic-imitative, soft-fur bodied)
  1. Dave's Swimming Shrimp, sizes 10–14
  2. Dave's Sowbug, sizes 14, 16
  3. Dave's Damsel Nymph:
      dark brown, sizes 8, 10
      tan, sizes 8, 10
      olive, sizes 10,12
  4. Dave's Dragonfly:
      dark black-brown, size 6
      light olive-brown, sizes 4. 6
  5. Whit Darkstone, size 4
  6. Whit Goldenstone, size 6
  7. Whit Yellowstone, size 10
  8. Hexagenia Wiggle-Nymph, size 8
  9. Brown Drake, size 10

WOOLLY WORMS

(weighted, chenille or fur bodies on 3XL hooks with saddle hackle wrapped sparsely. Design: tail/body/hackle/back)
  1. red wool/black chenille/soft furnace/peacock herl, sizes 4, 8
  2. grizzly tip/peacock herl/gold oval tinsel/grizzly, size 10
  3. short red marabou/golden yellow/grizzly/peacock herl, size 10
  4. grizzly tip/peacock herl/darkest furnace/no back, size 4
  5. fluorescent red yarn/bright insect-green and silver tinsel/grizzly/peacock herl, size 8

DRY FLIES

  1. Adams, sizes 12–16
  2. Royal Wulff, size 10
  3. White Wulff, size 12
  4. Humpy, sizes 10–16
  5. Deer-hair Caddis, sizes 12, 14
  6. Borger Tan-and-Grizzly Polycaddis, sizes 10–16
  7. Dave's Hopper, sizes 8–12
  8. Dave's Cricket, sizes 8, 12
  9. Black Deer-hair Ant, sizes 14, 16
  10. Muddler Minnow sizes 8, 10

STREAMERS

  1. Whitlock Sculpin (weighted), size 6
  2. Olive Matuka (weighted), size 8
  3. Muddler Minnow, sizes 4, 8
  4. White Marabou Muddler, size 8
  5. Yellow Marabou Muddler, size 8
  6. Thunder Creek Marabou (yellow and black, weighted), size 8
  7. Thunder Creek Marabou Black-Nosed Dace (weighted), size 4
  8. Silver Matuka Spruce (weighted), size 6
  9. Black Bunny Streamer (rabbit matuka, weighted), size 4

BOX NO. 2:
Match the Hatch

I rely on this box to fish most hatches, especially when trout are selectively feeding on these aquatic foods. It is my classic aquatic-insect life-cycle box.

MAYFLIES

Nymphs
  TYPE 1: weighted, imitative, soft-dubbed bodied, sizes 12-18 in olives, browns, tans, and black
  TYPE 2: suggestive imitations
      A. Hexagenia Wiggle-Nymph, size 8
      B. Brown Drake, size 10
      C. Green Drake, size 10
      D. Isonychia, size 12
  TYPE 3: emergers or floating nymphs, sizes 14–20 in olives and browns

Duns (No-Hackle type, wing/body)
  slate/yellow, sizes 14–22
  slate/tan, sizes 10–22
  dark slate/olive, sizes 16–22

Paraduns
  Hexagenia, sizes 6, 8
  Brown Drake, sizes 8, 10
  Green Drake, sizes 8, 10

Spinners (hen-spinner and hackle-spinner types, wing/body)
  clear white/reddish brown, sizes 14–22
  dun/olive dun, sizes 14–20
  clear white/cream yellow, sizes 14–22
  clear white/black, sizes 22–26
  grizzly/olive dun, sizes 14, 16

Paraspinner
  Hexagenia, sizes 6, 8

CADDIS

Larva: I do not carry larva imitations (as explained in caddis text)

Pupa: types 2A, 2B, and 3 fur-bodied, soft-hackle legs and duck-quill wing, weighted and unweighted, sizes 12–18, olives, tans, greens, cream, oranges, and browns

Adults: fished dry and diving, fluttering Polycaddis, wing/body/hackle
   1. tan/tan/grizzly tan, sizes 10–18
   2. tan/green/grizzly brown, sizes 12–18
   3. grey/olive/grizzly, sizes 14–18
   4. dark slate/dark olive/dark grizzly dun, sizes 14–18
   5. brown/orange/grizzly brown, sizes 8, 10

STONEFLIES

Nymphs: type B (weighted, impressionistic, soft-dubbed bodied)
   1. Darkstone, sizes 2–6
   2. Dark Goldenstone, sizes 4, 6
   3. Goldenstone, sizes 6, 8
   4. Yellowstone, sizes 10, 12
   5. Slate Olivestone, sizes 12, 14

Adults: because of their size and the infrequency of major hatches, I do not carry most of my larger adult stonefly imitations in this particular box
   1. Dave's Adult Goldenstone, size 8
   2. Dave's Adult Yellowstone, sizes 10, 12
   3. Slate Olivestone, sizes 12, 14

DAMSELFLIES

Nymphs: Type 2, weighted
   1. Dave's Tan Damsel, sizes 8, 10
   2. Dave's Dark-brown Damsel, sizes 8, 10
   3. Dave's Light-olive Damsel, sizes 10, 12

Adult: I carry these in the large-compartment plastic box that I carry the adult stones in

DRAGONFLIES

Nymph: Type 2, weighted (see earlier chapter on dragonflies and damselflies)
   1. dark olive-brown, size 4
   2. light olive-green, size 6

Adults: I do not carry adults

MIDGES

Pupae: large assortment of pupa in olives, greys, browns, reds, black, and cream, sizes 16–26

Adults: small assortment of adults in olives, black, grey, tan, and cream, sizes 16–26

BOX NO. 3:
Streamer Types

I use a Fly Rite plastic box with foam inserts or a fleece fly wallet for these flies. I carry one or two of each size, pattern, and design.
   1. **Whitlock Matuka Sculpin**, weighted
      A. olive, sizes 1/0, 4, 8
      B. Golden tan, sizes 3/0, 1/0, 6
   2. **Prismatic Streamers**
      A. Silver Shad, sizes 2, 6
      B. Golden Chub, sizes 4, 8
      C. Whitefish, size 2
   3. **Matukas** (wing/body/rib)
      A. olive grizzly/olive/gold, sizes 6-10
      B. dark furnace/red/gold, sizes 1/0, 4, 6
      C. badger/red/silver, sizes 2, 8
      D. black/black/silver, sizes 2, 6
      E. cree/yellow/gold, sizes 1/0, 6
   4. **Muddlers** (weighted and unweighted)
      A. standard mottled brown, sizes 1/0-10
      B. black, sizes 1/0, 4, 8
      C. white marabou, sizes 1/O, 4, 8
      D. yellow marabou, sizes 4, 8
      E. black marabou, sizes 1/0, 8
      F. multicolored marabou, sizes 3/0, 1/0, 6
      G. white rabbit muddler, size 1/0
   5. **Lefty's Deceiver**
      A. white, sizes 1/0, 4
      B. yellow, sizes 1/0, 4
      C. black, sizes 1/0, 4
   6. **Dave's Chamois Leech**
      A. olive, sizes 4, 8
      B. brown, sizes 4, 8
      C. black, sizes 4, 8
   7. **Dave's Lampeel**, size 2/0, 4
   8. **Omelet Series**
      A. Single Egg Glowbug design in fluorescent pink, light orange, dark orange, sizes 8, 12
      B. Double-Egg Sperm Fly
         1. fluorescent pink and silver, size 6
         2. fluorescent light orange and gold, size 6
         3. fluorescent dark orange and gold, size 6
         4. fluorescent chartreuse and silver, size 6
      C. Trout Yolk Fry, sizes 10, 12
         Salmon Yolk-Sac Fry, sizes 8, 10
      D. Trout Fry, sizes 8, 10
      E. Salmon Fry, sizes 6, 8

BOX NO. 4:
Terrestrials and Summer Midges

A small clip and compartment box I carry during the summer and early-fall months, especially when I fish small, low-water streams for selective trout.

1. Ants
   A. black deer hair, sizes 12–18
   B. fur ants (black or cinnamon), sizes 14–20
   C. flying ants or spent ants (black or cinnamon), sizes 14–20
2. Beetles
   A. black deer hair and peacock herl, sizes 10–18
   B. small assortment of brown, green, yellow (Japanese) beetles, sizes 6–16
3. Hornets and Bees
   A. spent wing (clipped deer-hair body), sizes 8–14
4. Jassids
   A. assortment of grizzly, tan, yellow, black, and green Jassids, sizes 12–20
5. Floating Worms, small assortment of deer-hair type in light green, olive, tan, and yellow, one-half to one and one-half inches in length
6. Small assortment of midget terrestrials, pupae and adults of midges and microcaddis, and mayfly duns and spinners, sizes 18–28
7. Dave's Shrimp and Sowbug, sizes 16, 18
8. Red Squirrel Nymphs, sizes 16, 18

BOX NO. 5:
Large Dry Flies

These include grasshoppers, crickets, caddis, adult stoneflies, and other large drys. I use a lightweight large-compartment box for these flies. I do not routinely carry this box; I bring it with me when I know these flies are necessary.

1. Dave's Hopper, grey, gold, and olive, sizes 4–12
2. Dave's Cricket, sizes 6–12
3. Dave's Stonefly Adult
   a. Darkstone, sizes 2–6
   b. Goldenstone, sizes 4–8
4. Adult Buck Caddis, sizes 4, 6
5. Damselfly Adult
   a. dun wing/tan body, size 8
   b. dun wing/bright-blue body, size 8
   c. black wing/dark-green body, size 6

BOX NO. 6:
Skaters, Spiders, and Variants

I use a small, single-compartment, durable, plastic box in which to store these long-hackled, fragile flies. They all lay flat in the box to preserve the hackle shape. I do not routinely carry this box. It includes an assortment (about two dozen) of dun, black grizzly, dun variants, brown and cream hackle flies, sizes 10–16 and the paracranefly series.

When I travel on extended trips I carry extra stocks of these flies if I think they will be needed. Tying flies on the road or at streamside is seldom easy or particularly fun for me. However, if I feel this is necessary here is how I prepare to do so.

If I travel in my camper, I load a tackle box that I use as a portable fly-tying kit with tools and supplies. (The tackle box I use is the Plano 777S box.) I carry extra supplies or bulky materials in a separate bag or another small box. If I fly to my destination, I usually carry a fly-tying setup that fits into a soft briefcase, and carry extra materials in a locking plastic bag. (The briefcase I use is made by Mark Pack.)

A durable, high-intensity, portable lamp and a vise that will work on any flat surface are worth their weight in gold on the road.

Over the years, most of the time I've been caught without the right fly or absolutely needed to match an important feeding situation, it has almost always concerned flies of size 14 and smaller. Occurrences of the smaller aquatic and terrestrial insects are the least predictable, and so it is a good idea to prepare for them as well as you can.

I do not tie flies at streamside. To me it is frustrating, time consuming, and a real nightmare. If I have to tie flies away from home, the table in my camper or in a motel is about as close to rising trout in a breezy stream that I will tie flies.

A well-conceived, conservative stock of flies, placed in an orderly, workable fly-box system, can make any day of trout fishing pure pleasure to experience. As I look over my boxes, they reflect to me a past of pleasure and a promise of a lot of wonderful fly-fishing ahead.

GLOSSARY

Andra Spectrum: an extra-fine synthetic dubbing material used for small dry-fly and nymph bodies. It is an excellent substitute for beaver-belly underfur. It is available in a wide variety of colors, including fluorescent colors.

Badger: a feather or hair color pattern in which there is a black base and white or light cream ends.

Bead-Chain eyes: these are made from a chain of small, hollow metal beads joined together with wire links. Two of the beads joined by a link are used for a pair of eyes. Bead chains are available in most hardware stores, in many fly-tying supply stores, and from catalogs.

Bead wire: this is a fine-gauge, stiff wire used to join wooden, glass, or metal beads together for jewelry or decorative design. This is available in most arts and crafts shops.

Buss Fuse Lead Wire: a lead fuse wire produced by Buss Fuse Company and often used by fly tiers to weight flies. One-half-, one-, two-, three-, and four-amp sizes are most practical for this purpose. One-half-amp size is ideal for hook sizes 16 to 20; one-amp for sizes 10 to 14; two-amp for sizes 4 to 8; three-amp for sizes 2/0 to 2; and four-amp for sizes 5/0 to 3/0.

Collar: the area of an artificial fly directly behind the head.

Cree: a cock hackle feather barred with three colors. The colors are usually white to light grey, tan to reddish brown, and dark grey to black.

CSE Single Strand Floss: a Danville product introduced and initially distributed by Creative Sports Enterprises. It is a heavy-duty, flat-floss tying thread.

Danville Single Strand Floss: same as CSE Single Strand Floss.

Dave's Bug Float: a silicone-based waterproofing paste and scent-masking agent.

Defeo style: a method of legging or bearding a fly in which a single feather is stripped of fibers so that an equal number of fibers remain on the left and right sides of the stem. The stem is tied in so that the fibers slope down and beneath the fly's body.

Dilly Wax: a soft, tacky, dubbing wax and fly float.

Dineer (Nylon Tow Floss): Dineer pertains to the size of the fibers, nylon tow refers to a particular material used for tying flies, especially steelhead attractor and egg patterns.

Dry-fly saddle: a hackle feather from the back of a rooster. The feather is relatively webless and very stiff. This feather is most suitable for tying larger (size 4 to 10) dry-fly collars, ribs, and tails.

Dubbing: natural fur or synthetic fibers or blends of the two that are spun by the tier to build fly bodies.

Dun: a color tone with a decidedly grey cast to it.

Five-minute epoxy: a two-part epoxy cement that usually begins to set or harden within five minutes of mixing. It is available in most variety, grocery, and hardware stores.

Flymph: describes the aquatic-insect emergence stage between nymph and adult. The term was first used by James Leisenring and Vernon S. Hidy in *The Art of Tying the Wet Fly and Fishing the Flymph*.

Flyrite: a synthetic-fiber tying material used for dubbing and wings.

Flyrite Poly II: fine-fibered synthetic dubbing and winging material available in sheets.

Furnace: a color pattern on hackle or hair in which there is a dark brown or black base and dark golden to dark brown edges or ends.

Gink: a silicone-based paste for waterproofing flies and fly lines.

Grizzly: a color pattern of distinctive bands or bars of black and white or light grey.

Guardhairs: the long, stiff outer hairs found on most animals.

Herb Howard Danville Special: an extra-strong, prewaxed, 6/0 to 7/0 nylon tying thread.

Herb Howard Flymaster: same thread as Herb Howard Danville Special.

Hobby (or Swiss) straw: a polypropylene or rayon raffialike straw that is sold in ribbon lengths. It is available in most arts and crafts shops and in some fly-tying supply stores.

Hook bend: the curved portion of a hook.

Hook gap: the distance between the hook point and the shank.

Hook shank: the portion of a hook between the hook eye and the bend.

Jig Hook: a hook with its eye and a short section of the shank bent at a ninety-degree-angle downward, over which is molded a lead or plastic head.

Kodel: a family of synthetic fiber materials.

Laggie's Glos Cote: a thin, clear, acrylic fly-tying cement that is fast-penetrating and flexible.

Latex: a natural rubber available in sheets from which sections are often cut for use in wrapping bodies or making nymph wingcases or legs.

Marabou blood feather: the very small, soft or stemless side and underfeathers from a chicken, turkey, or similar fowl.

Microweb: a synthetic, "veined" wing material made in very thin sheets for fly-tying.

Midge: a very small aquatic insect, or materials and tools used for tying midge-type flies.

Monocord: a flat, nylon medium-strong floss thread made by the Danville Thread Company.

Mucilin: a popular English waterproofing parafin wax paste or liquid compound for flies, leaders, and lines.

Mylar strips: a strong, ultra-thin, plastic film cut into strips for fly wings or body material.

Mylar thread: a nylon thread wrapped with Mylar plastic and used for tying thread, ribbing, or body material.

Orlon: a soft synthetic fiber. Orlon knitting yarn is particularly good for dubbing.

Orlon Sparkle Knitting Yarn: an Orlon knitting yarn with clear Gantron nylon fibers blended in to add sparkle. This is available in material and knitting shops.

Outrigger flotation: wings, body fibers, or tails extending to the sides of a dry fly to assist in support and flotation on the surface film.

Palmered: a hackle wound the length of the hook shank, usually over body materials.

Parachute hackle: dry-fly hackle that is wrapped horiziontally over or under the hook shank on a base of wings or feather stems to achieve a parachute effect on the fly's descent to the water and to provide outrigger flotation.

Pliobond: *see* Prairie Multi-Purpose Adhesive.

Poly Wing: a transparent synthetic wing material.

Poly XXX: extra-fine polypropylene dubbing material similar in texture to Andra Spectrum material and beaver underfur.

Prairie Multi-Purpose Adhesive: a latex-based, flexible cement.

Prismatic (or Prismalite) Mylar Tape: an adhesive Mylar tape that reflects light with a prism effect. It is available in many tackle stores and custom automobile stores.

Rubber Hackle: latex rubber strands from .03 to .12mm in diameter.

Scotchgard: a 3M Company silicone product used primarily as a water and oil repellent.

Sidewinder-style wings: quill wings tied to the sides of the fly's thorax to imitate mayfly wings and provide outrigger flotation.

Spade hackle: a hackle feather found on the shoulder of a rooster whose stiff fibers are ideal for tying tails and spider and skater patterns.

Sportsman's Goop Cement (or shoe goop): a waterproof latex glue that is strong and flexible. It can be found in athletic stores. Thin with toluene or laquer thinner.

Thorax-style hackle: a hackle wrapped at crisscross angles rather than perpendicular to the hook shank.

Tuffilm: a clear, flexible, plastic spray used in graphic arts. It is sold in art stores and some fly-tying supply stores.

Variegated cree: hackle feathers with an irregular three- or four-color pattern or barring. Feathers often differ in pattern and color on the same hackle neck.

XL: extra-long hook shank. Each X is one hook length.

XS: extra-short hook shank length. Each X is one hook shank length.